ADDITIONAL PRAISE FOR
Smart Couples Finish Rich™

"David Bach is the one financial expert to listen to when you're intimidated by your finances. His powerful and easy-to-use program will help couples of all ages learn to save and invest to afford their dreams."
> —Anthony Robbins, author of *Awaken the Giant Within*
> and *Unlimited Power*

"My husband and I read this book and found it easy to understand, compassionate, and full of simple financial tools that we could use together. *Smart Couples Finish Rich* takes the guesswork out of the complicated realm of joint finances and leads you down the path of true success."
> —Chérie Carter-Scott, author of *If Life Is a Game,*
> *These Are the Rules* and *If Success Is a Game, These Are the Rules*

"*Smart Couples Finish Rich* will help not just couples but financial advisers who work with couples. Bach's approach of looking at your values first and your 'stuff' second is right on the money."
> —Harry S. Dent, Jr., bestselling author of the *The Roaring 2000s*

"*Smart Couples Finish Rich* hits the perfect balance, and goes above and beyond to be a reference book and counselor. Its flexibility makes it a perfect reference guide as life changes. The clear and concise information is written conversationally. The format really makes it feel as though your finances have been reviewed by a professional. More important, you and your partner do it together, which ideally gets you talking."
> —*Pacific Coast Business Times*

"Bach does a great job convincing couples to think about money, talk about money, get a financial plan in order—and yes, spend less and save more."
> —*American Way*

"[Bach] specializes in commonsense advice and a clear-cut path for engaging your partner in fruitful discussions about your shared financial future . . . His advice serves to free you and your beloved from the stress of never being quite sure of exactly where you stand financially. You'll probably be surprised by how big a difference Bach's strategy can make in your relationship."
> —*Better Investing*

PRAISE FOR *Smart Women Finish Rich*™

"Inspires women to start planning today for a secure financial future. Every woman can benefit from this book . . . Bach is an excellent money coach."
—John Gray, bestselling author of *Men Are from Mars, Women Are from Venus*

"Straight-shooting, action-oriented tips for getting a handle on [your] spending and savings habits . . . presented in a straightforward, nonintimidating manner perfect for the personal finance newbie."
—ABC News.com

"Bach gets across some complicated stuff: how to organize a portfolio, keep the taxman at bay, invest in yourself, and earn more, all of which make this book one of the best overall."
—*Working Woman*

"*Finally* a book for women that talks about money in a way that makes sense. David Bach is not just an expert in managing money—he's the ultimate motivational coach for women. I can't recommend this book enough. It's a must-read!"
—Barbara DeAngelis, Ph.D., bestselling author of *Real Moments*

"If I had to identify one fundamental career skill that most workers lack, it would be how to manage their money so their salary goes further. This book by a Bay Area financial adviser offers a lot of sound information for people of both sexes."
—*San Francisco Chronicle*

"Finally, a financial planning guide that addresses the unique issues that women face today. But what I like the most is that David starts with the most important principle: aligning your money with your values."
—Harry S. Dent, Jr., bestselling author of *The Roaring 2000s*

"If you pick up this book, you'll be unable to put it down until you discover what you might have been doing wrong all these years—and how to remedy it. It's a seven-step plan to a secure financial future. If your parents didn't take you aside and tell you the secrets of life—the real money secrets—read this 242-page hardcover."
—*Carmel Times*

SMART COUPLES FINISH RICH™

ALSO BY DAVID BACH

Smart Women Finish Rich™

SMART

COUPLES

FINISH

DAVID BACH

RICH™

9 STEPS TO CREATING
A RICH FUTURE FOR YOU
AND YOUR PARTNER

BROADWAY BOOKS · NEW YORK

BROADWAY

A hardcover edition of this book was published in 2001 by Broadway Books.

First Broadway Books trade paperback edition published 2002

Designed by Richard Oriolo

The Library of Congress has cataloged the hardcover edition as follows:

Bach, David.
   Smart couples finish rich : 9 steps to creating a rich future for you and your partner /
David Bach.—1st ed.
    p. cm.
   1. Couples—Finance, Personal.   2. Investments.   3. Financial security.   I. Title.
HG179.B243 2001
332.024'0655—dc21   00-046755

ISBN 0-7679-0484-2

30 29 28 27 26 25 24 23 22

To my amazing wife Michelle . . .
you are my best friend, confidante, and safe harbor in the storm.
Thank you for always believing in me and my dreams.
I love you.

CONTENTS

ACKNOWLEDGMENTS xi

INTRODUCTION 1

WHY SMART COUPLES ARE TAKING
CONTROL OF THEIR FINANCIAL FUTURE

STEP ONE 13

LEARN THE FACTS AND
MYTHS ABOUT COUPLES AND MONEY

STEP TWO 33

DETERMINE THE TRUE PURPOSE
OF MONEY IN YOUR LIFE

STEP THREE 57

PLAN TOGETHER . . . WIN TOGETHER

STEP FOUR 85

THE COUPLES' LATTÉ FACTOR™

STEP FIVE 97

BUILD YOUR RETIREMENT BASKET

STEP SIX 143

BUILD YOUR SECURITY BASKET

STEP SEVEN 181

BUILD YOUR DREAM BASKET

STEP EIGHT 207

LEARN TO AVOID THE TEN BIGGEST
FINANCIAL MISTAKES COUPLES MAKE

STEP NINE 247

INCREASE YOUR INCOME BY
10 PERCENT IN NINE WEEKS

THREE WORDS THAT MAKE A DIFFERENCE 273

APPENDIX 1 275

APPENDIX 2 279

APPENDIX 3 284

APPENDIX 4 285

INDEX 295

ACKNOWLEDGMENTS

MANY PEOPLE MADE IT POSSIBLE for *Smart Women Finish Rich* and *Smart Couples Finish Rich* to become national bestsellers. Only because of the support and love of the following have I been able to take this incredible journey and reach so many people . . .

First, to the readers of *Smart Women Finish Rich* and *Smart Couples Finish Rich:* thank you, thank you, thank you. The best part of writing a book is hearing from readers who have been motivated to take action. To those of you who have e-mailed me or sent me letters, thank you for taking the time to let me know how I touched your lives. The knowledge that I've reached so many of you is what makes all this effort of writing, speaking, and traveling worth it.

To Suzanne Oaks, my editor at Broadway Books: we did it! Thanks again for your incredible feedback and support. Your ideas are always right on the money. To Claire Johnson, thank you for your patient help in putting the pieces of this updated book together. To my PR gurus Heidi Krupp and David Drake, thank you both for your tireless and incredible help promoting both of my books. Your teamwork on my behalf has been invaluable and I'm eternally thankful. To the outstanding sales team of Broadway, thank you for supporting my book, and selling it into the markets where my seminars take place. This extra effort has led to tens of thousands of additional book sales.

To Allan Mayer: working with you on these two books has truly been a joy. We are so "in synch," and I am so grateful to have you as a collaborator. Thanks for always doing what you say you're going to. You are a class act.

An enormous thank you goes to my team at Van Kampen Investments. As a result of our efforts, we have so far reached more than 250,000 women with Smart Women Finish Rich™ seminars—and we are just getting started! As we roll out Smart Couples Finish Rich™ seminars coast to coast in 2002, we will undoubtedly help thousands more. To Jack Zimmerman, Dominic Martellaro, Lisa Kueng, Scott West, and Gary DeMoss: thank you for believing in me and the power of this project. To the entire team of world-class wholesalers at Van Kampen who have collectively done thousands of seminars and to the thousands of financial advisors who now present my FinishRich™ seminars worldwide, thank you for delivering the message.

To Larry Rifkin at Connecticut Public Television: thank you for working so hard to bring my "Smart Women Finish Rich" special to PBS. A public television show needs an underwriter, and I was very fortunate to have three. First, thank you to Rick Sapio, the tireless founder of Mutuals.com. I will be forever grateful to you for being the lead underwriter. A big thank you also goes out to our other underwriters, Women.com and Van Kampen Mutual Funds.

To my world-class agent, Jan Miller: I will always be indebted to you for your guidance and shrewd deal-making. To Shannon Miser Marvin: thank you for returning all my calls, dealing with the contracts, and handling the hundreds of details that always need to be nailed down. You are the best!

To Harry Cornelius, thank you for your outstanding expertise in negotiating my financial service contracts. To Stephen Breimer, thank you for your excellent legal advice. I am truly grateful to you two gentlemen for helping me take FinishRich™ Inc. to the next level.

I also want to express my gratitude to my many mentors and coaches. To Bill Bachrach, the author of *Values-Based Financial Planning*: I will always be grateful for your TAC program and your permission to use your values conversation in *Smart Women Finish Rich*. To Bill Phillips, the author of *Body for Life*: your book has done amazing things to improve not only my health but Michelle's as well. To Dan Sullivan: thank you for *Strategic Coach* and for *Strategic Couples*. Your coaching program has dramatically changed the quality of our lives. To Tony Robbins: you are truly a world-class leader and coach. Thank you for creating "Date with Destiny"—it is because of you and your programs that I have been able to go for my dreams.

To Kathleen Price, my unbelievable "right hands" at The Bach Group: I will be forever appreciative for all that you do. Thanks for keeping The Bach Group growing, the clients happy, and me in good spirits while I write, speak, travel, and manage money—all at the same time. To the rest of The Bach Group team—Marty Bach, Emily Bach, Tom Moglia, Jeff Borges, Sharon Hundal, Geraldine Kobayashi, Leonore Pearsall, Patricia Brown—thank you all for making The Bach Group such a world-class money management group.

To my incredible parents, Bobbi and Marty Bach, words cannot express how much I love you both. I am truly grateful for your never-ending love and encouragement. Your belief in my abilities and your constant "cheering" through the good as well as the challenging times have allowed me to keep pushing forward. Thank you for providing me with an example of what a great marriage is and what it means to be a Smart Couple that works together to succeed in life.

To my sister Emily, congratulations on all your success. Thanks for doing "Smart Women Finish Rich" seminars and sharing the message. Most important, thanks for being such an amazing sister and such a great friend. To my brother-in-law Tom Moglia: thanks for making my sister so happy and being an all-around great guy.

To my "second family," Joan, Bill, Nana, and Michael: thanks for your constant love and encouragement and telling all your friends about my book. Most important, to Joan and Bill: thanks for having Michelle and letting me marry her!

To my incredible group of longtime friends—Betsey and T.G. Fraser, Jeff and Caroline Guenther, Donna and Jeff Odiorne, Jenny and Bill Holt, Steve Jones, Elliot Blumberg, David Kronick, Jeff and Dawn Adams, Tom Cooper, Andrew and Belinda Donner, Karen and Drew Warmington, Adam and Julie Young—thanks for your love and for being the best friends a guy could ask for.

Last, to my grandmother Rose Bach: thank you for being my original inspiration for writing *Smart Women Finish Rich*. I love you and miss you every day. Thank you for rooting for me up in heaven.

I am grateful to all of you from the bottom of my heart.

David Louis Bach
San Francisco, California
January 2002

Free! 30 Days of Personal Coaching

As one more way to say thank you for reading this book, I'd like to offer you a new program I've developed. It's called:

The 30-Day FinishRich™ Jumpstart

I created it to keep the readers of my books motivated to take action on their values, goals, and dreams. Please visit my website at *www.finish rich.com* and sign up today (it's free). And over the next 30 days you'll receive a personal message of financial inspiration. Each message will be short, inspiring, and action-oriented. Enjoy!

WHY SMART COUPLES ARE TAKING CONTROL OF THEIR FINANCIAL FUTURE

I'LL NEVER FORGET THE FIRST fight I had with my wife Michelle over money. We were just back from our honeymoon, and the bliss of getting married was still in the air. Our new apartment looked great. We were incredibly excited to be starting our lives together.

As Michelle began to unpack, I sat down at the kitchen table and started sorting through the mail. Since we'd been gone almost two weeks, there was a lot to go through. I began separating the important stuff from the junk mail, taking the bills that needed to be paid and placing them in piles. Nice, neat organized piles. In my mind, this bill-paying stuff would clearly be a nonissue. After all, both Michelle and I were financial professionals. I managed money for hundreds of couples; she helped corporate executives trade restricted stock. What's more, I'd spent the last five years teaching classes on financial management and had just started writing a book on money for women. Paying our bills and managing money as a couple were bound to be a breeze.

Neat and Simple?

As I sorted out the bills, I created a "David" pile and a "Michelle" pile. This was going to be so easy. I'd pay my bills (like my car payments and my cell phone) and Michelle would pay her bills (like her car and her cell phone). We'd split the household bills, which meant we needed a "we" pile. And . . . hmmm . . . who pays the insurance bills? Well, we'll figure that out. Maybe we also need a "to be discussed" pile. Let's see, that's four piles.

Oh, here's a bill for the cleaning lady. I guess that could go in our "we" pile. But what about this American Express bill with all the honeymoon expenses on it? Well, the card's in my name and I guess it's pretty much the guy's job to pay for the honeymoon, so that should probably go in the "David" pile. Dry cleaning? Well, even though we now get our dry cleaning done at the same place, the account is in my name, so I guess I can pay it. Let's see—how much does this cost? No way . . . this can't be right! How could my dry-cleaning bill have tripled in a month?

Michelle was in the bedroom organizing her closet. "Honey," I yelled to her, "do you know they charge $7 to dry-clean one of your sweaters? How can it cost so much to dry-clean women's clothing? And do you know you had them dry-clean *seven* sweaters this month? This is insane. We're going to have to get two dry-cleaning accounts, because I'm not paying these ridiculous prices for you."

Michelle stopped what she was doing and came into the kitchen. "Of course I know it costs $7 to dry-clean a sweater," she said. She looked down at my nice, neat piles of bills. "Hey, what's with all this?" she asked.

I grinned up at her. "Oh," I said, "I'm getting things organized. I'm separating our bills to see who pays what."

Michelle looked at me a little strangely. "Honey, you don't need to waste your time doing that. This is going to be easy. We are going to put all of our money in a joint checking account and pay everything together."

"We are?"

"Of course we are. We're married now, we love each other, and from now on everything we have is one and everything we do as one."

"Well, actually," I said, "that's not exactly what I had in mind." Sensing a little tension, I quickly added, "In the beginning at least, I think it might be easier if we sort of split this stuff up."

"But David," Michelle replied, "you make more and spend more than I do. You can't expect us to just split all these bills down the middle."

"Well, no, of course not," I said. "I thought I'd sort of split them up in a way that's fair."

"Well, what's fair?"

Good point, I thought. "Well, I need to think that through."

Michelle shook her head. "No, you don't. I'll tell you what's fair. What's fair is that we put all our money in one account and pay all the bills out of this account."

Something's Not Working

Fast-forward a few months. Michelle and I still hadn't totally agreed on who was responsible for paying what. Unfortunately, the bills kept arriving, just like clockwork, every 30 days. Only now they were starting to get paid late (and, as a result, we were getting hit with late fees).

Upset about all the money we were wasting on late fees, I began freaking out and blaming Michelle for the problem. In turn, she was telling me it was all the fault of my stupid "pile system." Needless to say, what we were doing wasn't working. And rather than sorting itself out, the problem was only getting worse. Instead of sitting down and discussing how we might reconcile our clearly different attitudes about handling money into one simple system that worked for both of us, we were running on "assumptions." I was assuming Michelle knew how I wanted our money to be managed, and she was assuming I knew what she wanted to do. We were each assuming the other was paying certain bills. We weren't on the same page—and the consequences were that this "money stuff" was creating more stress than it should.

The Good News . . .

Eventually, Michelle and I did come up with a system to manage our finances together. As a result, I'm happy to report that things are much, much better for us on the money front. We now work together on our finances, and instead of making assumptions about how the other one feels, we put our heads together and bounce ideas off each other. In short, we've learned to make a priority of discussing our finances and planning our financial goals and dreams together. Doing this changes everything: it ends the fights and it focuses the energy of a relationship on the positive instead of the problems.

Looking back, it's not surprising that as newlyweds Michelle and I had a hard time figuring out how to handle our finances. Even though we both had financial backgrounds, we had never taken a class or gotten any coaching about how to manage money as a couple. As a result, neither of us had ever thought about how different things become when you go from being two single people managing your money separately as individuals to a couple managing your money together.

Needless to say, what Michelle and I went through was hardly unique. Most couples have never been taught how to plan their financial future together. As a result, most couples rarely talk about money . . . unless they are fighting about it. My goal with this book is to change that. Having been a financial advisor for nearly 10 years, and a husband now for 4, I'm happy to report that it's both possible and fun to become a Smart Couple Who Finishes Rich. The key to being able to "win financially" is learning how to take the right actions in the right order. It's really not difficult at all—especially when you do it together as a couple.

In this book, we're going to work on how the two of you, as a couple, can both talk about and handle your money in a smart way.

Whether you're just starting out or are well into midlife, whether this is your first marriage or your fourth, this book will show you how to get your financial goals and your personal values in synch so they—and the two of you—can work together to make your dreams a reality! What's more, if you have financial fears—and most people do—you will learn how to address and overcome them as a couple.

Your Road Map to Living—and Finishing—Rich

My goal in this book is to provide an action-oriented road map that will enable the two of you to take control of your finances as a couple. In the chapters that follow, you will learn everything you need to do as a couple to both live and finish rich. Specifically, you will learn:

- How to learn to earn . . . together (without fighting!)

- How to look at your values and put what matters most in your life first

- How to use what I call the "Couples' Latté Factor" to transform any income into a million-dollar nest egg

- How to protect your family with a "security basket," provide for your future with a "retirement basket," and fund your dreams with a "dream basket"

- And finally, how to grow your income as a couple by 10 percent over the next nine weeks.

In the past, many of you may have read investment books that put you to sleep. I promise you, this one won't. The reality is that investing is a blast when you know exactly what to do and how to do it. The problem with most investment books—and most financial advisors—is that they talk over our heads. You won't find that here. That's because my approach to living and finishing rich involves some incredibly simple techniques that can be life-changing when you put them into action.

If My Grandparents Could Do It, So Can You

I learned how to invest from my grandmother, Rose Bach. It was Grandma Rose who helped me make my first stock purchase. I was just seven years old, and the stock was a share in the company that owned my favorite restaurant in the whole world . . . McDonald's.

Where did my grandmother learn to invest? That's an amazing story.

My grandparents had no money and no college education. During the Great Depression, they lived in Milwaukee, Wisconsin, and like many Americans of their time, they struggled to keep their heads above water. As my grandfather used to say, "You gotta watch the pennies because they add up to a dollar." Fortunately for my grandfather—and, ultimately, for me and my whole family—shortly after her thirtieth birthday my grandmother made a decision that transformed all our lives.

One day, tired of the never-ending struggle to make ends meet, she decided that someday she was going to be rich. It was a remarkable decision, for at the time, she was only earning $10 a week. And my grandfather was earning even less . . . just $5 a week.

The first step, she decided, was to build up a small nest egg. So, together, she and my grandfather began putting aside 10 percent of their paychecks each week, keeping the money in a coffee can in their kitchen.

After a month of saving, my grandmother took the money they had accumulated and went to a local brokerage office to open an account. She was not exactly welcomed with open arms. Scandalized that a married woman had come to see them on her own, the men running the brokerage told her to leave—and not come back without her husband!

Someone else might have been intimidated. But not my grandmother. She was a strong and feisty woman. "Gentlemen," she said, "if you don't want my money, I'll go next door and open an account with your competitor."

My grandmother got her account and she began to invest what she and my grandfather managed to save each week. To make a long story short, her investments eventually made her a millionaire. (Her investments also inspired a family tradition: her son—my father, Marty—

became a financial advisor, as did both of her grandchildren, my sister Emily and me.)

Of course, things didn't always go smoothly. A few years ago, I asked my grandmother how she did that first year. "I know how it turned out, Grandma," I said, "but how did it start?"

My question made her laugh. "David," she said, "I bought four stocks . . . and they all went to zero in less than a year!"

I was stunned. "Zero?" I repeated. "What did Grandpa say?"

Grandma laughed some more, her eyes sparkling. "I didn't tell him!" she replied.

"But what kept you going?" I asked her. "How did you keep investing after you lost all of your money after a full year of saving?"

She looked me straight in the eye. "David," she said, "I told you— I wanted to be rich, not poor." She went on to explain that she had quickly realized the problem was not the stock market or the stockbroker or even the particular stocks she had chosen. "The problem was me," she said. "I didn't know the first thing about investing. I had never taken a class on investing. Your grandfather didn't know anything about money. It was the blind leading the blind."

But then, she said, she realized something that then and there changed her life. "If we were going to get rich, I was going to have to *learn* how to get rich! I needed to take classes, read books, study the stock market, and make friends with rich people." This revelation of my grandmother's led to a lesson that has stayed with me ever since.

There are many things my Grandma Bach taught me about money, but none was more important than this:

If You Want to Get Rich, You Have to Learn to Earn

The fact is, anyone can become an investor. Indeed, today with the Internet, it's never been easier to get started. But becoming an investor and becoming wealthy are not the same thing. Had my grandmother not realized that she needed to get smart about money, she and my grandfather would more than likely have ended up like 90 percent of all Americans—struggling to survive during retirement.

My grandmother's story illustrates another lesson that's worth mentioning here—namely . . .

You Don't Have to Be Rich to Be an Investor

My grandparents started out with nothing, able to save only a few dollars a week. Yet over time they were able to build a million-dollar portfolio. How? By planning together, saving together, and investing together. Had they decided that because they were poor and didn't have college degrees, they would always be poor, that's just what would have happened. But that's not what they did. Instead, they decided to change their lives. They decided to be a Smart Couple Who Finishes Rich.

Okay, that was my grandparents and it was a long time ago. What about you today?

Can a book like this one really change the way you and your partner think about money and enable you to realize your financial dreams?

The answer is an unequivocal yes.

Can the process of working on your finances as a couple really be fun?

Absolutely. In fact, there are very few things in a relationship that can do more to solidify your bond and make you stronger as a couple than planning your financial future together. Think about it. Most couples decide to spend their lives together because they sincerely love each other and want to build a life together. I've never met a couple who said, "Wouldn't it be great to be together so we can fight on a regular basis about our finances!" But even though no one wants to fight about money, the fact is that most couples do. Either that or they flat out avoid the subject.

According to the experts, the number-one cause of divorce in this country isn't sex or religion or problems with the in-laws. It's fighting over money. Having advised hundreds of couples individually in my financial-planning practice, I can tell you from firsthand experience that working on your money together significantly improves the chances not only of your succeeding financially but of your staying together happily as a couple. The key is to take the journey together—not separately.

This book is meant for couples who want to do that. If you are looking for a book that will explain how to hide assets from your partner or create ways to keep your finances separate, you might as well stop reading now. My goal is to help you be the strongest couple you can be, and the best way I know to do this is to go on the journey together.

Taking Charge Together: The Secret to Your Success

You may have already noticed that I've been referring to your spouse or significant other as your "partner." I do this deliberately, for in a good relationship that's exactly what a spouse or significant other should be—a partner.

The vital importance of partners really acting like partners when it comes to money became apparent to me after I published my first book, *Smart Women Finish Rich*. One of the great things about writing a book is that you often get feedback from readers sharing with you what works and what does not. Within just a few months of the publication of *Smart Women Finish Rich*, I was getting dozens of e-mails daily from readers recounting the kind of impact the book was having on them.

Most of the messages were incredibly positive, but a few concerned me. For example, one woman wrote, "Your book has changed my life. I'm now totally motivated and taking charge of my own finances. The problem is, I can't get my husband to change. Without his support, I'm wondering if any of my efforts will be worth it." In a similar vein, another woman wrote, "Great ideas in theory, but my husband won't save, spends all of our income on 'male toys,' and won't listen to me about your ideas."

It wasn't just women complaining about irresponsible men. Even though *Smart Women Finish Rich* was meant for women, I got a fair number of e-mails from men who had purchased the book for their wives or girlfriends . . . only to find they weren't interested. As one man wrote to me, "I read your book before I gave it to my wife. Honestly, I hoped it would motivate her to become more involved with the family finances. Instead she said, 'You're doing a great job with our money and I'm not interested in this stuff.' "

Eventually, I got an e-mail that summed up the problem brilliantly. It came from a woman in Omaha, Nebraska, and it really struck a chord with me.

> *David [the woman wrote], after reading your book I became a supersonic jet engine on a plane. I'm striving to go forward, to reach my dream destination. Unfortunately, my husband's jet engine is going full steam in reverse. I know that this plane (our financial plan) is going to crash. You can't fly with one engine going forward and one engine going in reverse. I don't know what to do. I'm thinking of bailing out before we crash. Any suggestions?*

It was this e-mail that made me realize I needed to write a personal-finance book for couples. As the woman in Omaha said, a couple's financial plan is a lot like a plane with two engines. If both engines aren't pointed in the same direction or working at roughly equal power, you are going to have problems. Without teamwork, financial planning for most couples becomes a battle, not a victory. And ignoring the problem will only make it worse, for every month those bills are going to show up, whether you want them to or not. There's no getting around it. The bills show up, the monthly stress hits, the arguments start—and next thing you know it's the next month with the same problems all over again.

It's Time for the Two of You to Take Charge

So that's our basic premise: all couples should work on their finances together. And when I say all couples, I mean *all* couples. Age isn't a factor. Whether you're a brand-new couple starting out in your early twenties or a retired couple in your seventies, the process of planning your finances together is one you can begin today. All that's required for you to do this is for you to receive the tools. And that's what I intend to give you in this book.

Much of what you will learn as you read the nine chapters that follow will seem incredibly simple. You may even find yourself thinking, "I know that. I've heard that before."

Don't let this make you feel complacent. When it comes to money, just having heard of something isn't enough; you've got to know what it means. And just knowing what something means doesn't matter if you're not actually doing it. For example, even though nearly everyone is familiar with the concept of "paying yourself first," most couples don't know how much they should pay themselves first, or where the money should actually go. As a result, they don't do it.

One Plus One Equals Four

When two people work together to accomplish a goal, they can usually achieve it twice as fast as either of them would have working alone. This is certainly true when it comes to your money. The sooner you start working together, the more quickly you can dramatically improve your financial picture. The key is to truly believe that wherever you are starting from—no matter how bad or bleak it looks—things can and will get better. If right now you are badly in debt or living paycheck to paycheck, I am here to tell you as someone who has personally coached thousands of people on their finances that it can and will get better . . . if the two of you take action together.

By the same token, if you have already achieved financial success but find that for some reason the money in your life is not making your dreams come true, I am here to tell you that you shouldn't give up—that you can align your values with your dreams and live a fulfilling life . . . if you and your partner work on this money stuff together.

How Best to Use This Book

Before we get started, I want to give you some tips on how to get the most out of what this book has to offer. To begin with, you should think of this book as a road map—specifically, your personal financial road map to a financial destination you will shortly choose. As you use this financial road map, I'd like you to think of me as your personal financial coach, a friendly guide who can help you find your way through the obstacles and lead you quickly to the wealth and happiness you deserve.

You should also keep in mind that though taking control of your finances can be both easy and fun, it does require a real commitment. As I noted earlier, even though they are purchased with good intentions, most personal-finance books don't get read past the first few chapters. So as you start this one, do yourself a favor—make a commitment to yourself that you will invest the few hours necessary to really read this book and put the nine steps to work. I promise you that as easy as these steps are, if you just "go for it" and really do them, they will change your life. As I often tell my students and clients, if you do just two or three of the steps, you will be better off than 80 percent of the population. If you do five or six of the steps, you will be better off than 90 percent. And if you do all nine steps, you will end up in the financial elite—living in the top 1 percent.

I've deliberately organized things so that each of the next nine chapters covers a single step of our nine-step journey. Although each step is self-contained, they all build on the steps that went before. So my suggestion is that you read the chapters in order. You might even consider reading each chapter twice before you go on to the next one. Why read a chapter twice? Because when we're reading, we often miss something the first time around, and because repetition is the key to developing any skill.

One final suggestion: as you read this book, you may realize that you're not doing everything you should be doing with your finances. Don't use that as an excuse to jump all over your partner—or yourself. The purpose of this book is to improve your financial future, not to make you or your partner feel bad. As adults trying to make our lives better, we tend to be too hard on ourselves. If your financial life is not yet where you want it to be, that's okay—you're about to change that. Stay positive. Remember, the hardest part of changing things is . . . deciding to change. You've already made that decision. You've purchased this book and now you're reading it. So give yourself a break—and some credit.

The journey you and your partner are about to take together is meant to change your lives forever. So have fun with the process, and keep in mind that you've already taken the most important step toward controlling your financial destiny. You've decided to live smart and finish rich—together, as a couple.

Now let's get started!

LEARN THE FACTS

AND MYTHS ABOUT

COUPLES AND

MONEY

JOHN SAT IN MY OFFICE smiling from ear to ear. Indeed, he was practically glowing. After putting in more than 40 years as a successful salesman at a printing company, he was just two months away from retirement. He had come to my office with his wife of more than 30 years, Lucy, to make some plans. Excited about getting started on this new phase of their life together, the two were interviewing me to see if I would be the right financial planner for them. As I usually do in such situations, I began the meeting by asking a simple question: "With only 60 days to go, what does retirement look like to the two of you?"

John leaned forward confidently. "We're moving to South Carolina, where we own some land," he said, "and, we're gonna build us a little two-bedroom house on a lake and I'm going fishing every day!"

With that, he sat back in his chair, grinning like a school kid.

Lucy, however, had quite a different look on her face—a combination of anger and disbelief. Glaring coldly at John as if he were a stranger she was meeting for the first time, she asked him, "And who are you planning to move to South Carolina with?"

Now it was John's turn to look shocked. "Well, with you, of course," he said meekly.

Lucy laughed out loud. "John," she said, "if you think I'm leaving our kids, our grandchildren, and our five-bedroom house in Danville so you can go fishing in Timbuktu, you've got a screw loose!"

John looked at me helplessly, then turned back to Lucy. "But we bought that land in South Carolina to build our dream house on when I retired. Remember, honey?"

"John, that was 20 years ago!" she snapped. "You haven't even mentioned that land in the last 10 years. I was hoping you'd forgotten about it!"

PETER AND MARY *sat in my office, both completely happy. The day before, after five years of meticulous planning, the two of them—both in their early fifties— had taken early retirement from their respective employers. That's right—two retirements from two separate companies on the same day! They had spent the previous evening celebrating, first at his retirement party, then at hers. The excitement they both felt was contagious. They reminded me of two teenagers who had just graduated from high school.*

The couple had come to my office to take care of the paperwork for their 401(k) rollovers. Earlier in the day, they had met with their attorney and their accountant. Tomorrow, they would leave to fulfill a long-held—and long planned-for—dream of theirs: to move to an isolated village in Mongolia for two years as part of a church-sponsored program in which they would help build a new school for local children. An automatic payment program had been set up to take care of all their bills, their retirement accounts were fully and safely invested, and their expenses were covered for the next two years. Their kids were in college and the tuition payments were already arranged. Everything had been anticipated. Peter and Mary could not wait to catch their plane and start living out their dream.

I've started our journey with these two contrasting stories because they are both true—indeed, they both occurred in my office during the same week—and, taken together, they illustrate just how differently different couples can plan for their future. I'm confident that the first couple, John and Lucy, is not the model you want to follow. The second couple may not be your ideal either (especially if, like me, your idea of retirement isn't an isolated village in Mongolia). But the reality is that Peter and Mary's future does sound exciting. That's because it involves a dream they planned together and are now getting to live together. You can't hear about their story without becoming excited for them.

If you are in a relationship right now and have a significant other you plan to be with for a long time, it stands to reason that you want to have a bright future in which you live and finish rich together. But being smart and finishing rich doesn't just happen. It takes real action and positive commitment on your part.

It's Not Just About Money . . .

Here's another important part of Finishing Rich that many couples overlook: it's not just about the money. John and Lucy have money. What they don't have is a plan for the second half of their life together. Although they've been married for more than 30 years, neither has a clue as to how the other expects to spend his or her golden years. John thinks he's going fishing, and Lucy wants to know who he's going fishing with.

Having served as a financial planner for countless couples over the last 10 years, I can tell you from firsthand experience that way too many couples are like John and Lucy. They go through life without making any real plans for their future together; in many cases, they've never even discussed the subject. Each just assumes that somehow the other knows (and agrees with) what he or she happens to want. The result is invariably a disaster.

Then again, I've also seen the exact opposite. Every day I meet and work with couples who have been married for years, sometimes decades, who really do function as a team . . . as one. They really do communicate about their money and they really do plan for their financial future—in other words, they are Smart Couples who are living and finishing rich. This is my goal for you.

THE FACTS AND MYTHS
ABOUT COUPLES AND MONEY

The truth about money management is that it's not really that difficult. If you know what to do and what not to do, it's actually pretty easy. The challenge is that we're not taught about money in school. As a result, much of what we learn about it comes from friends, word of mouth, and marketing. This is why a lot of otherwise smart people spend their whole lives doing the wrong things with their money.

I often tell people it comes down to this . . .

> *It's not what you know about money—it's what you*
> *don't know that can wipe you out.*

Since so much of what people have learned about handling money is actually dead wrong, a big part of becoming a Smart Couple who finishes rich is about unlearning what the two of you think you know about the subject. To do this, I'm going to share with you some of the biggest myths about money and couples. By understanding these myths for what they are, and learning the true facts, you will instantly be better prepared to make better decisions about your finances.

MYTH NO. 1
If we love each other, we won't fight about money.

FACT NO. 1
**Money has very little to do with love . . . and a lot to do with
how much you fight.**

Repeat after me: love has nothing to do with money. It doesn't matter if you love your spouse or partner more than anything in the world. If the two of you have conflicting values about money and make financial decisions that fail to accommodate each other's feelings about the subject, you are going to have serious relationship problems.

Love does not conquer all. If it did, then one out of every two marriages would not end in divorce. Love usually gets you to the altar and creates passion for a few years, but a solid, long-lasting marriage takes more than just love. So please stop for a second and consider these basic facts:

1. How you spend money has nothing to do with how much you love each other.

2. The two of you were probably raised differently when it came to money.

3. The two of you probably value money differently.

4. The two of you probably spend money differently.

That's a lot of differences. So if the two of you happen to be fighting about money right now, I've got news for you: you're normal. And here's some even better news: you don't have to change who you are or what you value in order to finish rich. Nor do you need to become financial geniuses. As you will learn in this book, the things you need to do in order to become wealthy are basically quite simple. They don't require a lot of brains or education. They don't require positive-thinking exercises or memorizing mantras. All they require is what I call "positive action."

So if the two of you are fighting over money right now because your attitudes toward it are different, that's okay. Take a deep breath, exhale . . . and "let it go." By the time you're done with this book, you will see how quickly and easily you can transform both your lives and your relationship merely by following the nine simple steps I'm going to lay out for you. In the meantime, just remember—love's got nothing to do with finishing rich . . . nothing!

MYTH NO. 2
It takes money to make money.

FACT NO. 2
It takes very little money to make money . . . as long as you are patient and disciplined.

My grandparents had only a few dollars a week to invest. Nonetheless, over the course of several decades, they became wealthy.

I can see you rolling your eyes. That was then, you say; this is now. Well, not so fast. Let's look at the numbers. The nice thing about building wealth is that it's basically a numbers game, and the rules don't change much over time. Consider the following:

A Dollar Is Still Worth a Lot of Money . . . If It's Forced to Grow Up!

I want you to do an experiment. Go down to your local coffee shop one morning and for one hour count the number of couples buying cups of coffee. If it's a fancy franchise like, say, Starbucks, the price of a nice little cup of cappuccino will be about $2.50. Watch how many nice normal people spend that much every morning on coffee. Have you ever stopped to think about what the cost of those little cups of coffee can add up to over time? How much could you make if you spent $1 less on coffee every day and put what you saved into a good investment program? Let's take a look.

A Dollar a Day Can Grow Up to Be $1 Million . . .

Here's what happens if you start making a dollar a day work for you.

$1 a day at 5% =	$1 million in 99 years ("too long . . . won't work")
$1 a day at 10% =	$1 million in 56 years ("start at age 7, you're a millionaire at 63")
$1 a day at 15% =	$1 million in 40 years ("start at age 7, you're a millionaire at 47")

Now your brain is having a few thoughts. Okay, a dollar a day and compound interest are interesting and kind of neat, you are thinking, but where are we going to get annual returns of 10 or 15 percent? (The answer is the stock market, and we'll cover that in detail later on.) You're probably also thinking, "Hey, David, it looks great, but I'm not seven years old." That's right, you're not seven. But maybe you have kids who are. If so, do them a favor and show this to them.

Of course, that doesn't solve your problem. You're a lot older than seven, and try as we might, there's no way to turn back the clock. But there is a way to make up for lost time—namely, by kicking in more money. Since you're older than seven, you probably can afford to invest more than $1 a day. Let's see what happens if you put in a grown-up amount.

$10 Can Turn into a Million a Lot Faster Than $1

Here's a startling but probably true fact: if you can manage to save $10 a day, you can get rich.

I'll say that again: all you need to do in order to become wealthy over time is to commit right now to putting a fixed amount of money every day in growth investments. (Don't worry about what kind of growth investments; we'll cover that later on.)

$10 a day at 5% =	$1 million in 54 years ("still doesn't work great")
$10 a day at 10% =	$1 million in 34 years ("not quite so bad . . . we're getting there")
$10 a day at 15% =	$1 million in 25 years ("that's really just around the corner")

Now let's go crazy. What if *both* you and your partner saved $10 a day?

$20 a day at 10% =	$1 million in 27 years
$20 a day at 15% =	$1 million in 21 years

There are no tricks here. Becoming rich is nothing more than a matter of committing and sticking to a systematic savings and investment plan. How you set up and run that plan is something we'll deal with later on in this book. For now, I just want you to focus on the fact that you don't need to have money to make money. You just need to make the right decisions—and act on them. Check out the chart below on how to build a million-dollar nest egg.

Building a Million-Dollar Retirement Account

Building Your First $1,000,000
Daily or Monthly Investments Suggested to Build $1,000,000 by Age 65

$1,000,000
12% Annual Interest Rate

STARTING AGE	DAILY SAVINGS	MONTHLY SAVINGS	YEARLY SAVINGS
20	$ 2.00	$ 61	$ 730
25	$ 3.57	$ 109	$ 1,304
30	$ 6.35	$ 193	$ 2,317
35	$ 11.35	$ 345	$ 4,144
40	$ 20.55	$ 625	$ 7,500
45	$ 38.02	$ 1,157	$ 13,879
50	$ 73.49	$ 2,235	$ 26,824
55	$ 156.12	$ 4,749	$ 56,984

The purpose of this chart is to share with you how much money you should be saving daily, monthly, or yearly to accumulate $1,000,000 by age 65. It assumes you are starting with zero dollars invested and that you earn 12% annually. This chart does not take into consideration the impact of taxes.

There's Still Time . . . Even If You're in Your Fifties

Wherever you are right now in your life, a little extra savings can go an amazingly long way toward building a sizable nest egg. Consider the following simple plan for a couple in their fifties.

Say Jim and Maureen decide today to start using the Couples' Latté Factor (a technique we'll learn about in Step Four) to enable each of them to invest an extra $10 a day in their retirement accounts at work (a practice we'll discuss in Step Five). That amounts to an additional investment of $600 a month. Multiply that by 12 and we are now talking about a yearly increase in savings of $7,200. If they both start at age 50 and continue putting money away at that rate until they are 65, the results could be truly phenomenal.

Let's assume Jim and Maureen invest the extra money in a growth portfolio consisting of 75 percent stock-based mutual funds and 25 percent short-term bonds. With this sort of mix, it's reasonable to expect them to earn an annual return on their money of around about 11 percent. (It's not guaranteed, but that's what these investments have averaged for the last 30 years or so.) By the time Jim and Maureen reach 65, their extra savings should total nearly $275,000. And if their employers have a policy of matching, say, 50 percent of their retirement-plan contributions (which many companies today do), their total would be more than $412,000. Anyway you cut it, that represents a significant extra cushion for retirement.

Remember, the truth is that . . .

> *. . . most people overestimate what they can do financially in a year—and underestimate what they can achieve financially over a few decades.*

MYTH NO. 3
We don't make enough yet to be investors.

FACT NO. 3
Everyone makes enough to invest.

How many times have you heard someone say, "If only I could make a little more money, I could really get my financial act together"? How many times have *you* said it yourself? Ask most couples the source of their financial problems and they will tell you it's that they don't make enough money. The truth is that most couples don't have an income problem; what they have is a spending problem. If you don't believe me, think for a minute about how much you and your partner will probably earn over the course of your lifetime together.

To estimate how truly big a number this is, use the earnings chart below.

Earnings Outlook

How much money will pass through your hands during your lifetime and what will you do with it?

MONTHLY INCOME	10 YEARS	20 YEARS	30 YEARS	40 YEARS
$1,000	$120,000	$240,000	$360,000	$480,000
$1,500	180,000	360,000	540,000	720,000
$2,000	240,000	480,000	720,000	960,000
$2,500	300,000	600,000	900,000	1,200,000
$3,000	360,000	720,000	1,080,000	1,440,000
$3,500	420,000	840,000	1,260,000	1,680,000
$4,000	480,000	960,000	1,440,000	1,920,000
$4,500	540,000	1,080,000	1,620,000	2,160,000
$5,000	600,000	1,200,000	1,800,000	2,400,000
$5,500	660,000	1,320,000	1,980,000	2,640,000
$6,000	720,000	1,440,000	2,160,000	2,880,000
$6,500	780,000	1,560,000	2,340,000	3,120,000
$7,000	840,000	1,680,000	2,520,000	3,360,000
$7,500	900,000	1,800,000	2,700,000	3,600,000
$8,000	960,000	1,920,000	2,880,000	3,840,000
$8,500	1,020,000	2,040,000	3,060,000	4,080,000
$9,000	1,080,000	2,160,000	3,240,000	4,320,000
$9,500	1,140,000	2,280,000	3,420,000	4,560,000
$10,000	1,200,000	2,400,000	3,600,000	4,800,000

Source: *The Super Saver: Fundamental Strategies for Building Wealth* by Janet Lowe (Longman Financial Services Publishing: United States, 1990)

So what does your number look like? How much money are you and your partner likely to earn over the next decade or so? What if you take that out 30 or 40 years? My guess is that your joint lifetime disposable income probably adds up to something between $2 million and $4 million. Not quite so "disposable," is it? I suggest that from now on you stop thinking of your earnings as disposable income but rather as what I call "critical" income.

The bottom line is that you and your partner are trading precious time in your life for this income. To me—and hopefully to you—that makes it critically important to ensure that you don't waste what you earn, but rather that you manage it efficiently and intelligently. The key to doing this is to start saving now.

MYTH NO. 4
Taxes and inflation are now under control.

FACT NO. 4
Taxes and inflation are never going to be completely under control.

There seem to be two huge economic fallacies sweeping America today. One concerns inflation; the other, taxes.

According to the inflation fallacy, the fact that inflation rates have been low since the early 1990s means we've learned how to control it. That's absurd. As I write this, the cost of housing in my community has doubled in just five years. Gas prices have also doubled in the last five years. In my opinion, and in the opinion of most of the people I know, the cost of things is going up tremendously.

The five-bedroom, three-bath house in which I grew up cost about $100,000 when my parents bought it (brand spanking new in a nice area) a little over 20 years ago. Today, that same house goes for close to a million dollars. That's the reality of inflation. The truth is that a great many crucial commodities and services are not going to cost less in the future. They are going to cost more—in some cases a lot more. This means that your purchasing power (i.e., your available cash) is going to have to grow faster than inflation. If inflation averages 4 percent a year over the next 20 years—and that is probably a reasonable guess—then the dollar in your pocket today will have a purchasing power of only about 40 cents 20 years from now.

In a similar vein, many people assume that when they retire they will owe less in taxes because they won't be working. Really? Ask someone who's retired if they pay less in taxes than they used to. I'm very confident the answer will be no. Why? Because most of the income you will live on when you retire will be taxable. Specifically, when you pull your savings out of your deductible retirement accounts, you are probably going to have to pay income tax on those withdrawals. The same goes for the profits you've made on those annuities and insurance policies you've been funding for retirement.

The good news is that there is something you can do about it. Benjamin Franklin once said the only things in life that are certain are death and taxes. He was wrong. Death may be certain, but taxes can be delayed—and in the process reduced!

Many people pay way too much in taxes because they don't understand that there are many simple, legal ways to reduce their tax bite. One of the best involves a simple concept I call "pay yourself first." If you do it correctly, it can reduce your tax bill by thousands of dollars a year. We'll learn all about this concept in Step Five.

MYTH NO. 5

If we don't talk about money, everything will work out okay.

FACT NO. 5

**If the two of you don't start talking about money,
you'll more than likely die broke.**

I'm a very positive person, but when it comes to Americans and wealth management, the facts are frightening. The rich are getting richer and the poor are going nowhere fast. *Money* magazine recently reported that there are 7 million millionaires in America. Sounds like a lot of rich folks, right? Not when you consider that the population of the United States is almost 300 million. Do the math. Only about 2.3 percent of us are millionaires.

So what, you say? You don't have to be a millionaire to be doing all right—and most everyone else is still doing pretty well, aren't they?

Hardly. According to a study by Public Agenda, a nonprofit research organization . . .

Fully 50 Percent of Americans Under the Age of 50 Have Less Than $10,000 in Savings

And what of those baby boomers we keep hearing so much about? They're not so well off, either. According to the American Association of Retired Persons, only one in five baby boomers has more than $25,000 in assets. Moreover, according to the U.S. Department of Health and Human Services, 95 percent of Americans over the age of 65 still can't afford a retirement lifestyle that's the equal of what they enjoyed while they were working—a statistic that hasn't changed fundamentally in 20 years.

So what's the deal? How is it possible that in a booming economy, with an amazing stock market, where investing tips seem to be featured on every magazine cover and television show, most people are still watching *Who Wants to Be a Millionaire?* instead of being one? The answer is that while the economy as a whole may be roaring along, most people are not really taking advantage of the situation to accumulate wealth. People may be earning decent incomes these days, but most of us are not saving any money. As of February 2000, the U.S. savings rate was less than 2 percent.

Later on in this book, we will spend a great deal of time on how much money you and your partner will need to save in order to become wealthy and live rich. For now, rest assured that the average American is doing a pitiful job of saving for the future. So if the two of you feel like you're not doing enough right now to build a nest egg, there's no need to beat yourselves up about it. You are clearly not alone and you probably do a better job than your friends.

Then again, your goal is not to be average. It's to live and finish rich, and that means doing what most other people won't do.

So where do you start? That's easy. As in so many other aspects of life, the place to start getting your finances in shape is at home. Specifically, you and your partner must learn to talk about money together. The reason I say this is that in most families money is something of a "taboo" subject. Relatively few of us grew up in homes where Mom and Dad talked freely about the family finances with each other—let alone with the kids at the dinner table. As a result, most of us have grown up knowing nothing about money, including how to talk about it—even with the person with whom we've chosen to spend our life.

Smart Couples Talk About Money All the Time

The fact that most of us are not raised to talk about money is a real tragedy. Show me a couple who doesn't talk about money and plan their finances together, and I will show you a couple headed for financial trouble—if they're not already in it. When you work together on your finances, you can compound the results. When you don't, the same can be said for the mistakes you will invariably make. In general, two heads are always better than one. No matter what your specific goal happens to be, having a partner working on it with you, providing encouragement and ideas, makes achieving that goal much easier. More specifically, the two of you will probably find it easier to save more money together than either of you can save separately. Which leads me to one of the basic points of this book . . .

Couples Who Plan Together Have a Better Chance of Being Happy Together

This, in a nutshell, is what this book is all about. By planning your finances together as a couple, you will significantly improve your chances of becoming wealthy and being happier together.

Of course, nothing worthwhile comes without some effort. Because of the need for cooperation, it can sometimes seem more difficult for a couple to make financial plans together than for a single person to do the job on his or her own. But that's misleading. The trick is to get on the same page early on and then move forward as a team. So the place to start is by sharing your feelings about money with your partner.

Find Out How Your Partner Feels About Money

Being in a relationship is a funny thing. Once we find the person we've been looking for all of our lives, we begin to expect that this person should be able to "read" us. We think, "Gee, we know each other so well. I'm sure each of us knows how the other feels about *everything.*"

We all do this. But consider the following question: Do you really know how your partner feels about money? Do you know his or her values about money? In Step Two, you are going to learn a technique that will help you identify your values. In the process, you will discover how both you and your partner really feel about money at a core level. But that's for later. Right now, simply ask yourself this: On a scale of 1 to 10 (1 being "money is the root of all evil," 10 being "money is more important to me than anything else"), ask yourself, How important is money to me? Then ask yourself, How important do I think it is to my partner?

Record your answer below by circling the number that applies.

Money = Evil								Money = Most Important	
				YOU					
1	2	3	4	5	6	7	8	9	10
				YOUR PARTNER					
1	2	3	4	5	6	7	8	9	10

After you circle your own answers, ask your partner the same questions: How important is money to him or her? How important does your partner think money is to you?

How different were your responses from those of your partner? How different was your partner's response from what you expected it to be? How different was your response from what your partner expected?

The answers to these last three simple questions may lead to some very worthwhile conversations between the two of you.

I'm Not Sure My Partner Will Talk About Money with Me

Many people find it difficult to bring up the subject of money with their partners. As a result, the subject often gets pushed under the rug—over and over again. Maybe, they think, our money problems will just go away.

Trust me, they won't. They will only get worse. Dealing with financial matters is something any couple can do, but you've got to do the job yourselves, or it just won't get done. If the two of you don't make your finances a priority, they won't be one. Even if you hire a financial advisor, you've still got to make dealing with your finances a common goal that you both work toward together.

The couples who do the best financially are the couples who really work at it. They have done some soul-searching together, some dream-planning together, and they've put together a plan to make their goals and dreams a reality.

The Place to Start Is at Home—The Time to Start Is Now

The best way for the two of you to begin this process is by examining what you each know about your finances—and what you don't know. After all, before you can start planning how to get more out of your money and how to invest it wisely, you need to know exactly how much you've got, where it's currently parked, and just how accessible it is. You also need to understand what kind of financial commitments the two of you have—both separately as individuals and jointly as a couple.

To aid you in this task, I have created a simple true–false quiz that the two of you should both take. Take it separately—and be honest with yourself—then compare your answers. The goal isn't to get a high score or beat your partner; it's for both of you to discover how accurately (or inaccurately) you understand your current financial situation.

The "Smart Couples Finish Rich" Financial Knowledge Quiz

TRUE OR FALSE:

T [ ]　　F [ ]　　I know our current net worth (i.e., the value of the assets we have minus the liabilities we owe).

T [ ]　　F [ ]　　I have a solid grasp of what our fixed monthly overhead is, including property taxes and all forms of insurance.

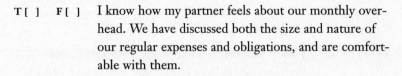

T [ ]   F [ ]   I know how my partner feels about our monthly overhead. We have discussed both the size and nature of our regular expenses and obligations, and are comfortable with them.

T [ ]   F [ ]   I know how much life insurance my partner and I carry. I know exactly what the death benefits are, how much cash value there is in our policies (if any), and what rate the money is earning (if applicable).

T [ ]   F [ ]   I have reviewed our life insurance policies sometime in the last 12 to 24 months, and I am comfortable that we are paying a competitive rate in today's insurance market.

T [ ]   F [ ]   I know the current value of our home, the size of our mortgage, the interest rate on the mortgage, and how much equity we have in our home. I also know the length of our mortgage-payment schedule and how much it would cost per month to pay down the mortgage in half the time.

OR

I know how much rent we pay, when our lease expires, how much of a security deposit we gave the landlord, and what renewal rights we have.

T [ ]   F [ ]   I know what type of homeowner's or renter's insurance we have and what the deductibles are. I know whether or not our policy would provide us with "today's replacement cost" or actual cash value, if our home and/or property were destroyed or stolen.

T [ ]   F [ ]   I know the nature and size of all of our investments (including cash, checking accounts, savings accounts, money-market accounts, CDs, Treasury bills, savings bonds, mutual funds, annuities, stocks and bonds, real estate investments, and collectibles such as stamps, coins, artwork, etc.). I also know where all the relevant paperwork is kept.

T [ ]   F [ ]   I know the annualized returns of all the above-mentioned investments.

T [ ]   F [ ]   I know the current value of all of our retirement accounts (including 401(k) plans, 403(b) plans, IRAs, Roth IRAs, SEP-IRAs, Keogh plans, company pension plans, etc.). I know where the statements for these accounts are kept and I have a solid grasp of how all our accounts performed last year.

T [ ]   F [ ]   I know what percentage of our income we are saving as a couple.

T [ ]   F [ ]   I know how much each of us is putting into our respective retirement accounts, whether that amounts to the maximum allowable contribution, whether our employers are making matching contributions, and what our respective vesting schedules are.

T [ ]   F [ ]   I know how much money each of us will be getting from Social Security when we retire, and what our pension benefits (if any) will be.

T [ ]   F [ ]   I know whether or not we have a will or living trust, what its provisions are, and how up-to-date it is.

T [ ]   F [ ]   I know whether our income would be protected by disability insurance should I or my partner become unable to work. If we do have disability insurance, I know the amount of the coverage, when the benefits would start, and whether they would be taxable. If we don't have disability insurance, I know why we don't have it.

T [ ]   F [ ]   I know what my partner's wishes are regarding medical treatment (including being kept alive by artificial means) in the event he or she falls seriously ill or is seriously injured. I know whether or not our will includes a valid power of attorney covering such situations. I also know how my partner feels about being an organ donor.

T [ ]   F [ ]   I know if my partner has taken an investment class in recent years.

T [ ]   F [ ]   I know how my partner's parents handled their finances and I know what effect that has had on how my partner feels about how we manage our money.

SCORING:

Give yourself one point for every time you answered "True," and zero for every time you answered "False."

14 to 18 points. Excellent! You and your partner obviously have been planning together, as a result of which you have a good grasp of the state of your finances and how you both feel about money.

9 to 13 points. The two of you are not totally in the dark, but there are some areas in which your knowledge is less than adequate.

Under 9 points. You and your partner don't make a habit of talking about money, do you? As a result, your chances of being hurt financially because of insufficient knowledge are enormous. You need to learn how to work together in order to protect yourselves from future financial disaster.

If you scored well on this test, congratulations! But don't go out and start celebrating just yet. Even among knowledgeable money managers, it's rare to find people who have a handle on *every* aspect of their own finances and what they could and should be doing to assure themselves secure futures. So even if you scored 12 or above, I guarantee you'll discover a few secrets and ideas that will be of enormous value to you.

So Much for the Bad News . . . From Here on in, It's all "Good"

If taking this quiz—or reading some of the myths and facts about money I presented earlier in this chapter—has left you feeling a little bummed out, I apologize. I personally can't stand negativity. In fact, I make it a policy to stay away from negative people. I believe they are like people with colds or the flu: if you spend too much time with them, you run the risk of "catching" what they have (i.e., their negativity).

But I started off this book with some cold, hard reality because I know that, as a couple, you want your life to be truly amazing. You want to live and finish rich, and you want to realize your dreams. You don't want money to hold you back; rather, you want it to lift you up. You believe in your relationship, and you believe in yourself, and you know deep down that you're smart enough to figure out how to make it all work for you.

Perhaps most important, you're looking to make a change in your life. That's why you purchased this book—because you are truly motivated to change for the better. But change takes action, and sometimes it takes pain to get motivated enough to take action. Sometimes it takes getting to a point where you say to yourself, "I've had enough. I want more out of life." Or you say, "Enough is enough, I'm not going to continue down the path I'm on."

Change is a funny thing. Although most people say they want to change—so they can have a better life, with more love, more dreams, and more fun—the fact is that many of us are afraid of change. Faced with the real prospect of it, we look at our lives and decide that being where we are right now isn't so bad, after all. Better the devil you know than the one you don't, we tell ourselves. Tony Robbins, the great motivational speaker (and a personal mentor of mine), calls this attitude a kind of "no man's land" of the soul. It's a place where your life isn't really that great, but it really isn't that bad, either. It's just so-so.

Well, I happen to think that life should be better than "not that bad" and more than "just so-so." Life should be exciting, challenging, and—ultimately—fulfilling.

By now, I hope this chapter has motivated you to start the process of taking action. Don't let those negative statistics I mentioned get you down. Remember, those averages don't have to be your reality. After all, you and your partner are not average! So stay motivated.

Now let's turn to Step Two, and continue your process of learning how to figure out what matters most to you and your partner when it comes to money.

STEP **2**

DETERMINE THE TRUE

PURPOSE OF MONEY

IN YOUR LIFE

AS A FINANCIAL ADVISOR, I specialize in doing what we call Purpose-Focused Financial Planning™. What this means is that before I start trying to figure out how much money my clients may need for their futures, I first help them try to get a clear idea of what they see as their purpose in life.

This concept often surprises people. The media and the investment industry have gotten us so focused on what they call "retirement planning" that everyone thinks personal finance is all about determining how much money you need at retirement. In fact, most people assume that when they meet with a financial advisor or planner the conversation should focus on specific investments, net worth calculations, tax rates, and how many years they will have to work before they can retire. While all these things are important, they are not what is most important. What I believe is most important is first having a conversation about what it is that matters *most to you*. What is it that you stand for and what it is that you care most deeply about? In other words, what are your values?

Your Life Values Should Determine Every Life Decision You Make

Stop for a second and really think about it: is there anything more important to you than your values? Where you live, how much you spend, what you focus your time and energy on—all are affected by your values. Your values color how you communicate with your partner, how you raise your children, and how you feel about what you have in your life. Your values can determine how hard you are willing to work to achieve your financial goals, how much money you currently spend, and how much money you will actually need at retirement. This is why I can tell you with total certainty that once you have a clear picture of what you value most in your life, you'll be able to create a truly meaningful Purpose-Focused Financial Plan.

To this end, Step Two of our journey to finishing rich involves learning how to understand what your values really are. Once your values are clear to you, it will be easy to decide what kind of "stuff" you want and what sort of things you want to do (which we will cover in Step Three). Perhaps most important, once you and your partner have clearly and specifically defined your values, you'll find yourselves much more motivated to put in the effort it takes to stick to your new Purpose-Focused Financial Plan.

The best way to explain the process of defining your values is to give you a peek at what it looks and sounds like when I explain the concept at one of my seminars.

Live from Hawaii—a "Smart Couples Finish Rich" Seminar!

Recently, I gave a "Smart Couples Finish Rich" seminar in Hawaii. The event was held on behalf of a company that wanted to reward its top employees and their spouses or significant others. When I walked into the seminar room, I found it filled with couples ranging in age from their mid-thirties to their mid-sixties. Some were newlyweds, while others had been together for more than 30 years and had multiple kids and grandchildren.

I began the seminar by introducing myself and asking a question. "My goal," I told the group, "is to share with you how you can do two things: (1) live rich, meaning live a life in line with your values, and (2) finish rich, meaning be able to retire with at least a million dollars in liquid assets."

Then I asked my question: "How many of you are basically in favor of both living and finishing rich?"

Just about everyone in the room laughed and raised their hands.

I then told them what I just told you at the beginning of this chapter—namely, that in order to figure out a sensible and meaningful plan for living and finishing rich, we first need to understand what our values are. "To do this," I said, "let me ask you all a really simple question:"

"What's the Purpose of Money in Your Life?"

"When you think about money in the context of your life and the things that are important to you, what purpose does it serve?"

The room was pretty much silent, so I repeated the question in a slightly different form. "When you think about the way you live, what are the values that money enables you to fulfill?"

Most everyone was still looking at me blankly. "Okay," I said, "I'm going to help you out a little bit with a cheat sheet." Using an overhead projector, I showed them a list of values. It included words and phrases such as "freedom," "happiness," "love," "health," and "making a difference."

"These are some examples of values," I explained. "Now let's see what each of you can come up with. When you think about your lives, what values are important to you? What is it that you're looking for in life?"

A woman in her early thirties raised her hand. "Teaching my children how to be good people," she said.

I turned to the whiteboard and wrote that down.

Then her husband chimed in. "Security," he said. "Knowing we are secure and our family is safe."

I wrote that down, too. "What about the rest of you?" I asked the group. "What is your purpose for being here on this planet? Why do you think you're here?"

"To have fun!" called out a woman in her fifties.

"Freedom!" a man shouted. "I want the freedom to do what I want to do when I want to do it."

"Yeah," agreed another man. "Like having the freedom to stay in Hawaii for more than five days."

Everyone laughed. " 'Having fun' and 'freedom' are values," I said, "but staying in Hawaii for more than five days is more of a material goal. The question is, if you could stay in Hawaii longer than five days, what value would that allow you to live by?"

The man's wife grinned broadly. "Viagra!" she shouted.

Now the room was cracking up. This guy turned bright red, and so did I. "Actually," I said, "you may be on to something. Maybe staying in Hawaii longer than five days would be good for your relationship. So the value here might be passion, love, or romance."

"Forget about romance," called out a sandy-haired man named Tom. "Staying in Hawaii more than five days would mean I could play more golf. That's what I want to do with *my* time."

I wrote "golf" on the whiteboard, but then I circled it. "Golf is a goal," I said to Tom. "The question is, what values does golf allow you live by?"

Tom shrugged. "Well, I don't know," he said, "but it's fun."

I wrote down the word "fun," then turned back to the group. "How many of you play golf?" I asked.

More than half the people in the room raised their hands.

"Okay," I continued, "those of you with your hands up, what values does golf provide you with?"

A fit-looking woman in her forties stood up. "It gives my husband and me a chance to spend four consecutive hours together," she said. "So it's a great way to have quality time with each other and also be outside doing something healthy."

"Great," I said. "So what values are those?"

"Well, for me, I guess it's the values of marriage and health."

"And the values of marriage and health are important to you?" I asked.

She nodded, and I wrote "marriage" and "health" on the board.

Then another woman spoke up and said, "I think spirituality is an important value. I think it's important to have a spiritual life."

So I wrote down "spirituality."

Yet another woman joined the conversation. "I like to spend time helping others and making a difference," she said.

No sooner had I finished writing down "make a difference and help others" then someone else called out another value, followed by another person, and then another. Within 10 minutes, we had filled two entire whiteboards with something like 30 examples of values people in the room said were important to them.

When things finally quieted down, I let everyone just look at the list of values for a minute. "That wasn't so hard, was it?" I asked.

Most everyone nodded in agreement.

"Well, now let's try something else," I continued. "Instead of coming up with values, let's think about the kind of stuff you want. What material things would you like to have that money can buy?"

The room just about exploded. "I want a new car!" a man called out. "No, jewelry!" his wife shouted. Everyone laughed. "That's right," another woman said. "More jewelry!" Then a second man said he wanted a new boat, followed by a woman who said she wanted a new kitchen. The guy who'd earlier talked about golf said he wanted to play more golf. And the woman who had mentioned Viagra yelled, "More Viagra!"

By now everyone was laughing and having a good time. And the suggestions kept pouring out. Whereas it had taken us a little more than 10 minutes to come up with 30 or so values, it took us less than three minutes to compile a list of maybe 30 different kinds of "stuff" that people wanted to buy.

"You know," I said, "it's always interesting to me how easy it is for us to list the kind of stuff we want to own versus the kind of values we want to live by. Yet the truth is that it's a lot more important to understand what your values are and to live your life by them than it is just to have stuff. Unfortunately, too many of us spend our lives pursuing stuff, without really looking at our values. And you know what that leads to?"

"Credit-card debt!" a woman called out.

We all laughed. "Well, that too," I said, "but actually I was thinking of something even more serious that happens when you spend 20 years focused not on your values but on getting more stuff. What happens is that it leads to a midlife crisis, which generally leads to all sorts of unhappiness, including divorce. The truth is that most midlife crises occur because people get to a certain age with all this stuff they've accumulated and suddenly it hits them that their stuff isn't really making them happy—that this stuff they've spent all this time and effort getting is actually the wrong stuff."

I went on to explain that this almost never happens to people who've got their values straight. "After all," I told the group, "how often does someone get to their fifties and look around and say, 'Well, I've lived my life in line with my values, but now I don't think I like my values anymore, so I guess I'll get divorced and start over'? Hardly ever."

In short, I concluded, values are the key to living smart and finishing rich. The sooner you and your partner start putting your values first—and stuff second—the sooner the two of you will start living a life that excites and empowers you both. That's because when you understand your values, you tend to live the life you really want almost automatically. Instead of having to "motivate yourself" to do the right things, you find yourself being pulled in the right direction by the power of your values. Stuff may be nice, but it rarely pulls us anywhere worthwhile. Only values can do that.

What's Really Important to You?

As a financial advisor, I've learned that when all is said and done money is good for three basic things. It helps people . . .

1) Be

2) Do

3) Have

Let me explain what I mean by this. When I say that money helps people be, I mean that it allows them to live in a particular way that defines who they are. When I say that money helps people do, I mean that it makes it possible for them to take actions that will help create the kind of lives they think they want. And when I say that money helps people have, I mean that it enables them to buy stuff.

Now, in an ideal world, the lives we lead, the things we do, and the stuff we buy would always be in line with our values. The challenge as I see it is that most people focus first on the "having," second on the "doing," and third on the "being." Which means that many people, even ones who use financial planners, go about it all backwards. Even worse, many people never even get to the "being" part. They spend so much time on the "having" and the "doing" that they never look up to see whether who they are is who they want to be.

In order to create a sensible Purpose-Focused Financial Plan, you must understand what money means to you, what values it can help you achieve. Once you know this, you can quickly focus your time and energy on what matters most to you—not what society, friends, or advertisers say matters, but what *you* say matters. To put it another way, the process is basically a matter of looking really deeply at what is most important to you, and then planning your finances around that. If it sounds like we're talking about more of a life-planning process than just a money-management process— well, quite frankly, that's what smart financial planning is really about.

Why Most Financial Planning Tools Don't Work

Consider this scenario. You are 45 years old, your income is currently $50,000 a year, and you've got $25,000 in the bank. You come to see me for retirement advice, and I plug those numbers into my fancy retirement-planning software. A nanosecond later, my computer tells me that you will need a lump sum of $1.5 million in order to be able to retire comfortably at age 65.

While you stare in disbelief, I ask my program what kind of savings and investment program you're going to need to set up in order to accumulate a lump sum like that. The computer hums silently, then tells us that if you can create a portfolio that generates an annual return of 8 percent, all you need to do to build an after-tax nest egg of $1.5 million is invest about $40,000 a year for the next 20 years.

"But David," you say, "I only *make* $50,000 a year—and that's before taxes."

"Hmm," I say, frowning. "That's a problem." I think for a moment, then brighten. "Well, don't worry. We'll just give your investment portfolio a higher return—say, 15 percent a year." I plug that into the program, and the computer decides that under these circumstances, you will need to save just $17,000 a year.

"But David," you say, "there's no way I can invest $17,000 a year—and, anyway, a 15 percent return is just not realistic."

"Oh," I reply. "I guess you've got a point." I think for another moment. "You know," I finally say, "any chance of an inheritance?"

Don't worry, I'm not really that ridiculous with my clients. The reason I created this scenario is to illustrate what can happen if you do financial planning strictly by the numbers, instead of by the life. What can happen is that you can all too easily convince yourself to not even bother trying. I constantly meet people in their fifties who gave up on their financial future in their late thirties because they felt it was already too late for them and there was no hope. That's sad, because it's never too late.

The point is that smart financial planning is more than a matter of numbers. It involves values first, and stuff second. Let's say you value security, but you and your partner are constantly spending more than you make as a couple. As a result, the two of you are living paycheck to paycheck. In other words, you are living your lives in massive conflict with your values, which creates massive stress. In a relationship, this can result in constant fighting and an end to passion.

Now, situations like this don't just happen. They are the result of repeated decisions and actions (like regularly spending too much money) that conflict with your value system. Your financial behavior simply doesn't match your personal values.

And don't think the problem is simply that you're not making enough money. Let's say your value is freedom, which to you and your partner means having the time to exercise every day and go on long walks together. Unfortunately, what you're actually doing is working 60 hours a week, which means you never have a chance to exercise or see your partner. Now, you may be enjoying financial success (in the sense that you're making a lot of money), but how likely is it that you're happy? Not very, because your life doesn't match your values.

Or consider this common dilemma. Your top value is family, but you are so busy working in order to be able to meet your mortgage payments that you never actually see your spouse and kids. Someone talked you into buying a bigger home than you could afford, and now you are paying the real price. No one (including you) considered your values when you purchased the house. Unfortunately, when you make big life decisions like that without considering your values, what you end up with is stress and unhappiness. No one wins.

So how do you get a clear picture of what it is you are looking for in life? Well, the good news is that you don't have to go into deep therapy, meditation, or be hypnotized. You don't have to delve back into your past and find out where you went wrong. You don't have to recite mantras ten times a day in front of a mirror. All you need to do is decide what you think your top five values are, write them down, and then start planning your life around them.

What is great about this process is that it's really not that difficult. In fact, it shouldn't take you more than 10 minutes or so. The reason it is so easy is that most people actually have a pretty good feeling—what I call "gut knowledge"—about what their values are. And to help you along, I've devised a simple technique using something I call the Value Circle™.

To get a feel for how this works, I'm going to let you eavesdrop on a real-life Purpose-Focused Financial Planning conversation I had with a client. By listening in, you should get a good sense of how the process works. Once you do, I'll show you how to create a Purpose-Focused Financial Plan for yourself.

Constructing Kim's Value Circle

Bill was 38; his wife Kim was 35. They had two little girls, ages 5 and 7. I started the conversation as I always do in such situations, asking, "Who wants to go through the Value Circle first?"

Kim immediately looked at Bill and then back at me. "I do," she said.

I nodded. "You know we're going to talk about money today," I began, "but before we do, let's talk about your values. When you think about your purpose in life and the things that really matter, *what's really important to you?* Specifically, what do you feel are the top five values you'd like to start focusing your time and energy on over the next 12 months?"

Having already attended one of my seminars, Kim didn't need a lot of prompting. "Definitely one of my biggest values is security," she said. "I was raised in a family that never had enough money, and I'm constantly in fear of not being able to pay our bills. So one of my top values is security."

I wrote down the word "security." "Now let's assume you had security in your life," I said. "What would be so important about having that security?

Kim said, "Well, if I had security, I would know that my family is always safe—that if anything happened to me, the girls would be taken care of. That is really important to me."

"So would you say family is a top value of yours?" I asked.

"Definitely," Kim said.

I wrote down the word "family." "And what's important about family to you?"

Kim smiled. "We have the most wonderful, beautiful girls, and I want to see them grow up to be happy, well-adjusted kids and, eventually, happy adults."

"Okay," I said, "let's see if we can turn that into a value you can focus on. Assuming your value of family is fulfilled and you raise great kids, what else is important to you?"

Kim immediately looked at Bill and squeezed his hand. "Well, Bill, of course," she said. "I want us to have a happy, lasting marriage like our parents did, where we grow old together. We already have friends who are getting divorced, and I don't want that to happen to us. So definitely a major value of mine is a strong marriage."

Bill smiled back at her.

"So one of your top five values is marriage," I said. I wrote that down, too. "Now let's say you are living in a way that really expresses your values of security, family, and marriage. What else is really important to you? If you were fulfilling those top three values and you could add two more to your Value Circle, what would you want to focus on?"

Kim looked hesitant. After a moment, she glanced at Bill. "Any ideas?" she asked.

I shook my head. "We'll get to Bill's values in a minute. Right now it's still your turn. If you could focus your time, energy, and passion on two more values, what would they be?"

Kim sighed and said, "Well, I guess I would also want to focus on my weight. I've gained about twenty pounds since I first had kids, and I feel bad about it. I know I need to lose weight, but I never seem to have the time to exercise, so let's put down exercise."

Again, I shook my head. "Exercise isn't really a value. It's something you do. Think about it this way: what's a value that exercise would promote?"

"Health," Kim said with certainty. "Health is definitely a top value I need to focus on."

"Health," I echoed, writing it down. "Great. And if you had health, what would be the last of your top five values?"

Kim frowned in concentration. "That's a tough one to answer. I think if I had really great health and all of those other values . . . I don't know—I guess I'd want to spend some of my time just having more fun."

"Well, fun is good," I said. "What does that value 'fun' mean to you?"

"Well, before Bill and I had kids, we used to be more spontaneous. We would go away on weekends and travel more. We had dates together. We did more things with our friends. It seems like a long time ago, and I'm not complaining because I love being a mom, but between my job, Bill's job, our house, and our two daughters, it doesn't seem like we have much time for ourselves anymore. I'd like to think there could be a way for us to start planning more fun time together."

"So fun would be a value you'd like to focus on?"

Kim nodded vigorously. "Fun sounds great. Let's definitely put that down as a value." She paused for a moment. "You know," she added, "I also really value my career, and we haven't put that down. Can we add career, too? Because I really want to focus on that, too."

"Kim," I said, "we can put down whatever you want. But for the purpose of this exercise, ideally I'd like you to focus on your top five values. So far we've put down security, family, health, marriage, and fun. Is your career an important enough value that it should replace one of these?"

She thought for moment. Kim worked for a software company that had recently gone public, and she earned a decent income. "To tell you the truth," she said finally, "if I focus on my career, the value of security is going to be taken care of. So I think I'd almost rather substitute career for security."

"Okay," I replied, "but let me ask you something. Is it your career that you value, or is it the security that your career brings you?"

Kim didn't hesitate. "Both," she said. "I consider it one value."

"Perfect," I said. "We'll put 'security/career' as one value in your Value Circle."

Constructing Bill's Value Circle

Now it was Bill's turn. He laughed when I gestured for him to start. "Can I just say 'ditto'?" he asked.

"No, Bill," I said with a smile, "you can't just say 'ditto.' "

"Well, you know," he replied, "Kim and I do have a lot of the same values."

"I'm sure you do," I said. "But we still need to do this. You need to think this process through, hear yourself talk about your values, and then see them written down on paper. So just play along for five minutes, okay?"

Bill nodded. "The truth is," he began, "when I think about all these things we're talking about—values and purpose and money— security isn't really something that I'd put at the top of my list. I know we'll always have a roof over our heads. We're making decent money and I'll always be able to find work." Bill was a contractor, and with the economy booming, his firm had more clients than it could handle. "What I really want is more freedom," he said. "My business requires me to work six days a week, watch over a crew of 20 men, and deal with all sorts of headaches. I want more freedom in my life."

"Okay," I said, "let's put down 'freedom.' Now assuming you had more freedom in your life, what would your next value be?"

"If I had more freedom, I would have more time. That's what I really want, you know—more time to do what I want to do, when I want to do it."

"Which would be what?" I asked.

Bill shook his head sadly. "I used to windsurf and play golf, and now I don't do either. You know, I haven't picked up a golf club in three years. That's pretty sad when you think about it. My company is doing well, but I don't have any time to do anything but work."

I nodded sympathetically. "And if you could play golf more and windsurf more," I asked, "what value would that promote in your life?"

"Well, just like Kim, I'd like to have more fun again," Bill said. "We are both doing well, we have a nice home, we've got two gorgeous girls, but we don't ever do anything fun anymore. Our life is boring."

"So what's the value, Bill?"

He looked at me and almost bounced out of his seat. "Excitement!" he boomed. "I want more excitement in my life."

Kim laughed. "Sure you do, Mister-watch-television-every-night-exciting-guy."

I had to laugh a little, too. "Okay," I said, "let's put down 'excitement.' Now what else, Bill? If you had freedom and excitement in your life, what other values would you want to be living by as well?"

Bill looked over at Kim. "Well, definitely family and marriage. But I consider those one value. To me, if I have a good marriage I'm going to have a good family. And if I don't have a good marriage, it's going to be hard to have a good family. So let's put them down as one value."

I nodded and did as he asked.

Then Bill turned a little sad. "You know what my next value would be?" he asked. "It would be friends. I barely see my buddies anymore.

I've got all these great friends, and we almost never talk or do anything together anymore, we're all so busy with our families. I really miss going out with them every once in a while and shooting the bull." ("Bull" wasn't exactly what he said, but you get the idea.)

I wrote down "friends." "You've got one more, Bill," I said. "What other value is important to you?"

"That's easy," he replied. "My parents. They live about a thousand miles away, and they can't really afford to visit very much, so my kids hardly ever get to see their grandparents. I'd really like to make an effort to talk to them more and see them more."

"So is 'parents' a top-five value for you?" I asked.

Bill looked at Kim. "I know we're really busy, honey, and the money is a little tight, but I do need to figure out a way to focus some more time on them. You know, they're not going to be here forever."

"Of course, that's fine with me," she said. "But you know, it's not just about us taking a trip to see them. There is a phone in our house, they have e-mail, and you can also write letters."

"I know," Bill said, almost guiltily. "You're right." He turned to me. "For now, let's put down 'parents.' "

"Great," I said. "Then you're done."

Does Your Financial Behavior Match Your Value Circle?

Now, while I was writing down Kim's and Bill's values, I wasn't just making a list. I was creating Value Circles for each of them. Here's what they looked like (see opposite page).

Notice that I wrote down Kim's and Bill's top five values not in a column but in a ring. There's a starting point to this ring, but there is no ranking. That's because we don't want to suggest that any one particular value is more important than any other. This reflects the fact that if you don't put a fair amount of effort into *all* of your top values, your life can become unbalanced. For example, we all know people who are great at creating security in their lives (that is, making lots of money) but who wind up getting divorced, their kids hating them, their physical condition a wreck—all because they didn't spend enough (or any)

THE VALUE CIRCLE ™

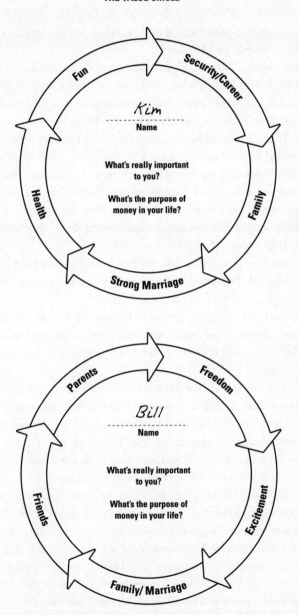

time cultivating any other values, like family, or fun, or health. The Value Circle not only allows you to see—and as a result, think about—what your top five values are, it also serves to remind you how important balance should be in your life.

Now, what does all of this talk about values have to do with money? Well, let's look at what we discovered when we compared what Kim and Bill said were their values to the way they were actually living their lives. The first value Kim mentioned as being important to her was security. When I pressed her on the subject, she explained that what she really wanted was to know that her kids would be protected if anything happened to her. As it turned out, however, when I looked into Bill and Kim's financial situation, I discovered that they had never bothered to draft a will or set up a trust, and that while they did have life insurance, they hadn't bought nearly enough coverage. In short, they were hardly living by their values of security and family.

When I pointed this out to them, they looked embarrassed. "Yeah," Bill said, "we know we've needed to do something about this. We've just procrastinated. Pretty dumb, huh?"

"Actually," I said, "it's perfectly normal. Wills and life insurance are almost always a 'do' item. Hopefully, now that you've looked at your values, they will become a 'must do' item, not a 'shoulda, coulda, woulda' item."

In a similar fashion, we worked through all the values they listed—looking to see whether their financial behavior was consistent with what they had identified as being most important to them. For example, when Kim admitted that the reason she wasn't working out was because she didn't feel like spending $50 a month on a gym, I pointed out that $50 a month was a small price to pay for a top-five value.

By the same token, when Bill thought about spending time with his friends, he realized that the main reason he didn't do it as often as he liked was because he always thought of it in terms of a major "guys' weekend," and most of his friends couldn't get away for that long or didn't want to spend the money. "You know," he finally said, "I don't know why I make such a big deal about this. I could just organize a monthly golf Saturday. We all like golf, and we can go to a public course." He grinned at Kim and me. "That gives me two values—friends and excitement—for the price of one."

"That's called value synergy," I said. "Often, promoting one value also helps fulfill another."

Kim, who had been sitting silently, lost in thought, suddenly spoke up. "Bill," she said, "you know how we're always complaining that we don't go anywhere because our big vacation costs so much?" She looked at me. "We generally take one big trip each year," she explained. "Last year we actually spent $3,000 going to Hawaii." Then she turned back to her husband. "You know, I'd almost rather go on three or four little weekend trips than a single big one. We could even just go camping. We'd get away more, we'd have probably the same amount of fun, and we'd spend a lot less money."

Kim went on to say that what she called "that 'spending money' thing" was a major source of stress for her and Bill. "I think we spend a lot more money than we need to," she said. "That's another reason I think we work so much. I'd like to see us get our expenses under better control so we could figure out a way to focus more on the things that matter to us—all this stuff we listed on those Value Circles."

Kim and Bill's Breakthrough

Kim and Bill got more out of the Value Circle process than just a few general ideas of things they needed to do. They actually got a complete, detailed Purpose-Focused Financial Plan. This consisted of a sheet of paper on which we listed the five values each had decided to focus on over the coming year. Next to each of the values, we wrote down five matching "do" ideas—that is, actions they needed to take in order to bring the way they lived their lives more in harmony with their values. (We'll cover how to do this in the next chapter, Step Three.) And next to those "do" ideas, we wrote down matching "have" ideas—that is, specific material goals that living according to their values would allow them to achieve.

This process may seem simple, but don't be fooled. It can also be very powerful. Indeed, within five weeks after completing their plan,

Bill and Kim finally had a lawyer draft a will for them—something they had talked about doing for nearly five years but never managed to get around to. They also increased their life-insurance coverage. Kim joined a gym. Bill planned his first golf Saturday with his buddies. And they worked out a plan to cut back on their spending.

The point is that doing this simple exercise got them to focus on what really mattered to them in life—to see through the clutter so they could concentrate less on having and more on being. Money is great to have, but all the money in the world won't make you happy if what you do with it conflicts with your values.

Creating Your Own Value Circle™

With this in mind, let's start to create your own Purpose-Focused Financial Plan™ by creating a Value Circle™ for both you and your partner. Although you can each do this exercise separately, it's much better to do it together. That way, if one of you gets stuck, the other can act as a prompter, asking questions such as "What does this value mean to you?" and "What's important about this value to you?" and so on.

So let's get started!

Pretend the two of you are arriving in our offices at The Bach Group in Orinda, California. You're going to meet with me in order to create your own personal Value Circle.

On the desk in front of you is a blank Value Circle sheet, waiting for you to tell yourselves and me (the recorder of the values) what matters most to you.

Here are some simple tips to get you through the process.

1. **First, relax.** This is not a test. It's meant to be fun. Our objective here is simple honesty. Write down only what feels right at a gut level. Don't put down a value just because you think it "looks" good. If it doesn't reflect how you feel in your gut, it won't really mean anything to you, and you won't focus or act on it.

2. **Start with the simple question,** What's really important to you? When you think about your life and the things that really

matter, what value is most important to you? What's the purpose of money in your life?

3. **Remember to stay focused on values**—not goals, not things, not stuff to do or buy. If, say, you worry a lot about money, you might be tempted to list as a value "having a million dollars." But that's not a value; it's a goal. The underlying value in this case would probably be security or freedom. The million dollars is just a way to fulfill one of those values. Similarly, many people say they want to travel. But "travel" is not a value; it's a thing to do. The value that travel promotes might be fun, excitement, or personal growth.

4. **As they occur to you,** write down values in the Value Circle until you have listed five core values that you can commit to focusing on over the next 12 months. You might find out that there are more than five values that you want to focus on. Some of my clients and students have come up with as many as 10 values. There's nothing wrong with that, if you are serious about your commitment. It's just that in my experience most people find it difficult to focus on more than five at a time.

5. **That's it.** You have completed the Value Circle. Give yourself a pat on the back.

THE VALUE CIRCLE ™

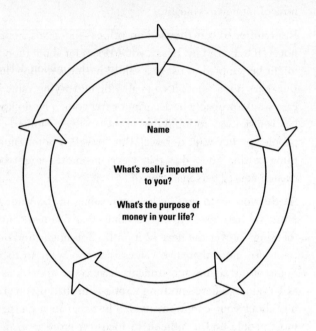

Name

What's really important
to you?

What's the purpose of
money in your life?

If You Find Yourself Getting Stuck . . .

Not to sound like a broken record, but your Value Circle needs to center on values or it won't work. Many people struggle with the difference between a value and a goal. Remember, values are about being; they define a way of life. Goals tend to be about doing and having; they involve stuff. To help you differentiate between the two, I've listed below some common values and some common goals. Use these examples to get yourself started, but don't just copy them down. In order for this exercise to be of any real use to you, you really have to care—at a gut level—about the values you choose.

Values vs. Goals

VALUES	GOALS
Security	Retire with a million dollars
Freedom	Pay off mortgage
Happiness	Be debt-free
Peace of mind	Not worry about debt
Fun	Travel
Excitement	Ski with friends
Power	Be the boss
Family	Spend more time with kids
Marriage	Plan more "date nights"
Friends	Annual "guys" or "girls" trip
Making a difference	Donate to charity
Spirituality	Go to church or temple
Independence	Stop working
Growth	Go back to school
Creativity	Learn to paint
Adventure	Take trip to Africa
Fulfillment	Stay married
Confidence	Exercise
Balance	Plan life better
Love	Have great marriage
Health	Lose weight

Please Don't Skip This Step

It's really easy to skip a step that requires you to stop, think, and act—especially when it involves something as unfamiliar as looking at your values. Some of my students—and even some of my prospective clients—think these value exercises are a waste of time, that they are nothing more than New Age, feel-good fluff. Well, believe me, there is nothing New Age about looking at your values. The Greek philosopher Socrates was talking about this exact type of thing back in 400 B.C. The key to human advancement, he taught, could be expressed in two powerful words: "know thyself."

So even if you and your partner would prefer to keep on reading, rather than stopping right now to create your Value Circles, I urge you to overcome your hesitation and carry out the exercise. The nine-step journey you are taking builds on itself. In the next chapter, we will look further at your Value Circle and come up with five "do" and "have" items to match your five values. So completing this step will make the next step much easier for you.

A Final Word About Values

It's amazing to me that so many of us can be with our partners for years, sometimes decades, and not know their most deeply held values. The fact is, there's just about nothing that can have more of an impact on a relationship than knowing what is really important to you and your partner. Unfortunately, they don't teach us in school how to look deep within ourselves and discover this knowledge. Nor do they teach us how to share it with the people who matter most to us.

If you have children, consider doing this exercise with them. There's no reason young kids can't start living life in line with their values. Think about the impact you could have on your children if you actually knew what their values were and helped make them real. Think about how much better your life would be if you had started doing this yourself when you were still a child.

There's also, of course, a very practical reason to define your values as clearly as you can. It's my experience that people will do more, and act more quickly, with regard to their finances when they understand how their actions relate to their values. The truth is that people will do more to protect their values than just about anything else in life. Certainly, values are a lot more powerful than any sense of obligation or responsibility. Values are not "to do" lists in disguise, nor are they New Year's resolutions such as "save more," "spend less," or "lose weight." People don't lose their motivation or get bored with their values. Once you've defined your top values clearly and written them down, they almost never leave you.

Ultimately, your values are what motivate you and shape your life. In fact, they have already motivated and shaped you, whether you know it or not. It's just that now you've chosen to be more proactive about them by consciously deciding which of your values you want to focus on.

Now that your Value Circles are complete, keep them handy because we're going to use them to start figuring out your specific financial goals. But before we do that, we need to look at where the two of you currently stand financially . . .

Because you can't plan where you want to go until you know where you are starting from.

PLAN TOGETHER . . .

WIN TOGETHER

NOW THAT YOU'VE CREATED your Value Circle, it's time to start creating your Purpose-Focused Financial Plan. To do this properly, you and your partner need to be on the same page—that is, both of you should be organized financially and planning for the future as a team. Teamwork is key to this effort. Over the years, I can't tell you how many times I've seen couples with modest incomes manage to finish rich simply by applying common sense and working together.

The best example of this I know involves a couple named Jerry and Lisa.

Jerry telephoned me on a Monday morning. That coming Friday, he said, after thirty years at a government job, he was going to be retiring. Could he and his wife come in on Thursday, he asked, to discuss his plans?

I called up his IRA account on my computer screen and reviewed his balance: $153,215. Jerry was 52.

Uh-oh, I thought. Either Jerry just inherited a lot of money or he's in for a rude awakening—and I'm in for a horrible meeting.

As it turned out, I was the one in for a shock. When Jerry and Lisa came into my office on Thursday, they were holding hands like newlyweds, literally bubbling with excitement. As Jerry talked about his plans and what he would do with his free time, Lisa kept exclaiming, "Isn't it great he can retire so young!"

After 10 minutes of this, I had to interrupt them. "What am I missing here?" I asked Jerry. "I only see $153,000 sitting in your retirement account. How can you possibly retire?"

Jerry smiled. "David," he said, "I can retire because Lisa and I have been planning this for the last 30 years." He went on to explain that right after they got married (he was 20, she was 18), he went to work for the government. He'd worked for the government ever since, bringing home an annual salary of about $40,000 in recent years. Lisa worked part-time as a hair stylist, earning about $17,000 a year.

Over the years, he continued, they'd purchased their home and a second house, a rental property, both of which they now owned "free and clear." They also had three cars and a boat, all fully paid for. "The kids are all finished with college," he concluded, "and Lisa plans to keep working for another 10 years. With her income and my government pension, I tell you, David—we won't be able to spend it all! We're set!"

I was stunned. As a financial advisor, I had plenty of experience with millionaires who were in constant financial trouble because they spent more than they made. Yet here was a couple who never earned more than $60,000 a year—sitting on top of the world.

"How did you do this?" I asked them. "How did you pay off your home, buy a rental property, save for college, put money away for retirement, and the rest—and do it all on a government salary and a hair stylist's income?"

Now it was Jerry and Lisa's turn to provide financial advice. What they taught me changed my life. It could also change yours.

A Little Planning Can Lead to Big Rewards

Jerry and Lisa's story begins with their parents. Both sets of parents were very conservative when it came to money, and they taught their children to use credit cards responsibly and never take on more debt than was absolutely necessary. "They told us that the way to buy a house was to get a 15-year mortgage and work toward paying it off as soon as we could," Jerry explained. "My father said if you don't have enough money to pay cash for something, don't buy it. My mom said that the time to start planning for our future was the first year we were married. 'Make your financial goals together each year,' she told us. 'Have fun making them and have fun sticking to them.' "

"But what about the rental property?" I asked. "How did you manage that?"

As Jerry told it, that was easy. "We bought our first house when I was 20, so it was paid off by the time I turned 35. Without any more mortgage payments to make, we had all this extra money each month. Lisa and I figured we could either waste it, or we could buy another house and rent it out. We realized if we bought another house, we could have it paid off by the time I hit 50, which is when I planned on retiring, and then we'd have extra income from the rental to live on."

And the three cars and the boat? They, too, turned out to be "easy." The cars are all used—none newer than seven years old, but all are well maintained so they drive like they are new. As for the boat, it was a long-held dream of Jerry and Lisa's that 10 years of disciplined saving made a reality.

Could it really be that simple? You just start planning at a young age, you work on your goals and dreams, you handle your money responsibly—and you get to retire in your early fifties? I looked at Jerry, still skeptical. "You know," I said. "You're pretty lucky Lisa still wants to work. If she didn't, you'd still have to."

Jerry shook his head. "It's not about luck," he replied. "Like I said, Lisa and I have been planning for this for a long time. About 10 years ago, I told her I didn't want to keep working for the government forever, and she said, 'Well, work until your pension kicks in and then I'll work part-time until I'm 60.' "

With that goal in mind, Lisa set about finding a job she loved, one that allowed her flexibility and the chance to be her own boss. It took a few tries but she finally found it with cutting hair.

"I'm telling you," Jerry said, "anyone can do what we've done. It's just a matter of planning it together."

I began this chapter with Jerry and Lisa's story because it is one of the best examples I know of a happy couple who never made very much money but who were still able to achieve all their goals because they planned their financial future together. The basic point can't be emphasized too much: if Jerry and Lisa could do it on a government salary and a part-time hair stylist's income, there's no reason you or I can't do it, too! All it takes is planning.

Failing to Plan Together Is the Same as *Planning* to Fail Together

Unfortunately, most couples are not like Jerry and Lisa. They don't plan together. Rather, they just let their financial life happen to them.

Letting your financial life just happen to you is like getting on an airplane with no clue as to where it's heading. It goes without saying that if you want to fly from San Francisco to New York, showing up at the Oakland airport won't do you any good. Likewise, getting yourself to the San Francisco airport on time but then getting on a plane bound for Los Angeles won't work either. Finally, even if you go to the right airport and get on the right plane, there's no guarantee you'll reach your destination unless you've got a pilot in the cockpit making sure you stay on course.

All this is obvious stuff when it comes to travel. Shouldn't it be equally obvious that the same principles apply when it comes to planning your financial life together?

There Are Three Fundamental Truths of Financial Planning

1) You can't plan your finances if you don't know where you're starting from.

2) You can't plan your finances if you don't know where you want to end up.

3) In order to stay on track from your starting point to your destination, you have to monitor your progress.

In this step—"Plan Together . . . Win Together"—we will discuss some simple tools and strategies to help us with that seemingly daunting task of getting our finances in order so that we can stay on track. We will also learn the importance of goal-setting in our relationships with our partners and in creating a rich financial future.

So . . . Do You Really Know Where the Two of You Are Right Now?

If I were to ask you and your partner right now to describe your current financial situation, could you tell me your net worth? Do you know what your assets and liabilities and expenses are? Could you easily list on a piece of paper what investments you own, how much equity you have in your home, and on what and to whom you owe money? Is all of this information neatly organized in some easily accessible place? Could you quickly get your hands on it if you needed to? Or would getting your records together be an impossible project?

Don't kid yourself about the answers to these questions. Be honest. Think back to that quiz you took in Step One. How well did you score? How well did your partner score?

If you're like most couples, you probably didn't score as well as you would have liked to. That's okay. In fact, it's normal. The goal right now is to start addressing those problems. Remember, you didn't buy this book to be normal, but to be above average—to be extraordinary, even. You bought this book—and are investing your time to read it—in order to finish rich.

Eight IRAs, Six Stock Certificates, Ten Credit Cards . . .

Bill and Nancy were a "normal" couple in their late thirties who came to my office because they wanted to get their financial act together. Married for 10 years, with two children, the two had been meaning to get their finances organized for years.

They brought with them a big file box of confusing paperwork—financial statements, annual reports, canceled checks, old receipts, you name it. "Here's everything," Bill announced. "Where do we start?"

Going through someone's financial records can be an amazing experience. It certainly was in the case of Bill and Nancy. For years, they had just thrown everything even vaguely financial into the file box. The good news was that they had kept a lot of records. The bad news was that they had clearly never bothered to look at most of what they had kept. Most of the reports and statements were still in the envelopes in which they had been sent—and most of the envelopes had never been opened.

After going through the contents of their box for a while, I discovered that between the two of them Bill and Nancy had at least eight separate independent retirement accounts. Eight IRAs for a couple still in their thirties. They also had five bank accounts, 10 credit cards, a home mortgage, several savings bonds, six stock certificates, and on and on. It took us the better part of an afternoon to figure out finally how much money they had and where it all was.

Insane, right? Totally the exception, right?

Wrong.

While you may not be this disorganized, I've learned the hard way that most couples don't really have a great system for getting and keeping their finances organized. This stuff is not taught in school, and most people are too busy working during the week to figure it out on their own. So they don't.

Don't worry, though. After one too many meetings like the one I had with Bill and Nancy, I sat down and created a system to help couples get their financial house in order quickly and easily. Over the years, thousands of people have used this system to take charge of their financial lives, and now I am going to share it with you.

Give Yourself a Financial Cleanup

When someone calls my office at The Bach Group to schedule a consultation about their finances, the first thing we do is send them my

FinishRich Inventory Planner™. This is a tool I developed to help people get their financial documents organized. Getting organized—what I call having a "financial cleanup"—is the first thing you need to do when you decide to get serious about financial planning. You have to clean up the mess before you can move forward.

In Step Two, I showed you how to identify your values when it comes to money. Having done that, now it's time to roll up your sleeves and get to work on the "task stuff." At the back of this book, in the Appendix, you will find a copy of my FinishRich Inventory Planner. Turn to page 279 and read through it. Don't fill it out right now. Just take a look at it.

Filling out the FinishRich Inventory Planner is one of the most important exercises in this book. It's a task that can literally change your life. But I don't want you to stop reading now. I want you to postpone filling out the form until after you both finish reading this book. Think of it as a "homework assignment" that the two of you will do later.

Even though I don't want you to stop and fill out the Planner, I do want you to take some action now. What I want you to do is to get your financial records in proper order so that filling out the Planner won't take you forever.

If you're like most of the students who take my investment classes, I'm sure you already have all of your investment information alphabetized in color-coded files with neatly typed labels. Since you have everything carefully stored in a nice, clean, easy-to-reach file drawer, locating everything you need to fill out the Inventory Planner is going to be a breeze. It probably won't take you more than 15 minutes or so. Right?

Just kidding. I'm well aware that most people's filing system consists of a shoe box or old book carton into which you toss all those bank statements, stock certificates, insurance policies, and other financial "stuff" you know you should keep but really don't feel like dealing with. Well, don't worry about it. Even if you keep your "files" in a ratty shopping bag hidden at the back of your clothes closet, I'm going to give you a system that will make managing your financial paperwork so simple that you'll never be disorganized again.

It's Time to Find Your Stuff

Before I explain the details, I want to say something to you from the heart. This book might be able to entertain you and get you thinking about some important issues, but there's no way it's going to change your life unless you are willing to take some real action yourself. The system I'm about to show you is so simple that the two of you will probably be able to set it up in less than 30 minutes. But because it's so simple you're going to be tempted to read right through the next few pages and say to each other, "Oh, that makes sense—we'll do it later."

Don't do it "later." Make a commitment to each other right now that you will get this exercise done in the next 48 hours. Do it while it's still fresh in your minds and you are motivated. Remember, the whole point of doing this is to improve your financial lives. I could care less about what your filing system looks like. What I care about is that you have an easy-to-use way of keeping track of your financial information—and that you have a clear understanding (meaning you've got it down in writing) of what you own, owe, and spend.

If you are one of the rare couples who bought a money-management software program like Quicken and actually used it for more than 90 days, then this process will be easy because you already have things pretty well organized. If not, don't worry. As I said, it shouldn't take you much more than half an hour. If it takes you longer, that's good. It means you really needed to do it.

THE FINISHRICH FILE FOLDER SYSTEM™

So here's what I want you to do. First, I want you to get yourself a dozen or so hanging folders and a box of at least 50 file folders to put inside them. Then I want you to label the hanging folders as follows:

☐ 1) Label the first one **"Tax Returns."** In it, put eight file folders, one for each of the last seven years plus one for this year. Mark the year on each folder's tab and put into it all of that year's important tax documents, such as W-2 forms, 1099s, and (most important) a copy of all the tax returns you filed for that year. Hopefully, you've at least saved your old tax returns. If you haven't but used a professional tax preparer in the past, call him or her and ask for back copies. As a rule, you should keep old tax records for at least seven years because that's how far back the law allows the IRS to go when it wants to audit you. I recommend hanging on to them even longer, but that's up to you.

☐ 2) Label the second hanging folder **"Retirement Accounts."** This is where you're going to keep all of your retirement-account statements. You should create a file for each retirement account that you and your partner have. If the two of you have three IRAs and a 401(k) plan, then you should have a separate file for each. And don't forget to write whose IRA it is on the top of each file. The most important thing to keep in these folders are the quarterly statements. You *don't* need to keep the prospectuses that the mutual-fund companies mail you each quarter. However, if you have a company retirement account, you should definitely keep the sign-up package because it tells you what investment options you have—something you should review annually.

☐ 3) Label the third hanging folder **"Social Security."** You should put your most recent Social Security Benefits Statement in this folder. If you haven't received one in the mail, get online and go to *www.ssa.gov* to request one. If you don't have Internet access, telephone your local Social Security office (the number is listed on the front of most phone books under "Federal Government").

☐ 4) Label the fourth hanging folder **"Investment Accounts."** In this folder you put files for each investment account the two of you have that is not a retirement account. If you own mutual funds, maintain a brokerage account, or own individual stocks, each and every statement you receive that is related to these investments should go in a particular folder. If the two of you have both individual and joint accounts, create separate files for them as well.

☐ 5) Label the fifth hanging folder **"Savings and Checking Accounts."** If you have separate checking and savings accounts, create separate file folders for them. Keep your monthly bank statements here.

☐ 6) Label the sixth hanging folder **"Household Accounts."** If you own your own home, this one should contain the following file folders: "House Title," into which you'll put all your title information (if you can't find this stuff, call your real estate agent or title company); "Home Improvements," where you'll keep all your receipts for any home-improvement work you do (since home-improvement expenses can be added to the cost basis of your house when you sell it, you should keep these receipts for as long as you own your house); and "Home Mortgage," for all your mortgage statements (which you should check regularly, since mortgage companies often DON'T CREDIT YOU PROPERLY*). If you're a renter, this folder should contain your lease, the receipt for your security deposit, and the receipts for your rental payments.

☐ 7) Label the seventh hanging folder **"Credit Card DEBT."** Make sure you capitalize the word "DEBT" so it stands out and bothers you every time you see it. I'm not kidding. I'll explain later how to deal with credit-card debt. For the time being, my hope is that this won't be one of your larger hanging folders. You should create a separate file for each credit-card account you and your partner have. For many couples, this folder may contain more than a dozen files. I've actually met couples with as many as 30. However many files you have, keep all your monthly statements in them. And hang on to them. As with tax returns, I keep all my credit-card records for at least seven years in case the IRS ever decides to audit me.

---

*I once saw a TV news report about how mortgage companies regularly make mistakes, so I went back and checked my mortgage statements. Sure enough, I discovered that 8 out of my past 12 monthly mortgage statements were inaccurate! It took me months to get my account corrected. Learn from my experience. Don't ever file your monthly mortgage statement without opening it. Make sure you always give these statements a close inspection!

☐   8)   Label the eighth hanging folder **"Other Liabilities."** In here go all of your records dealing with debts other than your mortgage and your credit-card accounts. These would include college loans, car loans, personal loans, etc. Each debt should have its own file, which should contain the loan note and your payment records.

☐   9)   Label the ninth hanging folder **"Insurance."** It will contain separate folders for each of your insurance policies, including health, life, car, homeowners or renters, disability, long-term care, etc. In these folders put the appropriate policy and all the related payment records.

☐   10)   Label the tenth hanging folder **"Family Will or Trust."** This should have a copy of your most recent will or living trust, along with the business card of the attorney who set it up.

☐   11)   If you have children, put together a folder labeled **"Children's Accounts."** It should hold all statements and other records pertaining to college savings accounts or other investments that either or both of you have made for your kids.

☐   12)   Finally, create a folder called **"FinishRich Inventory Planner."** Here's where you're going to put the worksheet on page 279 after you've filled it out. This folder will also contain a file in which you keep a running semi-annual total of your net worth—a vital record that will help you keep track of your financial progress.

That's it. You're done. A dozen folders—11 if you don't have children. Not so bad, is it?

As you begin the process of putting together your file-folder system, you may find you are missing some documents. In some cases (e.g., your Social Security Benefits Statement or your will), this may be because you never received or created the document in question in the first place; in others (e.g., copies of old tax returns), you may have inadvertently thrown them out. Whatever the reason, don't worry about it. Just put the files together as best you can and simply make a note of what you don't have. By the time you reach the end of this book, you will be totally organized and well prepared to fill in all the gaps.

Right now, you should feel great about the progress you've just made. Now that the two of you have started the process of getting your financial house in order, you're already in much better shape than when you first picked up this book.

What If My Partner Doesn't Want to Do This Exercise with Me?

Let's face it. Even if you're in a serious relationship right now (married or otherwise committed), the chances are slim that you and your partner simultaneously woke up one morning and said to each other, "You know what? We should head down to the bookstore and find a book about how couples can learn to manage their money together. Then we should read the book and get our finances totally organized. It will be a ton of fun and really help our future."

More than likely, one of you purchased this book on his or her own because he or she is concerned about your financial future as a couple. Chances are that this partner is really eager to get going on these exercises, while the other partner is a bit less motivated—maybe a lot less motivated.

Why do I say this? Because, for whatever reason, the fact seems to be that opposites attract. This is certainly true for most of the couples I know. Neat people wind up with people who are messy. People who understand how important it is to squeeze the toothpaste from the bottom of the tube marry people who are "middle squeezers."

I'm not going to try to be a therapist and pretend I know why we do this . . . we just do. And while differences can add real spice to a relationship, they can also cause real problems. Indeed, nothing motivated me to write this book more than that story I related in the Introduction about the woman who told me her marriage felt like a plane with one jet engine going full force ahead while the other was going full force in reverse. She wanted to bail out of the plane before it crashed. That story was really sad. And it's more common than not.

The Best Place to Start with Your Partner Is By Getting Organized

People always ask me what's the best way to start if you and your partner have never worked on your finances together. More to the point, they want to know, is there a way to get started without inevitably winding up in a fight?

My answer is simple. You set up what I call a "clean out the money files" date. That's what the FinishRich File System is all about. You say to your partner, "Hey, it's time we got our money files organized." Think of it the same way you think about cleaning out the garage: it's one of those chores that's so easy to put off, but don't you feel great after you finally get it done!

So here's what I recommend if this book wasn't a joint purchase but rather the result of one of you feeling it's time to get serious about your finances: approach your partner with this chapter and suggest that the two of you schedule two hours to put together a new file system. Now here's a sneaky suggestion. If your partner isn't interested in working with you on this, just start doing it without him or her. Just sit down at the kitchen table (or wherever) and start setting up the files. You'll be amazed how fast your significant other will come around and want to get involved.

Pulling together all your financial records and setting up a new filing system tends to spark the interest of even reluctant spouses and partners. After all, it's a little more serious—and important to their futures—than cleaning out the garage.

Don't Be too Aggressive: Offer Honey . . . not Vinegar!

Enthusiasm is a great thing. But too much can be counterproductive. One of the worst things you can do when you want to move forward positively in a relationship and deal with your finances is to start jumping all over your partner about what he or she is not doing.

I learned this the hard way when I first started doing my "Smart Women Finish Rich" seminars. Women would leave my seminars so excited and motivated that when they got home they would announce to their partners or spouses things like, "We are doing everything wrong. I just had this class with this financial advisor and now I know that you're going to die before me or divorce me for some bimbo, so show me where all our money is right now so I can fix the mess you put us in!"

Which was not quite what I had in mind.

After a few concerned phone calls from angry husbands and boyfriends wanting to know what I had been telling their wives or girlfriends (to which I would meekly reply, "Um, all I said was that they should do their financial homework and get their financial files organized"), I realized the importance of diplomacy.

As my Grandma Bach used to say, "You catch a whole lot more flies with honey than with vinegar." In other words, if you want to make planning and managing your finances a fun process that the two of you will undertake together, you should take care to raise the issue nicely.

That's just what a client of mine named Betsy did. She had attended one of my seminars and realized immediately that she needed to talk to her husband Victor about organizing their records, which by her own description were "a total mess." Fortunately, she also realized that if she jumped all over Victor about it, he probably wouldn't react well.

"What I did," she told me later, "was say to Victor, 'Honey, I've got a huge homework assignment from this seminar I took and I know I'm going to need your help. Do you think we could work together on it this weekend, because I'm not sure I can do it without you?' "

This proved to be the perfect way to raise the subject. No one was accusing anyone of anything (like letting their finances fall into disarray). Nor did it look like one partner was trying to take sole control of the couple's money. Because Betsy presented it as something she needed to do but couldn't without Victor's help, he was more than happy to work on it with her. What's more, she added, "When I showed Victor what the assignment was, he readily admitted it was something that we should have done years ago."

In the end, Victor wound up being grateful to Betsy for getting them to clean out their financial garage—and for realizing that they should be handling their finances together, as a team. "I have to admit it really felt good when we finished filling out the inventory worksheet that weekend," he told me. "For the first time in years, Betsy and I really discussed where our financial life was. By getting all of our assets and liabilities down on paper, we were finally able to see in black and white where we actually stood and how much our family was worth. While I always sort of had a running total in my head, filling out the inventory made it clearer and easier to deal with. I have to say, it's quite a weight off my shoulders to have Betsy now involved with our money. It takes some of the pressure off of me."

So remember to go for it and really do this project!

Small Successes Build Confidence and Momentum

Creating a filing system at home for your finances is not a big deal. In fact, it's such a small thing that it's easy to rationalize not doing it. You can say to yourself, "Yeah, sure, it sounds like a good idea, but we've got that stuff pretty much handled."

But stop for a moment and imagine what would happen if you actually went ahead and did it. Imagine if you actually made a "money date" with your partner to work on your finances together, and then the two of you got everything organized. Imagine how it would feel if every month when it came time to deal with your bills and other financial obligations, you could simply open up a file drawer and know where everything was.

If all this simple exercise does is give you a little more financial confidence, it's worth its weight in gold. The average American spends over seven hours a day watching television. All I'm asking is that the two of you plan to spend just two hours sometime in the next few days to get all of your financial information organized.

Believe me—sometimes all it takes to change your life massively for the better is a small action and a small success. I know from having helped so many couples with this filing system that it really can get you motivated to take massive financial action in your life . . . and that's what the remainder of this book is about.

TAKING YOUR VALUES AND MAKING THEM REAL

Now that you're getting organized financially, let's get started on your goals. Having given more than a thousand speeches and workshops over the last seven years, I know from experience that nothing can change a person's life faster than defining a number of specific, meaningful goals and then putting them down in writing. Believe me, simply writing down a few meaningful goals can literally transform your future in just a matter of days.

There is one problem with this approach. The idea of "goal-setting" is such an overexposed concept that the minute they hear it, most people almost automatically shut down. Their brains go, "Oh, not that goal-setting stuff again! Give me some other secret." If you are thinking this right now, I do understand. But hear me out, and then take 10 minutes to try out my suggestions. You've come this far. What's a few more minutes?

So why do you need to set goals? Here's the bottom line . . .

Life Is Difficult

The fact is that it's not easy to get good grades, or graduate from college, or find someone to love and then have a great relationship (or marriage). It's not easy to succeed in work or business. It's not easy to become wealthy. It's not easy to raise good kids. It's not easy to stay thin.

I could go on and on, but you get the point. Life is not easy. But that's not the only truth that matters in this context. It also happens to be true that it takes just as much effort to have a "bad life," in which you don't get what you want, as it does to have a "good life," where you do. So given the choice, why not go for the good life?

Even if you wind up falling short in the end, it's still worth trying for a good life. After all, whether or not you win in the end, if you "show up for the game," at least you get to play. Unfortunately, most people are not in the game. They simply let their lives happen to them. They live as if they were in a raft heading downstream without a paddle. Wherever the river of life takes them, that's where they go. And you know where most of these people end up? On the rocks!

It's sad but true. Most people who just "go with the flow" wind up complaining about where they "floated." They go around saying life is not fair. Well, I disagree. Life is totally fair. You get what you go for. Go for nothing and you get nothing. Go for something, and even if you miss your main goal, you might still achieve a lot of good stuff along the way.

I'm not just saying this. Goal-setting works. It's a fact. The world is filled with people who started out with nothing and wound up with more than they ever dreamed—simply as a result of having set goals for themselves. One phenomenal example of this is a woman we all know and love named Oprah Winfrey. Here's someone who grew up poor, was sexually abused as a child, was told she'd amount to nothing, and yet became one of the greatest role models of our time. Now, Oprah didn't wake up one morning when she was a teenager and say, "I think tomorrow I'll have my own TV show and influence the lives of millions of people every day." She worked for decades, setting goals and battling against all kinds of obstacles to make it happen.

The same could be said of a man we all know named Michael Jordan. Arguably the greatest basketball player of all time, Michael didn't suddenly wake up in his late twenties and say, "I think I'll be the greatest basketball star who ever lived." This was a guy who couldn't even make his high school varsity team when he first tried out. People told him to forget basketball when he was young. But Michael had dreams, he had goals, and he worked against all challenges to make them real.

So how does this impact the two of you? You don't have to want to be Oprah or Michael Jordan. I'm not asking you to decide right now to change the world or become the "greatest ever." I'm simply suggesting that you and your partner sit down, take the five values we looked at in Step Two, and set yourselves five specific goals (at least one of which should have something to do with your finances) that the two of you intend to achieve over the next 12 months. In this way, you'll create for yourselves that Purpose-Focused Financial Plan I've been talking about.

DESIGNING YOUR PURPOSE-FOCUSED FINANCIAL PLAN™

So what is a Purpose-Focused Financial Plan? A Purpose-Focused Financial Plan is nothing more than a list of things to do (your goals) to enable you to live a life in line with the values that are most important to you. Here are seven tips on how to define those goals, followed by a worksheet that will help you create your plan.

RULE NO. 1
Make sure your goals are based on your values.

As we discussed in Step Two, identifying your top five values may not sound like much, but doing this simple exercise can transform your life. That's because the clearer you are about your values, the easier it is to base your goals on them—and the more you base your goals on your values, the more likely it is that you will achieve them. After all, can you think of anything better or more exciting to plan your spending and investing around than the things that really matter to you? And what could matter more than the values by which you and your partner want to live and grow?

Of course, living the life you want based on your values doesn't just happen. You have to make it happen. You have to design it. This means using the Value Circle from Step Two and getting your top five values clearly defined. And remember, don't get hung up on perfection here. There are no "perfect" values or even "right" values. The idea is simply for you and your partner to start thinking and planning proactively on the basis of what is most important to you.

Ideally, each of these top five values should lead you to a specific key goal. You'll write down a value and then, right next to it, a related goal on which you want to focus your time and energy.

RULE NO. 2
Make your goals specific, detailed, and with a finish line.

I can't emphasize enough the importance of making your top five goals as specific as possible. On the worksheet, you'll find five boxes designed to help you do just that.

Many couples want to be wealthier. Others want to be more romantic. Still others want to build a strong family. Practically all of us want something we don't currently have.

Unfortunately, wanting something and getting it are two different things. In order to achieve a goal, you must know precisely what it is that you're after. In other words, you need to take those vague ideas and thoughts you have about what sort of life you'd like and make them specific.

For instance, I would love to have a vacation home. Now I could say that one of my goals is eventually to buy one, and I could write down on my worksheet: "own a second home." But what would that accomplish? Not much, because a general phrase like "own a second home" doesn't help my wife or me focus on what we really need to do to get where we want to go. Where would this second home be? How much would it cost? What would it look like? When would I buy it? How long would it take us to save up for it?

On the other hand, what if I were to think my goal through and describe it this way: "Within the next three years, I intend to buy a five-bedroom, three-bath vacation house on the west shore of Lake Tahoe with a dock from which Michelle and I can go swimming"? Well, that's something we can literally see. We can visualize exactly what this second home of ours looks like. We can also find out what a property like that would cost. We can figure out whether it's a realistic dream for us. We can design a plan to start saving for it.

We can even draw up a timetable. For example, we might decide that our intention is to purchase our Tahoe house no later than the spring of 2003 and later that year spend the months of July, August, and December there.

Now our goal is starting to feel real, to feel exciting. Perhaps most important, because we've included a timetable, we can tell if we're on the road to making it happen or if we're just fooling ourselves. If we get to, say, the middle of 2002 and we haven't yet begun to put money away for the down payment on our vacation home or to do any research on what sort of properties are available in the areas we like, that's a pretty good indication that we need to rethink how serious we are.

Needless to say, your goal doesn't have to be buying a dream house in Lake Tahoe. Getting your credit-card bills paid off over the next 12 months can be a specific and measurable goal. So can going to Hawaii on a dream vacation sometime in the next two years. Or cleaning out the house from top to bottom in the next three months.

RULE NO. 3
Put your top five goals in writing.

I know it's a cliché, but it also happens to be true: people who write down their financial goals get rich. It's a fact. Study after study has shown that writing down your goals makes it much more likely that you'll achieve them. Having been a goal-writer for years, I can tell you from experience that when you write down a goal on paper, even if you put the paper in a drawer and don't look at it for a year, the chances are that what you've written down will come true.

Writing down goals is truly an amazing thing. It does something to you subconsciously that often brings the goal to you. For one thing, writing down your goals helps you make them more specific. For another, it makes your goals seem more real to you. The more real your goals are, the more excited the two of you will get—and the more excited you get, the more likely it is that you'll make it to the finish line.

When you write down your goals, you make them important. When you write down important goals, you make your life purposeful.

RULE NO. 4
Start taking action toward your goals within 48 hours.

I learned the power of action at a seminar called "Date With Destiny" run by Anthony Robbins. "It's not enough to write down your goals," he told us, "you've got to act on them." His rule of thumb was that you should never leave a goal just "sitting there" without taking some action toward achieving it within the next 48 hours. The idea, he explained, was that if you don't get moving immediately toward your goal, even if only in a small way, chances are you'll never get moving at all.

Nothing I've ever learned about goal-setting has ever had as much impact on me—and on the results I've achieved—as this simple tip. What I've learned from Tony Robbins over the last 10 years is that a cause set in motion becomes a life set in action. This is why our Purpose-Focused Financial Plan worksheet includes a box that asks you to write out your "48-hour action step." This can be anything—but it has to be something.

Let's go back to my example about purchasing a home on Lake Tahoe. Even if I don't think I'm actually going to be able to buy it for five years, there are still things I can do to start moving toward my goal right away. I can get on the Internet and start reading about Lake Tahoe. I can contact a few realtors in the area and ask them to send me information on homes that meet my criteria. I can subscribe to a Tahoe newspaper in order to be able to check out the real estate ads. I can plan to rent a home in Tahoe for a few weeks so Michelle and I can see how much we enjoy being up there for more than a few days.

The point is I can "do something," and I can do it within the next 48 hours. By taking this sort of specific immediate action, my goal becomes even more real to me and thus even more exciting. It's this excitement that will ultimately create the lasting energy the two of you will need in order to see your goal through to reality.

RULE NO. 5
Enlist help.

There's a huge myth out there that I'd like to bust: the myth of the "self-made" person. People typically use this phrase when they're talking about some success they have achieved or the wealth they have accumulated, and to be fair, they often do it in order to differentiate themselves from people who inherited their wealth or position. That's fine, but the truth is that there is no such thing as a "self-made" person. No one ever reaches a really important goal without some sort of help from some other person. No matter what the situation is, human beings need other human beings to help them move forward.

So when it comes to achieving your goals, stop and think for a second. Whom can the two of you turn to for help in achieving your top five goals? Don't assume you and your partner need to do all this by yourselves. There are all sorts of wonderful resources out there just ready and waiting to help you make your goals a reality. Some of them are probably living right in your own home. If you have kids, perhaps they can help you. What about friends who may be able to offer assistance? Now move beyond the people you know and start thinking about people you may need to *get* to know.

While there's nothing more important than sharing your dreams and goals with the people you love and trust, it also doesn't hurt to share them with strangers either. You never know—the person you're sitting next to at a dinner party or a lecture may be in the perfect position to help you make your dream a reality. If you keep your goals to yourself, you could miss your big chance.

I once had a woman in one of my seminars who worked as an administrative assistant for an adult education company but whose dream was to be an animation artist. Following the rules I've just laid out for you, she made her goal specific, gave herself a deadline, wrote it down on paper—and began telling everyone she met just what she was after. Sure enough, someone she met at a party told her about a job opening, and just four weeks later she was hired as a creative director at a start-up company designing online greeting cards. I promise you, it wasn't a fluke. It's just a matter of sharing your dream—and not being afraid to go for it.

Later on in this book, we're going to cover things like retirement accounts, wills, insurance, systematic investment plans, how you can increase your income in just nine weeks, and on and on. Many of these things will require you to enlist help. That's great. There is nothing wrong with asking for help. So make sure you include on your worksheet a list of the people whom you should be enlisting to help you achieve your top five goals.

RULE NO. 6
Get a rough idea of how much money it will cost to achieve your goals.

As you define your top five goals, you're going to find that some may have nothing to do with money, while others are all about money. Some goals will take almost no time to save for, and some goals may take a lot of time and investing to reach. Since it's important to know which is which, part of creating a Purpose-Focused Financial Plan involves estimating how much money you think you will ultimately need to pay for your top five goals.

So ask yourself, What is this goal going to cost? How much do I need to start putting aside each week or month to help me get there?

If a goal is going to cost money, and you don't start planning and saving for the cost, you are not going to achieve it. Later, in Step Seven, I'll discuss which types of investments you should use to pay for your dreams and goals. For now, just note in the appropriate box on the worksheet a rough estimate of how much money you think you're going to need. (If you don't have a number in mind right now, don't worry about it; you can fill it in later.)

The reason this box is so important is that you may find some of your biggest goals require almost no money. Which means you can get started on them right away. On the other hand, you may discover that some of your top five goals are so expensive that it's not even realistic to put them down on paper. That's not to say you should forget about them, but it may be a sign you should do some rethinking. Some goals that at first glance seem impossibly pricey might on closer inspection turn out to have cheaper solutions. For example, you may find that owning a beach house is so expensive that short of winning the lottery, you'll never be able to afford it. But renting one for a few weeks each year may not be out of the question—and, indeed, it may be a better way to get you started on the road toward your ultimate goal.

The point here is that you need to get a sense of what it is going to take in dollars and cents to achieve your various goals. This will enable the two of you to do two things: (1) understand how realistic (or unrealistic) your goals may be, and (2) get yourselves started on a systematic savings and investment plan to accumulate the money you are going to need to achieve them.

RULE NO. 7
Make sure your goals match your values . . . as a couple.

I can't stress enough the importance of making sure your goals reflect what *both* you and your partner want. Remember that goal I mentioned of someday owning a vacation home in Tahoe? It's something I've personally wanted since I spent a summer up there when I was 18. But now that I'm married, goal-setting is not just about me anymore . . . it's about "us." And just because I want something badly doesn't mean Michelle wants it (and vice versa).

Michelle and I don't have kids yet, and we've talked for a long time about doing some serious traveling before we become parents. But guess what? Like so many couples, we've talked about doing something and not done it. We've both been working so much that we've managed to take only two weeks of vacation in almost two years. Recently, when Michelle and I were discussing our top five goals, she pointed out to me that we weren't getting any younger and that if we were going to travel, the time to do it was soon.

Viewed in this light, my goal of buying a house in Tahoe in the next three years doesn't make a lot of sense. And indeed, after discussing it thoroughly, Michelle and I agreed that my dream of owning a second home would have to wait. Right now, we needed to focus on our goal and dream of traveling.

It never ceases to amaze me how many couples don't set goals together or share their dreams with each other. What's the point of being with someone if we don't share our most intimate dreams and thoughts with them? Some people, of course, have partners who aren't supportive, partners whose dreams and goals are so different from their own that they just can't get together on them. If that's your situation, you've got a problem—a problem this book can't solve. Fortunately, most people who tell me their spouses or significant others don't support them aren't really in that fix. They're just not giving their partners enough credit.

So don't keep your top five goals to yourself. Share them with your partner. If you've got kids, share your dreams with them, too. Ask them what they'd like to see the family doing over the next three years. Ask them about their values, and then work together on a family list of five things that you all want to accomplish together. Nothing brings a family closer like planning major goals together. By discussing our goals, values, and dreams together, Michelle and I began the process of creating our future together. You can do the same thing with your family.

Okay, enough talk about the tools. It's time to go to work and set some goals.

Let's Get Started!

Use the Purpose-Focused Financial Plan worksheet that follows to get yourself thinking about what five key things you would like to accomplish over the next 12 months. Remember, you want these goals to be specific and measurable—things like paying off your credit-card debt or saving up the down payment for a house. In the back of the book, you'll find two additional worksheets—one for your partner, the other for the two of you to fill out together as a couple.

While you are thinking about the five key things you'd like to accomplish in the next 12 months, your partner should be doing the same with his or her goals. Once you've both finished, sit down together and use the third worksheet to figure out your goals as a couple.

To put yourself in the right frame of mind to define your goals, use what I call the Clarity Question. It's exactly what I ask in my seminars to get my students to get started on their action plans.

> *"Twelve months from now, what five specific things would you need to have accomplished in order to feel you have made great financial progress in your life?"*

PURPOSE-FOCUSED FINANCIAL PLAN™
Designing a Proactive Year

The goal of a Purpose-Focused Financial Plan is to write down what you are going to focus your energy on in the next 12 months. To do this, follow the six steps below and fill in the worksheet on the following page:

1. List your top five values. Ideally you already did this in chapter three when we covered the concept of creating your Value Circle. Remember you are writing down values first to address the issue of who you want to "be" as a person.

2. Based on your top five values . . . write down specifically what you want to "do." Your top five "to do's" will be your top five goals for the next 12 months.

3. Now it is time to make these goals specific and measurable. Remember the more detailed and provable, the better.

4. In the fourth box on the next page, it's time to hit hard the "action plan." What action can you take in the next 48 hours to move toward your goals? Remember that "I don't know" is not acceptable. The answer to "I don't know" is . . . "I know you don't but if you did, what would you do in the next 48 hours to get moving?"

5. Who are you going to go to for help? Be specific. You will need help if your goal is big and worth going for. In this box, write in who could help you reach your goal.

6. When are you going to start and when is your deadline to finish?

PURPOSE-FOCUSED FINANCIAL PLAN ™

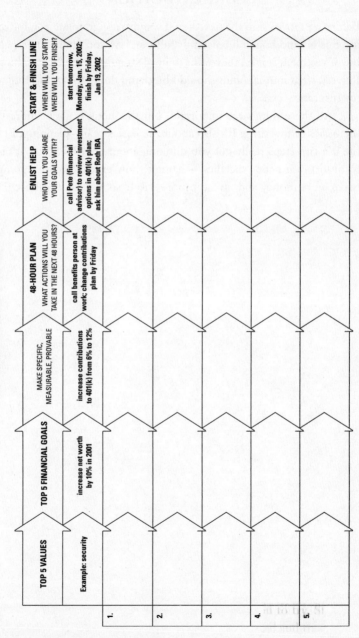

TOP 5 VALUES	TOP 5 FINANCIAL GOALS	MAKE SPECIFIC, MEASURABLE, PROVABLE	48-HOUR PLAN WHAT ACTIONS WILL YOU TAKE IN THE NEXT 48 HOURS?	ENLIST HELP WHO WILL YOU SHARE YOUR GOALS WITH?	START & FINISH LINE WHEN WILL YOU START? WHEN WILL YOU FINISH?
Example: security	increase net worth by 10% in 2001	increase contributions to 401(k) from 6% to 12%	call benefits person at work; change contributions plan by Friday	call Pete (financial advisor) to review investment options in 401(k) plan; ask him about Roth IRA	start tomorrow, Monday, Jan. 15, 2002; finish by Friday, Jan 19, 2002
1.					
2.					
3.					
4.					
5.					

CONGRATULATIONS!

Before we move on to the next step, I want to congratulate you for reading this far and hopefully playing "full out." All too often, when people buy investment books, they want to head straight to the "facts": how do I invest, what mutual funds should I buy, am I doing the right thing with my insurance, etc.

All these things are important, but this book is about more than the basics of investing. It's also about the basics of life-planning. I hope the last two steps really got you thinking about your life. Now it's time to head toward the "specifics"—namely, how exactly are you going to make more money and invest it more wisely so you can finish rich?

THE COUPLES'
LATTÉ FACTOR™

The Problem Is Not Our Income . . . It's What We Spend!

IF YOU REMEMBER ONLY ONE THING from this book, it should be the sentence above. The reality of life is that just about everyone in America makes enough money to be wealthy. So why aren't we all rich? The problem isn't our income; it's what we spend.

What do most Americans do with their hard-earned money? They waste a lot of it. That's right—they simply waste a lot of it every day on "small things." I put that phrase in quotes because, as we shall see, it is quite misleading. So-called "small things" can add up very quickly to some amazingly large amounts.

In this, the fourth step of your journey to becoming a Smart Couple who finishes rich, you are going to learn how anyone can become wealthy on practically any income. In the process, you're also going to learn to appreciate the power of your money and the importance of the wealth for which you work so hard.

Most of us don't really think about how we spend our money—or if we do, we focus solely on the big items. At the same time, we ignore the small but steady expenses that drain away our cash. We don't think about what it cost us to earn our money and we don't realize how much wealth we could have if, instead of wasting it, we invested it. By understanding what I call the Couples' Latté Factor, you're going to change all that. The point is, you work hard for your money, and your money should work just as hard for you!

Americans Have a Spending Problem

I know *you* don't have a spending problem, do you? But trust me on this—if you don't, your friends and neighbors probably do. The fact is, U.S. consumer debt is at record highs, currently totaling more than $1.3 trillion! Upward of one million people a year declare bankruptcy in America. It's almost patriotic to spend yourself into poverty.

It's not hard to figure out why so many people have been going broke. These days you can buy just about anything without actually having to pay for it . . . at least not until later. You can go to a furniture store and decorate your whole house, and the nice people there won't bill you for 18 months. Or maybe you want a new car or a boat, or both. No problem. You just go to the showroom, smile, and—presto!—you've got yourself a brand-spanking-new BMW or Mercedes with low monthly payments.

You can even buy a house with no money down. Heck, there are banks that will let you buy a house with no money down and then loan you some extra cash so you can pay off your credit cards. (These are known as 110 and 125 percent home-equity loans and, no, you don't want one.)

With all these opportunities—all these temptations—all over the place, who wouldn't give in? Gosh darn it, we're working hard. The world is a tough place. We deserve nice stuff. Not only that, but we deserve it now! Forget about saving. Give me my stuff today. *FedEx* me my stuff. And, oh yeah, while we're at it, make sure to put it on the credit card that gives us frequent-flyer points. Don't they have some sort of special promotion this month where we can earn extra miles? Maybe we should spend a little more and get a little more stuff.

Now if you think I'm starting to sound a little silly here, you're right—this is silly. But does it sound at all familiar? Do you know these people? Maybe intimately?

Okay, not everyone is that bad. Not everyone is out there leasing a new BMW every two years. You're probably not. But does that mean you should pat yourself on the back? Not necessarily.

All too often, being careful about the big things makes us feel as if we can afford to forget about the little things. We don't like to admit it, but it's true. There's a tendency to say to ourselves, "I'm not wasteful with my money, but gosh darn it, I should at least be able to buy myself a nice cup of coffee and a bagel in the morning. I ought to at least be able to rent a few videos tonight and pick up a pizza. Five dollars here and $5 there isn't such a big deal, is it?"

Well, maybe it is. Maybe $5 here and there can become a million-dollar deal if you invest it right.

Got your attention, didn't I? Well, I'm not exaggerating. It's true. There is a simple and sure way of turning your small savings of $5 here and $5 there into big results. It's so simple, in fact, that I can sum it up in just three words—three critical words in a Smart Couple's vocabulary . . . they are . . . The Latté Factor.

THE COUPLES' LATTÉ FACTOR™

What's a Latté Factor? The Latté Factor is a simple concept that evolved from a seminar I did where a couple suggested to me that they simply did not have $5 to $10 a day to save for retirement. What we learned over the course of a conversation was that this couple actually had more than enough income to become wealthy. As I said in the beginning of this chapter, the problem wasn't their income, it was what they were spending. The best way to explain this powerful yet simple concept is to share with you their story.

Jim and Susie Learn About the Couples' Latté Factor

At one of my financial-management seminars, a guy named Jim stood up at the end of the third day of a three-day class and in a few words nearly wiped out nine hours of teaching on my part.

Jim was in his mid-thirties. He had come to the class with his wife, Susie. "David," he said, "your class has been great, and your stories are cute, and your idea about putting your money into a retirement plan makes sense. But in the real world, it just won't work. You talk about putting aside $5 or $10 a day like it's no big deal. In the real world, we don't have an extra $10 a day to save. In the real world, we live paycheck to paycheck. In the real world, we're broke."

Completely deflated, I looked at him in disbelief. My financial-advisor brain thought, "You've got to be kidding. Everyone can manage to save $10 a day."

But then I looked around the room and noticed that a lot of people were nodding in agreement with what Jim had just said. They, too, were feeling like there was no way they could save an extra $10 a day.

Was I wrong? Was it completely unrealistic to think that everyone could find an extra $10 a day to put into a retirement account? There was only one way to find out. I turned back to Jim and asked him to take me through a typical day of his and tell me how he spent his money.

"Let's start in the morning," I said. "Before you go to work, do you drink coffee?"

Jim looked around nervously, as if I'd asked him a trick question. "Well, yes," he finally said.

"Great," I replied. "Where do you get it? Do you make it at home or do you get it at work for free?"

Jim shifted in his chair and glanced at his wife, Susie, who was sitting next to him. "We get our coffee on the way to work," he said.

"Oh really. You both get coffee together on the way to work? Well that's nice. Do you go somewhere fancy to get this coffee?"

Before Jim could answer, his wife spoke up. "Of course not," she exclaimed. "We go to Starbucks!"

The class cracked up.

"Right," I said. "Nothing fancy. Just Starbucks. So what do you get at Starbucks?"

It turned out they both got grande nonfat lattés.

"Very good," I said. "And how much do these nonfat lattés at this nonfancy coffee shop cost you each morning?"

Jim looked at Susie. As far as he was concerned, this was her show now. She said the lattés totaled about $6.

"And do you get anything to eat with them?" I asked.

"Well, usually we get a bagel or a muffin," Susie replied.

"And what does that cost?"

"Well, the muffins usually cost about $1.75 each. So I guess that's $3.50."

"Three-fifty, for muffins?" I asked.

Susie said, "Well, they are nonfat muffins!"

"Oh, that explains it," I said. "Do you get a newspaper?"

Susie nodded.

"Okay," I said, "let's add this all up. Six bucks for two lattés. Three-fifty for the nonfat muffins, and let's say 50 cents for the newspaper. So we're at $10 between the two of you, and you haven't even gotten to work yet. Interesting."

Over the next several minutes we went through the rest of Jim's and Susie's day. As they listed each expenditure, I wrote it down on the chalkboard. Here's what their daily spending habits wound up looking like:

Jim

Double nonfat latté: $3.50

Nonfat muffin: $1.75

Newspaper: $0.50

Candy bar and a Coke before noon: $2.00

Lunch (usually a burrito, chips, and a Coke): $8.00

Parking: $10.00 a day

Rental of two videos for the kids: $7.50

Susie

Double nonfat latté: $3.50

Nonfat muffin: $1.75

Juice and protein bar before noon with friends: $6.25

Lunch (usually a salad and an iced tea): $9.50

A double latté around 3 P.M.: $3.50

Takeout dinner for her, Jim, and the kids: $25.00

Late fee for not returning last night's videos on time (Jim puts this expense on her): $3.00

When I added it all up, the total came to $85.75. Figuring in the sales taxes, Jim and Susie were spending more than $90 a day—all on so-called "little stuff"!

By this point, the rest of the class was looking at them as if they were the worst kind of spendthrifts imaginable. But you know what? There were at least six other people in this class with fancy cups of coffee in their hands! They were sipping and laughing at the same time.

Now the point here is not that you should stop drinking coffee or even stop going to fancy places like Starbucks. I happen to enjoy Starbucks myself. The point is that here we had a typical couple who thought they couldn't afford to save any money, and yet there they were spending more than $90 on what were really extravagances.

Of course, when I suggested this to Jim and Susie, their first reaction was to get mad. "What do you mean, extravagances?" Jim questioned. "Since when is morning coffee and lunch an extravagance?"

"Calm down," I replied. "No one wants you two to starve to death. But what if you made your own coffee at home and ate an apple instead of buying a muffin? Instead of spending $10 at Starbucks, my guess is that it would cost you about 50 cents a day. You might also think about bringing your lunch to work a few times a week. And what about skipping the nightly video rentals? And if you have to rent a video, at the very least you could make darn sure to return it on time."

By this point Jim looked as if he couldn't decide whether to punch me out or thank me.

"Look," I continued, "my point isn't to criticize how you and your wife live. My point is that if the two of you really took a hard look at how you handle your money, I know you could each find at least $10 a day that you could be saving instead of spending."

What finally clinched it was when I explained how much that $10 a day could be worth to them. The math is really quite amazing. Saving just $10 a day (excluding weekends) amounts to roughly $200 a month, or $2,400 a year. If Jim and Susie (who were both in their mid-thirties) each put that much into a pretax retirement account that earned an annual return of 12 percent, by the time they were 65, they'd have a nest egg of *more than $2.3 million!*

As I finished scribbling the figures on the chalkboard, Jim and Susie both looked at me and then stared at each other. Finally Susie said, "David, are you trying to tell us that our lattés could wind up costing us $2.3 million?"

The class laughed, but Susie had it exactly right.

Society Is Now Designed to Help You "Latté" Your Future Away

There's a reason so many of us "latté" away our futures. It's that it's so easy. You can't go two blocks in any city or town in America without coming across a fast-food restaurant or a juice bar or a fancy place to have a fancy cup of coffee. Stop in any one of them on a regular basis and you can easily wind up spending $5 a day. Drink just two Cokes a day, and that's $2. And I haven't even touched on things like cigarettes, which can cost people $5 a day, or stopping by the bar for an after-work cocktail and quickly dropping an additional $10 a day.

There's no getting around it. Money is easy to waste. It's especially easy to waste on the small stuff. That's what the Latté Factor is all about. It's simply a metaphor for all the small amounts of money we spend on little things. The challenge is that the small stuff adds up—and before you know it, you've cost yourself millions.

The Smart Couples' Seven-Day Financial Challenge™

With this in mind, here's an exercise I'd like you to try. Starting tomorrow, I want the two of you each to get a small pad and track your expenses for the next seven days. This is not complicated. You simply write down every expenditure you make, no matter how large or small.

In order for this to be useful, you've got to promise me—and yourselves—two things.

1) You'll write down everything you spend money on for one week.

2) You won't suddenly change your spending habits because you're embarrassed about what you might find. Just be the wonderful human being that you always are and spend like you always spend.

Why do I suggest seven days? Because seven days is enough time to get a really clear picture of how you spend money—and it's not so long that you'll get tired of keeping your list.

At the end of the week, you should sit down with your partner and go over each other's lists, with an eye toward finding simple things you can each eliminate from your regular spending patterns. By the way, when you sit down with your partner, start by sharing what you are going to start cutting out, not what you suggest your partner cut out. Remember, you get more with honey than vinegar here!

That's the Dumbest Idea I Ever Heard . . .

The Seven-Day Financial Challenge is another one of those ideas that you can easily blow off because it seems so simple. But don't—at least not before you consider the following story.

Not too long ago, I was in New York being interviewed—live—on a major radio show with literally millions of listeners. In the middle of the interview, the host proceeded to tell me that my Seven-Day Financial Challenge was the dumbest idea he had ever heard. "David," he said incredulously, "you're telling me and my listeners that if we track our expenses for seven days, we're going to be able to change our lives financially. Give me a break. I can't tell you how dumb that is."

"Really?" I replied. "Why don't you just try it? If you still think it's a dumb idea after seven days, I'll pay you a hundred bucks."

He phoned me a week later. Unfortunately, this conversation

wasn't broadcast live on the radio. "I'm really embarrassed," he said, "but I had to call you. You were right. I tracked my expenses for seven days, and just like you predicted, I was stunned by what I found out."

"Which was what?" I asked.

"Well," he said, "this past week I spent almost $500 eating out." (For those of you wondering how anyone could spend $500 in a single week eating out—believe me, in Manhattan, which is where the radio host lives, it's easy.)

Anyway, he went on to tell me how he'd worked out the math and realized that $500 a week amounted to $2,000 a month. In other words, he was spending $24,000 a year on dinners out! And yet at the same time, he was not participating in the 401(k) plan his radio station offered or taking advantage of his company's stock-purchase program. Why? Because even though he was pulling down a six-figure salary, he always felt short of cash!

As a result of what my Seven-Day Financial Challenge made him realize, the radio host cut back eating out from six nights a week to three nights a week, and he signed up for his 401(k) plan.

The moral of this story should be obvious. Don't judge this simple idea too quickly. Try it out. Spend a week tracking your expenses. Then be brutally honest with yourself. How much money are you wasting each day? Each week? Each month? What about you and your partner combined? In other words, what is your Couples' Latté Factor?

Take a few minutes and really think about this. The reason this simple concept is so important is that if you can get yourself to believe you can find an additional $10 a day to put away in a retirement account (which is exactly what we're going to cover in detail in the next chapter), you can began to take advantage of the concept called the "miracle of compound interest."

What's the Miracle of Compound Interest?

Albert Einstein, widely considered one of the greatest minds of all time, was once asked to name the most amazing phenomenon he had ever come across. He replied that it was the power of compound interest. It was truly "miraculous" when you looked at it, he said, and even more so when you actually put it to work.

Einstein wasn't kidding. The miracle of compound interest is unbelievably simple yet life-changing. It comes down to this . . .

Over time money compounds.
Over a lot of time money compounds dramatically!

You don't have take my word for this. On the pages that follow are some powerful charts that illustrate this concept. Take a good look at them and think about your Couples' Latté Factor. Now that each of you has hopefully found a way to save $5 to $10 a day (or more), let's consider what this "small" amount of saving can do to transform your financial future. Without worrying about what specific investments you might make (we'll get to that later), just look at what saving money "systematically" each month can do for you.

TO BUILD WEALTH . . . PAY YOURSELF FIRST AND DO IT MONTHLY						
YOUR MONTHLY INVESTMENT	YOUR AGE	TOTAL AMOUNT OF MONTHLY INVESTMENTS THROUGH AGE 65	AT A 4% RATE OF RETURN	AT A 7% RATE OF RETURN	AT A 9% RATE OF RETURN	AT A 12% RATE OF RETURN
$100	25	48,000	118,590	264,012	471,643	1,188,242
	30	42,000	91,678	181,156	296,385	649,527
	40	30,000	51,584	81,480	112,953	189,764
	50	18,000	24,691	31,881	38,124	50,458
$150	25	72,000	177,294	393,722	702,198	1,764,716
	30	63,000	137,060	270,158	441,268	964,644
	40	45,000	77,119	121,511	168,168	281,827
	50	27,000	36,914	47,544	56,761	74,937
$200	25	96,000	237,180	528,025	943,286	2,376,484
	30	84,000	183,355	362,312	592,770	1,299,054
	40	60,000	103,169	162,959	225,906	379,527
	50	36,000	49,382	63,762	76,249	100,915

Now think about it another way. What if you systematically put this money into a retirement account such as a Roth IRA? Take a look at this next chart. Remember, to make this chart work you have to save only $5.50 a day! It's not a big deal . . . if you do it!

THE TIME VALUE OF MONEY

Invest Now Rather Than Later

BILLY — Investing at Age 14 (10% Annual Return)

AGE	INVESTMENT	TOTAL VALUE
14	$2,000	$2,200
15	2,000	4,620
16	2,000	7,282
17	2,000	10,210
18	2,000	13,431
19	0	14,774
20	0	16,252
21	0	17,877
22	0	19,665
23	0	21,631
24	0	23,794
25	0	26,174
26	0	28,791
27	0	31,670
28	0	34,837
29	0	38,321
30	0	42,153
31	0	46,368
32	0	51,005
33	0	56,106
34	0	61,716
35	0	67,888
36	0	74,676
37	0	82,144
38	0	90,359
39	0	99,394
40	0	109,334
41	0	120,267
42	0	132,294
43	0	145,523
44	0	160,076
45	0	176,083
46	0	193,692
47	0	213,061
48	0	234,367
49	0	257,803
50	0	283,358
51	0	311,942
52	0	343,136
53	0	377,450
54	0	415,195
55	0	456,715
56	0	502,386
57	0	552,625
58	0	607,887
59	0	668,676
60	0	735,543
61	0	809,098
62	0	890,007
63	0	979,008
64	0	1,076,909
65	0	1,184,600

SEE THE DIFFERENCE

SUSAN — Investing at Age 19 (10% Annual Return)

AGE	INVESTMENT	TOTAL VALUE
19	$2,000	2,200
20	2,000	4,620
21	2,000	7,282
22	2,000	10,210
23	2,000	13,431
24	2,000	16,974
25	2,000	20,871
26	2,000	25,158
27	0	27,674
28	0	30,442
29	0	33,486
30	0	36,834
31	0	40,518
32	0	44,570
33	0	48,027
34	0	53,929
35	0	59,322
36	0	65,256
37	0	71,780
38	0	78,958
39	0	86,854
40	0	95,540
41	0	105,094
42	0	115,603
43	0	127,163
44	0	139,880
45	0	153,868
46	0	169,255
47	0	188,180
48	0	204,798
49	0	226,278
50	0	247,806
51	0	272,586
52	0	299,845
53	0	329,830
54	0	362,813
55	0	399,094
56	0	439,003
57	0	482,904
58	0	531,194
59	0	584,314
60	0	642,745
61	0	707,020
62	0	777,722
63	0	855,494
64	0	941,043
65	0	1,035,148

SEE THE DIFFERENCE

KIM — Investing at Age 27 (10% Annual Return)

AGE	INVESTMENT	TOTAL VALUE
19	0	0
20	0	0
21	0	0
22	0	0
23	0	0
24	0	0
25	0	0
26	0	0
27	$2,000	2,200
28	2,000	4,620
29	2,000	7,282
30	2,000	10,210
31	2,000	13,431
32	2,000	16,974
33	2,000	20,871
34	2,000	25,158
35	2,000	29,874
36	2,000	35,072
37	2,000	40,768
38	2,000	47,045
39	2,000	53,949
40	2,000	61,544
41	2,000	69,899
42	2,000	79,089
43	2,000	89,198
44	2,000	100,318
45	2,000	112,550
46	2,000	126,005
47	2,000	140,805
48	2,000	157,086
49	2,000	174,094
50	2,000	194,694
51	2,000	216,363
52	2,000	240,199
53	2,000	266,419
54	2,000	295,261
55	2,000	326,988
56	2,000	361,886
57	2,000	400,275
58	2,000	442,503
59	2,000	488,953
60	2,000	540,048
61	2,000	596,253
62	2,000	658,078
63	2,000	726,086
64	2,000	800,895
65	2,000	883,185

Total invested = $10,000.
Earnings beyond investment = $1,174,600.

Total invested = $16,000.
Earnings beyond investment = $1,019,148.

Total Investment = $78,000.
Earnings beyond investment = $805,185.

Billy earns $1,174,600   Susan earns $1,019,148   Kim earns $ 805,185

Billy invested $68,000 less than Kim and has $369,415 more!
START INVESTING EARLY!

Are you motivated yet? How could you not be? By the way, you have my permission to copy these charts and show them to your friends. I truly wish that when I was younger, someone had shown them to me. I started working when I was 16, but I didn't open a retirement account until I was 24.

Keep Going . . . You're Doing Great

While you are really motivated, let's head to the next chapter (Step Five) and get specific. We are now going to take a look at exactly where you should put your Latté Factor money. Because it's not enough to just save money and spend less, you need to know what to do with these newfound savings. That's exactly what Step Five is all about. In Step Five, the retirement basket, we're going to discuss two concepts that make Americans rich. The first concept is the power of "pay yourself first," and the second concept is where this money actually goes . . . specifically, pretax retirement accounts. Combine the Couples' Latté Factor with the power of Step Five and you will be an unstoppable couple on your road to wealth. So keep reading . . . you're doing great!

BUILD YOUR
RETIREMENT BASKET

On June 7, 2001, President George W. Bush signed into law a massive new tax-reform bill known as the Economic Growth and Tax Relief Reconciliation Act of 2001. Among the more than 400 changes it made in the tax code, the new law significantly improved what Smart Couples (and everyone else) can do to save more money for their futures. As confusing as many of these changes may seem, it is crucial that you understand how they can affect you in 2002 and beyond. So please read this section carefully. What you will find is that you can now put significantly more money than ever before into tax-deductible and tax-deferred retirement accounts. And if you are fifty years old or older, you are in even better shape because of the new law's numerous "catch-up provision." Happy savings!

BY NOW, I HOPE YOU'VE REALIZED at a gut level that the two of you really can afford to put money away for your future. Now it's time to move beyond gut-level thinking to gut-level action. As I said in the introduction, this book is not about positive thinking—it's about positive doing. Remember, you can't think your way to wealth; you must *act* your way to wealth.

My grandmother used to say that you should never put all your eggs in one basket. She was right. As I see it, there are *three* baskets into which you should put your eggs. I call them the retirement basket, the security basket, and the dream basket. The retirement basket safeguards your future, the security basket protects you and your family against the unexpected (such as medical emergencies, the death of a loved one, or the loss of a job), and the dream basket enables you to fulfill those deeply held desires that make life worthwhile. This three-basket approach may sound simple, but don't let that fool you. If you fill the baskets properly, the two of you can create for yourselves a financial life filled with abundance and, most important, security.

The first basket we're going to discuss is the retirement basket. Specifically, in Step Five, you and your partner will learn what you need to do in order to accumulate a million-dollar retirement nest egg. Needless to say, the two of you can go beyond a million dollars—and, in fact, you may need to, depending on your ages—but whatever amount turns out to be right for you as a couple, the goal here is the same. Over the course of this chapter, you will learn exactly what the two of you must do to build a substantial retirement account—in other words, how to fill your retirement basket.

The Government Is Not Going to Fill Your Retirement Basket . . . You Are!

Depending on Social Security to provide for you after retirement, is asking for trouble. At best, Social Security will just keep your head above water. According to the government, the average wage earner who retired at age 65 in 2000 received just $987 a month in Social Security benefits. I suppose that's better than nothing, but it's certainly not enough to maintain a comfortable lifestyle.

For more than a decade now, politicians have been talking about the "crisis" facing Social Security and the need to modernize the system. Well, don't hold your breath on this one. As my grandmother realized some 55 years ago, if you want to be rich, forget about the government's help—you need to plan for your own financial future. In other words, you and your partner need to make building a retirement basket a top priority.

Pay Yourself First!

There are only a few ways of amassing substantial wealth in America today. You can inherit it, you can win it, you can marry it . . . or you can pay yourself first. Chances are if you're reading this book, you and your partner missed out on the first three possibilities. So you're going to need to build your wealth together on your own. That means paying yourself first.

I Know You've Heard This Before . . . but Stay with Me for a Second

"Pay yourself first" is a phrase we've probably all heard. That can be a problem, because often when you're hearing something for the second or third time, your brain goes, "Hey, I've heard that idea already, so how good can it be? Give me something new."

Well, this time at least, don't let your brain do that. Just because we've all heard of something doesn't mean any of us really knows anything about it or has any genuine experience with it. When I ask people in my seminars or at my lectures to raise their hands if they've heard of the concept of "paying yourself first," just about everyone does. But when I ask how many of them have actually done it, most of the hands go down.

The fact is, most people don't really know what "pay yourself first" means. They don't know how much they should pay themselves, and they don't know what they should do with the money once they've got it.

Maybe you are one of those people. Maybe your partner is. Whatever the case, let me explain it to you.

THE THREE PRINCIPLES OF PAY YOURSELF FIRST

1. What "Pay Yourself First" Really Means

Paying yourself first means putting aside a set percentage of every dollar you earn and investing it for your future in a pretax retirement account.

While that may seem simple—and sensible—enough, the fact is that most people do exactly the opposite. We take our hard-earned dollars and pay everyone else first. We pay the mortgage, our car-loan payment, the utility bill—you name it. And at the head of the list, the one we pay before everyone else is . . . the government.

Thanks to the miracle of payroll withholding estimated tax payments, every time we earn a dollar, we immediately run to the IRS (figuratively speaking, of course) and say, "Here I am—please take a third of my paycheck." And if we happen to live in a state like California or New York that imposes its own income tax, we say, "Oops, I don't want to leave you out either—here's another 8 percent of my income."

Add up all that generosity and you've given away nearly half of your hard-earned money to the government *before you've even seen it!* That's about as generous as you can get.

Now, I'm as patriotic as the next guy, but I think offering to pay the government close to half your wages in taxes is just downright dumb! Why? Because you don't have to. The reality is that there is an entirely legal way to avoid—or at least significantly reduce—the big bite the government takes out of your paycheck. Which leads us to the second principle.

2. Where the Money You "Pay Yourself First" Should Go

The bad news is that the government loves to take our money. The good news is that it's also interested in encouraging people to save. With that in mind, Congress has passed a series of laws over the last 20 years under which smart people can minimize their tax burden—and, at the same time, create a nest egg for their future—by putting part of their earnings into what are known as *pretax retirement accounts.*

To Finish Rich, You Should Pay Yourself First By Contributing as Much as You Can to a Pretax Retirement Account

There are many different types of pretax retirement accounts: 401(k) plans, 403(b) plans, SEP-IRAs, traditional IRAs, and so on. Later on, I'll detail how they all work, along with the best ways of using them. For now, all you need to know is that these accounts all work basically the same way: money you put in them is not subject to any taxes (income or capital gains) until you take it out. The catch is that, in most cases, you can't take it out before you reach retirement age without incurring a stiff penalty.

The great thing about pretax retirement accounts, of course, is that by making use of them, you can put your money to work without first losing 40 cents or more of your hard-earned dollar to taxes.

Here's how it works. Let's say you take $100 out of your paycheck every month and put it into a pretax retirement account. Well, that's $100 a month that won't be subject to income taxes—not federal taxes, not state taxes!

Normally, of course, if you earn $100, you've got to give close to $35 of it to the government. You'll pay roughly $28 in federal taxes, and depending on where you live, as much as another $5 to $9 in state taxes. That leaves you with just $65 or so to invest, and whatever capital gains or dividends you happened to earn from that would also be reduced by taxes.

By contrast, with a pretax account, you get to put the entire $100 to work for you, and as long as you keep the money in the account, you won't have to pay any taxes on whatever capital gains or dividends it happens to earn. In fact, you won't have to pay any taxes on the money—no matter how large your nest egg grows—until you start to take it out of the account. (Of course, in most cases, you've got to leave your money in the account until you reach the age of 59$\frac{1}{2}$. If you don't, in addition to paying all the taxes that are due, you'll also get hit with a penalty. More about this later.)

Think about it. Earn a dollar and pay taxes first, and you're left with only about 65 cents to invest. Put it in an IRA or some similar retirement account that allows you to defer taxes, and you've got the full dollar to play with.

Which would you rather invest—a dollar or 65 cents? If your investment grows at an annual rate of 10 percent, your pretax dollar will have swelled to $1.10 within a year. Your after-tax investment of 65 cents, on the other hand, will be worth just 72 cents. Quite a difference, isn't it? Now multiply this by some real money and then take it out 20 years, and pretty soon you're talking about a difference that may total some tens of thousands of dollars. Run it out 30 or 40 years and we're in six-figure territory.

Here is a simple chart that illustrates the power of pretax investing. Once you get your head around this concept, you'll never want to pay the government first again.

| | TAX-DEFERRED VS. TAXABLE INVESTING | | | | |
AGE	MONTHLY INVESTMENT THROUGH THE AGE OF 65	RATE OF RETURN	TAXABLE ACCUMULATION	TAX-DEFERRED ACCUMULATION	DIFFERENCE OF TAX-DEFERRED INVESTING
30	$100	4%	72,581	91,373	+18,792
		7%	115,762	180,105	+64,343
		9%	162,036	294,178	+136,142
		12%	277,603	643,096	+365,493

The above example is for illustrative purposes only. It shows a 30-year-old individual investing $100 a month through the age of 65 and compares the growth of the money invested in a taxable account vs. a tax-deferred one. The taxable account assumes a 28% tax bracket.

3. How Much Should You Pay Yourself?

Here's a simple rule of thumb: if you don't want to have to struggle to keep your head above water when you retire, you should be saving 10 percent of your pretax income each year. Period.

That's right—10 percent of your *pretax* income. Not your after-tax or take-home pay, but your gross pay. If you and your spouse jointly earn $75,000 a year, the two of you should be putting aside at least $7,500 a year for retirement. And I mean just for retirement. Any savings you're doing so you can buy a house or a new car or take that dream vacation should be *on top of* the $7,500. That 10 percent you're paying yourself first is not for anything else but your retirement.

If You Are Not Paying Yourself the First 10 Percent of Your Income, You Are Living Beyond Your Means

Maybe that sounds brutal, but it's true. If you and your partner are not currently putting 10 percent of your pretax income into a pretax retirement account, you are heading for trouble. I don't mean to sound overly gloomy or harsh. By now, I hope you have learned to trust that I really do care about you and I appreciate the opportunity to be your "financial coach." And I want you to let this coaching sink in.

I know plenty of people who seem to be very well off, who live in nice homes and drive nice cars, wear nice clothes and belong to country clubs with more nice people who also have and do nice things—and none of them are saving 10 percent of their income. As I said before, this is true of many Americans. Well, guess what? Many Americans, when they reach retirement age, won't have enough money to maintain their comfortable lifestyles through what are supposed to be their "golden years." This is because most people who look rich really aren't. In fact, they are working their tails off, and once you peel back the facade, what you find isn't wealth and security but stress and debt.

You and your partner deserve more than that. But it won't just happen. You've got to decide to act and make it happen.

If You Want to Be Really Rich, You Should Save 15 Percent of Your Income

What do I mean by "really rich"? Everyone has his or her own definition, but here's a fairly straightforward standard: to be considered really rich, you should have at least $1 million in liquid assets, above and beyond the value of your home.

Obviously, that's not Bill Gates rich. Or even your average dot-com IPO jackpot-winner rich. But it is a nice comfortable nest egg. And it's something anyone can accumulate. You don't have to be lucky, you just have to be disciplined enough to put aside 15 percent of your income.

You want more? Then put aside more. If you'd like to enter the ranks of the richest 1 percent of Americans, you'll need to save 20 percent of your income.

It's important to note that the younger you are when you start saving, the better off you'll be. In fact, the best time to become a massive saver and investor is when you are in your twenties. Unfortunately, this also happens to be the time in our lives when we are the least motivated to save money. When most of us get out of college, get our first job, and start having a family, we generally find ourselves stretched pretty thin. A savings and investment program isn't our top priority. We tell ourselves it's something we'll get around to when things aren't so tight.

Before we know it, of course, we're in our forties or fifties and we're still telling ourselves that we'll get around to it eventually.

Now, if you happen to be in your forties or fifties and you're just getting started, I don't want you to panic. Still, I do want you to recognize that you've got some serious catching up to do. It won't necessarily be easy, but it can be done.

The Time to Commit to Saving—to Paying Yourself First—Is Now

Whatever else you do, I hope that you and your partner don't finish this chapter without having a serious conversation about this idea of paying yourself first. As a couple, you should set yourselves a "pay yourself first" goal. It should be a percentage of your pretax income that you both can handle, can stick to, and can increase a little each year.

Let's say you start this year with a "pay yourself first" target of 10 percent of your income and agree to increase the amount by 1 percent each succeeding year. Within 10 years, you'll be saving 20 percent of your income. At that rate, you won't ever have to worry about your financial future. You'll be set for life.

Building a Nest Egg with Free Money

Putting aside 10, 15, or even 20 percent of your income may sound like a lot, but over the next few pages you will see that it can be both easy and fun. Why is it fun? Because when you pay yourself first into a retirement basket, you wind up paying less in taxes up front *and* your money grows tax-deferred. The results of this can be truly amazing. It's like getting free money from the government!

If you don't understand exactly how this works, you're not alone. Millions of Americans don't—and as a result, they fail to take advantage of all the different retirement accounts and programs available to them. As far as I'm concerned, this is one of the great shames of American education. Every child should be taught about basic financial planning in junior high or high school. If we learned this stuff early, we'd all be much better off. Unfortunately, personal finance has never been part of the curriculum, so you need to learn it now. Anyway, the fact is that paying yourself first into a retirement basket is really quite simple.

How to Save $5,000 a Year Without Giving Yourself a $5,000-a-year Pay Cut

Before I describe all the different types of pretax retirement accounts there are, I want to go over something I know is probably bothering you.

Let's say you and your partner earn a combined total of $50,000 a year. In order to follow my suggestion that the two of you save a minimum of 10 percent of your pretax income, you'd have to start putting aside at least $5,000 a year. Now if you've never done this before, I know how you're going to react. You're going to say, "There is no way we can do this! We're living paycheck to paycheck. No way can we afford to take a $5,000-a-year pay cut. And don't tell me the Latté Factor is going to save us $5,000 a year."

Is this what you're thinking? Well, don't worry. The two of you *can* save $5,000 a year without giving yourselves a $5,000 pay cut.

That's right. You read that correctly. If you are not currently saving 10 percent of your income, you can start doing so tomorrow—*without decreasing your spendable income by 10 percent!*

How can that be?

It's simple. Normally you earn $50,000 a year, right?

Wrong.

Assuming you've got a combined tax rate of 35 percent or so (the average for most Americans), what you actually bring home is about $32,500 in spendable income. Now, despite what you might think, putting $5,000 into a pretax retirement account will not reduce your spendable income from $32,500 to $27,500. Remember, you're paying yourself first—*before* you pay the government. In other words, the $5,000 you're saving comes off the top. What gets reduced is your gross income, which will drop from $50,000 to $45,000.

So let's do the math: $45,000 taxed at 35 percent leaves the two of you with a spendable income of $29,250. Before, you had a net spendable income of $32,500. Now you're getting $29,250. The difference is $3,250 a year. Divide this by two (there are, after all, two of you) and it comes out to a pay cut of $1,625 a year each. Divide that by 12 months, and that comes to a pay cut of $135 a month. Divide that by 30 days a month and it comes to $4.51 a day—an amount the Latté Factor can easily cover!

Of course, most couples who earn a combined income of $50,000 a year are not saving 10 percent of their income. If they were, millions more of us would be millionaires.

I grant you, the math can be a little confusing. If I were explaining it on a chalkboard at one of my seminars, it might take 15 to 20 minutes before everyone got it. So don't worry if you don't understand it right away. Just keep rereading the explanation until it sinks in. It's simple, basic math that can change your life forever.

If, after all this, you still don't feel you can save 10 percent or more of your income right now, do what I did when I started paying myself first. I was 25 at the time, and I didn't fully realize how important paying yourself first was. I also didn't believe that I could handle the pay cut. So instead of putting aside 10 percent of my gross income, I started by saving an amount that I figured I'd barely notice: in my case, it was 3 percent. At the same time, I made a commitment to myself, which I put in writing, to bump up my contributions to my 401(k) plan by another 3 percent at the end of six months.

I figured if I increased my contributions by 3 percent every six months, I'd be fully maximizing my 401(k) plan within two years. What actually ended up happening is that I quickly realized that putting money aside wasn't as difficult as I thought it would be. As a result, in less than a year, I increased my contributions from 3 percent to 6 percent, and then from 6 percent to the maximum. I was doing what I needed to do, but because I had gotten there gradually, I barely felt the difference in my spendable income.

The Ins and Outs of Retirement Accounts

There are basically two types of retirement accounts: the kind your company provides for you (called employer-sponsored retirement accounts) and the kind you provide for yourself (known as individual plans).

Over the next few pages, I will review how these plans work and how you go about setting them up and contributing to them. If you work for a company that has a retirement plan in place, you won't need to worry about the retirement accounts I describe for self-employed people. Then again, in this constantly changing economy where more and more people are becoming self-employed, it may be worth reading about these plans even if you are currently covered by a company program.

THE MOTHER OF ALL RETIREMENT ACCOUNTS: THE 401(K)

By far the most popular retirement program U.S. companies make available to their employees is the 401(k) plan; nonprofit organizations can offer employees a similar program known as the 403(b). The 401(k)—it takes its name from the section of the law that brought it into being—is what is known as a self-directed plan. This means that while the plan is administered by the employer, it is directed by the employee. In other words, it is up to you to tell your company whether or not you want to participate in the plan, how much you want to contribute to it, and where you want your money to be invested.

The Basics of 401(k) Investing

The first thing you need to know if you work for a company is whether or not your employer has a 401(k) plan in place. It constantly surprises me how many people don't know if their company offers this sort of retirement plan. You really should find this out before you accept a job with a new employer. Not having a 401(k) plan puts your financial future at risk, and you might want to think twice before you go to work for a company that refuses to provide one.

Assuming your company does have a 401(k) plan, the second thing you need to do is make sure you're signed up for it. Enrolling shouldn't cost you anything. It's a benefit that is provided by the company to the employee. What normally happens when you start a new job is that you get a ton of paperwork handed to you. This generally includes what is known as the "sign-up package" for the 401(k) plan.

Many people mistakenly assume that signing up for a 401(k) plan is automatic. IT'S NOT! Sadly, many companies find that fewer than half of their eligible employees participate in their 401(k) plans. It's not hard to understand why. As a new employee, you are handed this huge package of material and you're so busy getting used to your new job that you simply don't have time to read it all. The next thing you know, six months have gone by and you are still not signed up for the plan.

So here's my recommendation. If you work for a company that offers a 401(k) plan, first thing tomorrow check with the benefits person in your company's personnel department to make sure you are properly signed up. If it turns out that you are not enrolled, ask for a sign-up package. (This goes for your partner as well.)

Some companies won't let you join their 401(k) plan until you've worked there for some minimum amount of time, usually 6 to 12 months. This is not a legal requirement but a matter of corporate policy. If you ask "loudly" enough, sometimes they will waive the rules and let you join early. If not, find out when you will be eligible and mark the date on your calendar. As soon as it arrives, run (don't walk) to the benefits department and get signed up. Believe me, no one from benefits is going to remind you to sign up for the plan. Not to be negative, but they aren't watching this stuff. That's why you have to.

If You're Already Signed Up . . .

If you and your partner are already signed up for a 401(k) plan, the most important question to ask is whether you are "maxing out." That is, are you taking full advantage of the "pay yourself first" system by making the maximum contribution your plan allows?

Please don't assume for one second that you are doing this. It's simply too important not to double-check. *Paying Yourself First* as much as you can into your 401(k) plan is essential if you and your partner are really serious about getting—and finishing—rich. You both need to be doing this.

By law, the maximum dollar amount you can contribute to a 401(k) plan in 2002 is $11,000. With the new tax legislation, the amount is now raised each year by a specific amount (see chart below); so keep checking with your benefits department to make sure your contribution level is up to date. Keep in mind that just because the government has raised the amount you can contribute to a 401(k) plan doesn't mean your employer will raise your contribution accordingly. Most likely, you will have to go back to your benefits department and give them specific instructions to increase the amount. This may sound like a bother but, believe me, it's worth it. Keeping an eye on these sorts of details is what makes the difference between having to struggle at retirement and finishing rich.

If you do just one thing tomorrow after finishing this chapter, please let it be that you contact your benefits department to make sure you are truly maximizing your contributions to your 401(k) plan. If it turns out that you're not, make it a goal to increase the size of your contribution immediately, even if it's by only a few percentage points. Remember my story about how I managed to ramp up my contributions gradually without it hurting. Believe me, it's worth doing. In the long run, a small increase in your 401(k) contributions can make a huge difference in your wealth.

401(k) and 403(b) Contribution Limits		
YEAR	MAXIMUM ALLOWABLE (IF AGE 49 OR YOUNGER)	MAXIMUM ALLOWABLE (IF AGE 50 OR OLDER)
2002	$11,000	$12,000
2003	$12,000	$14,000
2004	$13,000	$16,000
2005	$14,000	$18,000
2006	$15,000	$20,000

Note: After 2006, increases are adjusted for inflation in $500 increments.

Now That Your Money Is in the Plan, How Do You Get It Out?

Another concern that keeps people from contributing to a company retirement plan is the mistaken notion that once they put their money in the plan, they will lose control over it. Nothing could be further from the truth. It's true that you're not supposed to take any money out of a 401(k) or similar retirement plan until you reach the age of 59¹/₂. But that doesn't mean you can't. It's your money, and in most cases you can get hold of it if you really need to.

Of course, as soon as you take money out of a 401(k) plan, it becomes subject to taxes as ordinary income. And if you're younger than 59¹/₂, you'll generally have to pay an additional 10 percent penalty to the government. (There are ways you can avoid this penalty. I'll tell you about them later.) In any case, I don't recommend that you withdraw your retirement money prematurely.

You Can Borrow from Your 401(k) Plan . . . But I Don't Suggest It

If you're really strapped, one way to make use of your 401(k) money without actually making a withdrawal is to borrow against it. Most plans allow you to lend yourself a portion of what you've saved, up to a maximum of $50,000. While this can be a simple process (in fact, some companies now allow you to do this over the phone), it is a very serious decision. First of all, any money you borrow from the plan must be paid back with interest. Second, most companies require you to repay the loan within five years. Third, if you are ever laid off, your company could force you to move your 401(k) money out of the plan. If this happens and you can't pay back the loan, it's considered a withdrawal and you could be hit with taxes, penalties, and interest charges. I've seen this happen, and it can be very sad and stressful.

Because of this, even though borrowing against your 401(k) can seem like a painless way of getting money out of the plan, you should regard it as a last-resort option.

Unfortunately, a lot of people don't. According to *Kiplinger's Magazine*, one out of every five Americans with a 401(k) account borrows against it. Even worse, according to the *Wall Street Journal*, people are doing this to fund all sorts of short-term projects, such as vacations, second homes, and even boats.

In my view, these people are asking for trouble. Remember, you put money into a retirement account for one reason and one reason only: for your retirement. If you take 401(k) money out early (or borrow against it) to pay down your credit-card debt or buy some luxury you couldn't otherwise afford, you're only cheating yourself. Smart Couples who want to finish rich don't borrow against their 401(k) plans; they let the money grow for retirement!

And don't worry about locking yourself into a burdensome commitment. Any decision you make now regarding the size of your 401(k) contribution can always be changed. If you suddenly find yourself in a financial squeeze, you can reduce your contribution. Indeed, most companies will allow you to change the size of your 401(k) contributions just by making a phone call.

Two Couples, Same Plan . . . a $700,000 Difference!

If you think I'm being a broken record here, going on about the importance of maxing out your retirement plan, consider this story of two couples who came into my office a few years ago.

The first couple, Marilyn and Robert, had spent 30 years focusing their retirement efforts on funding Robert's retirement account at work. When Robert's employer, an oil company, first began offering a retirement account that would allow workers to put away as much as 12 percent of their income, Robert and Marilyn figured it made sense for Robert to participate, but they weren't sure they could afford to put so much of Robert's paycheck aside. In the end, Marilyn's father put it in perspective. "Robert," he said, "the two of you can't afford *not* to do this. Just make the sacrifice now, and you'll be very glad later on that you did." With that sensible advice ringing in his ears, Robert elected to make the maximum contribution of 12 percent.

At the same time, Robert and Marilyn's best friends, Larry and Connie, were wrestling with the same issues. Larry had a job very similar to Robert's, and the two men earned roughly the same amount of money.

But Larry and Connie made a different decision. After a great deal of discussion, they decided to put away just 3 percent of Larry's income. They simply didn't feel they could afford to put away any more than that.

Thirty years later, when Robert and Larry were in their mid-fifties, they were both downsized. Shortly after that, they and their wives attended one of my retirement seminars. Later, they made appointments to come see me (separately) in my office.

Robert and Marilyn were excited when they showed up for their appointment. They were ready to retire and they knew they had saved enough to be able to do it. Indeed, when I looked at their 401(k) records, I saw that they had more than $935,000 in their account.

"I Blew It . . ."

Not so for Larry and Connie. When they came into my office the day after Robert and Marilyn, they were plainly worried. In fact, the first thing Larry said to me was, "I blew it." Larry and Connie had only about $250,000 in their 401(k) account—almost $700,000 less than Robert and Marilyn.

To her credit, Connie refused to let her husband take all the blame. "It really wasn't Larry's fault," she said. "I was worried about our bills and I thought we would eventually put more money away, but we just never did. Things came up—college costs, a new kitchen, a few trips—and the next thing you know, we're sitting here facing retirement. Now we're in trouble. We know we can't afford to retire and we are seriously worried about whether Larry can find a new job at 56."

Learn from Larry and Connie's example. Don't make the same mistake they did. Maximize your retirement contribution now.

Now That I'm Contributing to the Plan, How Do I Decide Where to Invest It?

Another big question concerning 401(k) and 403(b) plans is, how do I invest the money I'm putting into my account? It's actually quite simple. Included in the sign-up paperwork for your plan is a list of different investments for you to choose from. A typical 401(k) plan will offer at least three types of investment options: (1) a guaranteed fixed-rate investment; (2) a selection of mutual funds; and (3) stock in your own company (if it happens to be public). Generally speaking, you can put all your money into one of these choices, or divide it up as you see fit.

The single biggest mistake people make when it comes to 401(k) plans is not spending enough time reviewing their investments options before they decide which ones to pick. Often what happens when we get the huge pile of sign-up materials is that we let it sit unread on our desk until the sign-up deadline arrives. At that point, we've got to make a decision. The problem is, we have no information on which to base it.

So what do we do? We do what we used to do when we were in school and hadn't done our homework. We ask the guy or gal at the next desk what he or she signed up for.

This works great if they know what they're talking about. Unfortunately, all too often they don't have a clue.

Beware of "Cubicle Copying"

When I make this point in lectures, people always laugh because so many of them know they are guilty of this sort of "cubicle copying." (That's what I call the practice of turning to the person in the cubicle next to yours and asking, "Which box did you check off?") The problem with this system is that those little boxes you are checking off determine where your money will be invested—and that, in turn, may determine whether you wind up being rich or poor. What's really scary is that even though this decision can determine your family's entire financial future, many people spend less than 15 minutes making it.

So here's my suggestion. If you're already signed up for your company's 401(k) plan (or 403(b) plan if you're at a nonprofit), pull out your last quarterly statement and review the investment choices you made. Then call the benefits department and ask them for a current list of investment options and a summary of how each of these investments has been performing recently. In addition, ask your benefits person if the firm that administers your company's plan has an advisor who will go over the investment options with you. Most likely, the firm that set up your company's 401(k) plan promised to provide "free financial advice" to all plan participants. Unfortunately, most employees are not aware that this valuable advice is available at no cost, and so they never take advantage of it.

I also strongly suggest that you review your investment options with your partner, and if you have one—which I hope you do—with a personal financial advisor as well. Most financial advisors will review your 401(k) plan options with you at no cost.

It's Time to Do Your Own Research

Finally, do your own research. Today, with the Internet, gathering information about fund performance is a snap. There are literally thousands of Web sites that offer financial information. To make it easier for you to find a good financial Web site, I've listed some of my favorites below. At these sites, you can review everything from stocks to bonds to mutual funds and learn a lot about overall financial planning:

1. *www.morningstar.com* Morningstar is the company that really started it all in terms of ranking mutual funds, and its Web site is probably the best one of its type around. The Morningstar site not only allows you to review your portfolio and find top funds quickly and easily, it also provides general descriptions of the funds, along with an in-depth analysis that is nothing short of incredible. One of the things I like best about this site is a page called Fund Quickrank, which allows you to quickly screen funds based on their performance, their Morningstar ratings, or their volatility. To find Fund Quickrank, simply go to the Morningstar home page and scroll down to the "Tool Box" section. There you'll see a link to Fund Quickrank. Click over to the page and it will take you through the process in three easy steps. You can also screen for stocks on this site.

2. *http://finance.yahoo.com* Yahoo Finance is probably the most popular financial site on the Web, and for good reason. This is a true full-service financial portal, offering stock analysis, portfolio tracking, message boards, research, and online bill-pay-

ing. To get detailed information on mutual funds, click on the link labeled "Mutual Funds." It will take you to a list of all the different types of fund categories. From there, you can quickly run a search. Once you've found a fund that interests you, a click on the "Profile" link next to the fund's symbol will summon up a quick analysis courtesy of Morningstar.

3. *www.mfea.com* This is a great site with a lot of educational information on mutual funds. Among other things, it includes a list of funds that accept initial investments of $50 or less. (As of this writing, there were 242 mutual funds on the list.) The site also ranks funds by performance and provides a detailed information sheet on each fund.

4. *www.financenter.com* This site offers the best collection of financial tools anywhere on the Internet. There are calculators for just about everything you could imagine—from how long it will take you to pay down your credit-card debt to how much it will cost you to retire. Wondering if you should lease a car versus buy one? Want to figure out how much of a house you can afford? One of Financenter's calculators will tell you. When you need to crunch numbers, this is the place to go.

5. *www.quicken.com* Quicken gets it. It's that simple. This company makes the best retirement and expense-tracking software in the world, and their Web site is equally phenomenal. It's both easy to use and well-integrated . . . not only with Quicken's own personal-finance software, but with just about everyone else's as well. If there's a mutual fund you want to analyze quickly, click on the "Analyze a Fund" button on the site's home page for a detailed analysis.

6. *www.gomez.com* This Web site compares online brokers, banks, insurance companies, and just about every financial institution you can think of. In other words, it's basically an Internet *Consumer Reports* for financial services. If you're considering using an online brokerage, clicking on the "Brokers" button will give you an instant ranking of the top 20 firms plus an explanation of why they deserve the rating they got.

7. *www.mutuals.com* This site offers easy-to-digest information about more than 10,000 mutual funds. It also sells and manages them. To do mutual fund research on this site, click into the "Research Center." The site's data on funds is provided by *valueline.com*, which is another great Web site worth checking out.

Don't Let Anyone Talk You Out of Joining Your Company's 401(k) Plan

Many people make the mistake of not enrolling in their company's 401(k) plan because someone they know tells them it isn't any good. This is by far the number-one reason people cite at my seminars and lectures when I ask them why they haven't signed up. Some nice person will raise his or her hand and say, "I don't use my 401(k) plan because a friend told me that the investment choices it offers are lousy and I can do better on my own."

That may sound reasonable, but the truth is that it's not. The fact is, even if you're a phenomenal investor, on your own—that is, investing outside a tax-favored plan like a 401(k)—you would be hard-pressed to outperform even a mediocre 401(k).

Why do I say this? Because every dollar you invest in your 401(k) investments is a *pretax investment*. When you invest on your own, you lose that advantage. Moreover, many companies will supplement your 401(k) contributions with a contribution of their own, kicking in as much as 50 cents for every dollar you contribute. Some even match you dollar for dollar. That's *free money* from the company you work for.

Let's do the math. Let's say you invest $100 in your 401(k) plan. If your company is typical, it will contribute an additional $50—which means now you've got $150 working for you in your 401(k) account. If the plan generates an annual return of just 10 percent, at the end of a year you'll have a balance of $165.

To do better than that investing on your own, you'd have to generate an annual return of nearly 154 percent! Remember, you'd be working with after-tax dollars, which means that right off the bat your $100 in earnings would be reduced by income taxes to just $65 or so. If you think you know an investment that will consistently turn $65 into

$165 in just one year, you don't need this book. The reality is that the stock market has generated an average return of about 12 percent a year since 1926.

Of course, you will have to pay ordinary income tax on your 401(k) money when you start withdrawing it after you reach the age of 59¹/₂. But having been able to grow tax-deferred, your nest egg will be so large by then that you'll still be way ahead of the game.

Another reality is that most 401(k) plans today provide employees with an excellent series of investment options, offering participants as many as 10 to 15 mutual funds from which to choose—generally including an index fund (whose performance will match that of the stock market as a whole). So ignore that naysayer at your office who complains about the lousy investment options in your 401(k).

What Happens to My 401(k) Money If I Change Jobs?

Recent surveys indicate that most of us will work for 10 or more different employers over the course of our lifetime. Talk to someone in their thirties, and chances are they have already held half a dozen different jobs. In the midst of all this job changing, many people leave their 401(k) money behind, in their old employer's plan, when they go to a new company. This is a huge mistake. What they should do in most cases is "roll it over" into their own Individual Retirement Accounts (IRAs).

Here's why.

1. **Money you leave behind in an old employer's plan is out of your control.** Once you're gone, your former employer can legally move your money without your permission. For instance, say your old 401(k) plan had been managed by Charles Schwab but now your company decides to move the plan to Fidelity. If the company can't find you, it will move your money into its new Fidelity plan automatically. However, since the company is not allowed to make investment decisions for you, your money will be put into a money-market account, where it will sit until the company hears from you. Which may not be for years. In the meantime, your money is earning a lot

less than it could or should be. Trust me, you want to keep control over your money. So take it with you.

2. **By not rolling over your 401(k) money into an IRA, you're limiting your investment options.** With an IRA, there is almost no limit to the sort of investments you can make. You can put your money into stocks, bonds, mutual funds, or just about any recognized investment vehicle that strikes your fancy. This is generally not true of 401(k) plans.

3. **An IRA offers you better beneficiary options than a 401(k).** Most 401(k) plans allow you to name only a spouse as your beneficiary (that is, the person who will inherit your account if you should die). You may, however, want to do more elaborate estate planning, in which you name a trust as a contingent beneficiary. Generally speaking, you can't do this with a 401(k) plan. Also, most 401(k) plans don't allow you to make your kids contingent beneficiaries. Why does this matter? Because in the event you and your spouse die together, if your children aren't contingent beneficiaries of your retirement account, the money might have to be distributed and they could have to pay income and estate taxes on the proceeds. That could cost them as much as 70 percent of what you managed to put away.

To be fair, there is one advantage to leaving your money in a former employer's 401(k) plan: you don't have to make any decisions or think about any of these issues. But that's not how a Smart Couple operates—not if you want to finish rich.

If Your Company Doesn't Have a Retirement Plan . . .

In my view, companies have a moral obligation to offer employees 401(k) or similar retirement plans. I find it incredibly sad when I meet people who have worked for the same company for decades and don't have any money for retirement because their bosses never bothered to put a self-directed plan in place.

The fact is, there is simply no excuse. Setting up and administering a 401(k) plan is both simple and inexpensive. Indeed, for a company with fewer than 100 employees, it shouldn't cost more than a few thousand dollars a year.

If, for some reason, your current employer does not have a 401(k) plan in place, I strongly recommend that you and your fellow employees make it known—in writing—that you are concerned about your future and feel that the company's unwillingness to offer a retirement plan puts your financial future in jeopardy.

I also recommend that you make it as easy as possible for your employer to do the right thing. Do the basic research for him or her. Contact a few of the many companies that offer "turnkey" 401(k) plans for small businesses and get them to send you some information about how the process works. Then pass it along to your boss. Among the companies that can help you with this are Administaff (reachable at 800–465–3800 or *www.administaff.com*), Fidelity Investments (at 800–343–9184 or *www.firsco.com*), the Vanguard Group (800–984–5925 or *www.vanguard.com*), GoldK (781-693-4600 or *www.goldk.com*), and T. Rowe Price (800–422–2577 or *www.troweprice.com*). This is only a starting point, but by doing some of the groundwork, you stand a better chance of getting your company to set up a plan. In addition, you may even end up impressing your boss with your initiative.

If There Is No Way You Can Get Your Employer to Offer a 401(k) Plan . . .

If all your efforts are in vain, and your employer simply won't (or, for some reason, can't) set up a 401(k) plan for you and your fellow workers, then you have no choice—you *must* open an Individual Retirement Account.

Fortunately, opening an IRA has never been simpler. As a result of the massive Taxpayer Relief Act of 1997 and the IRS Restructuring and Reform Act of 1998, it is easier than ever to become eligible to open a traditional tax-deductible IRA. In addition, there are now more ways to take advantage of all the benefits IRAs offer. And there is even a brand-new type of IRA, called a Roth IRA.

THE TRADITIONAL IRA

Starting in 2002, with a traditional IRA, both you and your spouse can each put up to $3,000 a year into a tax-deferred investment account. Depending on your tax situation—that is, how much you make and whether or not you contribute to a 401(k) plan—the entire $3,000 contribution may be tax-deductible. And whether or not it's deductible, once your contribution is in the account, it will grow tax-free until you take it out.

Maxing Out Your IRA

As a result of the 2001 tax law changes, you can now put more money than ever before into a traditional IRA or a Roth IRA. These accounts are now starting to really get exciting!

Traditional and Roth IRA Contribution Limits		
YEAR	MAXIMUM ALLOWABLE (IF AGE 49 OR YOUNGER)	MAXIMUM ALLOWABLE (IF AGE 50 OR OLDER)
2002	$3,000	$3,500
2003	$3,000	$3,500
2004	$3,000	$3,500
2005	$4,000	$4,500
2006	$4,000	$4,500
2007	$4,000	$4,500
2008	$5,000	$6,000

Note: After 2008, increases are adjusted for inflation in $500 increments.

Who's Eligible to Use a Traditional IRA?

Anyone under the age of 70$1/2$ who earns income from a job (as opposed to interest or investment income) or is married to someone who earns income from a job can open and contribute to a traditional IRA.

How Much Money Can I Deposit in a Traditional IRA?

By law, an eligible individual is allowed to invest up to $3,000 a year in a traditional IRA. Depending on your income and whether or not you participate in a company-sponsored retirement plan, you may be able to deduct your entire $3,000 contribution.

What Are the Tax Advantages of a Traditional IRA?

There are two big tax advantages to a traditional IRA. Depending on how much you earn and the extent to which you participate in a company-sponsored retirement plan, part or all of your IRA contributions may constitute a pretax investment (that is, one that is tax-deductible). In any case, regardless of whether of not your contribution is deductible, the money you invest in an IRA account grows tax-deferred—meaning that as long as you keep your nest egg in the account, you don't have to pay any income or capital gains taxes on any dividends or investment profits it may earn. This ability to defer taxes allows your money to grow much faster than it otherwise would—and makes it possible for you to finish rich!

Can a Spouse Who Doesn't Work Invest in a Traditional IRA?

Yes, if you work and participate in a 401(k) plan, your nonworking spouse can still contribute up to $3,000 a year to a traditional IRA account. If your combined annual income is less than $150,000, this contribution may be tax-deductible. This is an awesome new benefit that resulted from the tax law changes of 1997. Under the old law, the maximum annual contribution to a spousal IRA was a mere $250. Unfortunately, many spouses miss out on this new benefit because they don't realize the law has been changed.

What If I Use a 401(k) Plan?

Even if you participate in a 401(k) plan at work, you can still fund an IRA if you wish. Depending on your marital status and income, your contribution may even be tax-deductible. Things get a bit more complicated if you are married and filing separate tax returns. If this is your situation, I suggest you consult a tax advisor. In addition, you can read IRS Publication 590 ("Individual Retirement Arrangements") or visit the IRS Web site (www.irs.gov).

What's the Deadline for Funding a Traditional IRA?

The deadline for making contributions to a traditional IRA is the date your tax returns are due for that year—April 15 of the year following the one for which you're making the contribution. However, don't wait until the last minute to fund your IRA. The sooner you take care of it, the more time you'll have to take advantage of the tax-deferral benefit.

When Can I Take Out My Money?

The basics of withdrawing money from a traditional IRA are quite simple. To begin with, the money you put into the account is supposed to stay there until you reach the age of $59\frac{1}{2}$. At that point, you can start taking out your contributions without incurring any penalties. You will, of course, have to pay income taxes on the money you withdraw. If your contributions were after-tax contributions (that is, if they weren't tax-deductible), you'll owe tax only on any gains your original investment may have made, not on the original investment itself.

What Happens If I Take Money Out of My Traditional (Deductible) IRA Before I Reach $59\frac{1}{2}$?

If you take any money out of a traditional (deductible) IRA before you reach $59\frac{1}{2}$, in addition to paying income tax on the withdrawal, you may have to pay a penalty fee amounting to 10 percent of whatever interest or investment earnings your initial deposit generated over the years. For example, say you invested $10,000 and it grew to $15,000. If you withdrew this $15,000 prematurely, you would have to pay income taxes on the entire $15,000, plus a penalty of 10 percent of the $5,000 gain ($500). However, no taxes or penalties are due on a premature withdrawal if you put the money back into an IRA within 60 days.

Are There Any Other Exceptions to This 10 Percent Penalty Rule?

Yes, you can make penalty-free withdrawals to pay for certain special expenses. These include higher-education bills for you, your spouse, your children, or your grandchildren, as well as up to $10,000 of the cost of your first home. You can also take money out of your IRA without penalty to cover medical expenses due to long-term illness or disability, to pay for health-insurance premiums, and to effect a property separation in the case of a divorce. Of course, in all these situations you will still have to pay income tax on the money you withdraw.

Are There Any Other Exceptions?

There is one other way you can avoid the early-withdrawal penalty—although to qualify for it, you must be in your early fifties and planning to retire early. According to an obscure section of the tax code known as Internal Revenue Service Rule 72(t) 2(A) iv—generally referred to as "72T"—you don't have to pay the penalty if you take your money in what the IRS defines as "substantially equal and periodic payments that are based on life-expectancy tables." In plain language, the IRS allows you to take a fixed amount of money out of your IRA early without penalty provided you work out a withdrawal schedule in advance and then stick to it. This is an extremely complicated undertaking that you shouldn't attempt without professional guidance. Done correctly, however, it can be hugely valuable to prospective early retirees. So if early retirement is a possibility for you, make a point of finding a financial specialist who knows the ins and outs of rule "72T." It could save you a bundle in tax penalties.

Can I Leave My Money in a Traditional IRA as Long as I Want?

No. With a traditional IRA, you must start taking money out when you reach the age of 70$\frac{1}{2}$. IRS Publication 590 ("Individual Retirement Arrangements") explains how to calculate your "mandatory withdrawal"—i.e., how much you are required to take out and when. This can be a complicated procedure, and so once again I recommend that you get a financial and/or tax advisor to help you figure things out. If you have older parents, make sure they are doing the same because if you fail to make your mandatory withdrawal, or if you get it wrong, you can get hit with a penalty amounting to 50 percent of the total you were supposed to withdraw.

THE BRAND-NEW ROTH IRA

When the Roth IRA was introduced in 1997, many experts were skeptical that it would really be worthwhile for the average American. In the years since then, however, skepticism has been replaced by enthusiasm.

The Roth IRA—it's named for Sen. William Roth, who sponsored the legislation that created it—is quite similar to the traditional IRA, except for two things. The first difference is that with a Roth IRA, your contributions are not tax-deductible. Once your money is in the account, however, it grows tax-deferred, just as it would in a traditional IRA. And when you take it out, you encounter the second big difference: provided you're older than 59$\frac{1}{2}$ and the money has been in the account for at least 5 years, it's *totally tax-free!* That's right—you pay no income taxes, no capital gains taxes, nothing!

Now if you're just learning about the Roth IRA for the first time and you are at all like me, you're probably wondering, "What's the catch?" Why would the government give us this incredible tax break? Well, remember, contributions to a Roth IRA are not tax-deductible, and that deductibility is what originally made the traditional IRA so popular. If you're one of the many people for whom the tax deduction is important, a Roth IRA may not make sense for you. But before I discuss which kind of IRA may be right for you, let's go over the specifics of the Roth.

Who Is Eligible for a Roth IRA?

As with a traditional IRA, you need to have earned income in order to be eligible to open a Roth IRA. But you can't earn too much. For singles, the cutoff point starts at a modified adjusted gross income (known as a "MAGI") of $95,000. Below that level, you can contribute up to $3,000 a year to a Roth IRA. Above it, the maximum allowable contribution begins to drop. If your MAGI is more than $110,000, you can't contribute anything. For married couples, the cutoff starts at a joint MAGI of $150,000 and tops out at $160,000 (that is, below $150,000, you can contribute up to $3,000 a year each; above $160,000, you can't contribute anything; between those two numbers, you're allowed a partial contribution). These numbers may change upward in 2002 and beyond (review the chart on page 120).

If I Participate in a 401(k) Plan at Work, Can I Still Open a Roth IRA?

Yes! I love pointing this out at my seminars because so few people are aware of it. My suggestion is that you and your partner first make sure that the two of you are maxing out your contributions to your 401(k) plans. Once that's taken care of, if your joint income is less than $160,000 a year, you should look into funding a Roth IRA. Couples who maximize their 401(k) plans and then contribute to Roth IRAs are setting themselves up to Finish Rich! I strongly recommend this.

What Are the Tax Advantages of a Roth IRA?

As I've explained, your contributions to a Roth IRA aren't deductible, so they will not reduce your current taxes. On the other hand, the money you put in a Roth IRA will grow tax-deferred. Most important, when you take it out, it's totally tax-free—provided it's been in the account for at least five years and you are over the age of 59$^{1}/_{2}$. It's this tax-free withdrawal that makes the Roth IRA such a good deal.

What's the Deadline for Funding a Roth IRA?

The deadline for making contributions to a Roth IRA is the same as the deadline for a traditional IRA—the date your tax returns are due for that year (April 15).

So Which Would Be Best for Us—a Traditional IRA or a Roth IRA?

Without knowing your personal situation, it's hard to say which plan might make the most sense for you. But there are some general guidelines you might consider.

GUIDELINES FOR FUNDING ROTH VS. REGULAR IRAS

1. The first priority for both of you should always be to max out your contributions to a 401(k) or similar tax-deductible company-sponsored plan.

2. If you're not eligible to participate in a 401(k) plan and you are more than 10 years away from retirement, my personal recommendation is that you go with the Roth IRA. The reason is that in the long run, the benefit of being able to make tax-free withdrawals from your retirement account is enormous.

3. If you don't like worrying about things like the cost basis of your IRA contributions or whether they were pretax or after-tax, then go with the Roth IRA. Why? Because none of these things matter with a Roth, since there won't be any tax to calculate when you take the money out after you reach retirement age.

4. If you don't intend to touch your IRA money and you want to leave it to your heirs, go with a Roth IRA. With a Roth, you are not forced to make mandatory withdrawals.

5. If you feel strongly that you need the tax deduction in order to justify funding an IRA, then use a traditional IRA.

What About Converting Our Traditional IRAs to Roth IRAs?

Over the last few years, many tax and financial consultants have been advising their clients to convert their old traditional IRAs to new Roth IRAs. The reason, of course, is the fact that once your money has been in a Roth IRA for five years, it can be withdrawn tax-free. But while this is a great selling point for converting your traditional IRA to a Roth, there's a big catch here. *When you convert a traditional IRA to a Roth IRA, you've got to pay income taxes on the money in the account.*

For example, say you decide to convert a traditional IRA in which you've got a current balance of $50,000. In order to do so, you've got to declare that $50,000 as ordinary income earned during the year in which you're making the conversion. Chances are this will bump you up into a higher tax bracket.

Now, some financial advisors will suggest that if you have the money to pay the extra taxes, you should do it, because you'll come out ahead in the end. The idea is that by paying a bit more now, your tax bite will be much lower down the road when you eventually take the money out of your Roth IRA. Unfortunately, what I find is that most people don't have extra money sitting around. And if they do, they don't want to spend it on income taxes.

Typically, what happens is that people pull money out of their IRAs in order to pay the extra tax they've incurred by converting to a Roth. And in most cases, that makes no sense. Take our $50,000 example. If you withdrew $20,000 from your retirement account to pay the tax bill resulting from the conversion, that would leave you with only $30,000 invested in your new Roth IRA. That's a 40 percent reduction in your wealth. Is the Roth's tax advantage worth that much? Probably not.

Keep the following thought in mind. Regardless of what everyone says, *the government is not stupid!* It created the Roth conversion option to generate more tax revenue for itself.

That doesn't mean converting is never a good idea. For example, if you know you are going to leave your money in a Roth IRA for at least 15 years and you have the extra cash (outside your IRA) to pay the extra taxes you're going to face, you might want to look into converting to a Roth.

Also, if you are in your sixties or seventies, and you have a huge IRA, it can make sense for estate-planning reasons to do a Roth conversion. Let's say you are not planning to live on your IRA money, but rather intend for your kids to inherit it someday. In this case, you can justify converting a traditional IRA to a Roth IRA. For one thing, unlike a traditional IRA, with its mandatory withdrawal requirement for people over 70$^1/_2$, you can leave money in a Roth IRA for as long as you live. For another, when your children inherit your Roth IRA, they won't be forced to withdraw the money the way they would with a traditional IRA. Rather, they can leave the proceeds in the account and watch their money continue to grow, free of taxes, for decades. And then when they are finally ready to withdraw it, it will still be tax-free.

Whatever your situation, if you are thinking of converting your traditional IRA to a Roth, check out *www.rothira.com*. It's a great Web site devoted to Roth IRAs, complete with a calculator designed to assist you with conversion decisions.

Working Teens Can Open a Roth IRA

Because of their long-term advantages, Roth IRAs are great for teenagers. And if you think involving teenagers in this sort of thing is unrealistic, think again. I believe strongly that everyone with teenaged children or grandchildren should do everything they can to get them investing now. Teaching your kids about the importance of investing while they're still in high school can make the difference between their eventually becoming rich or having to struggle.

I can't think of a better gift parents or grandparents can give their children or grandchildren than a Roth IRA. I'm not talking just about the account and the money to fund it, but the knowledge and habits the child can acquire as he or she starts learning about the importance of saving for retirement.

Imagine the impact you could have if you helped your 16- or 17-year-old open a Roth IRA. Take a look again at the chart on page 95 illustrating the power of compound interest. I include this chart in all of my seminars, and I tell my students, "Show it to your kids!"

So How Would I Do This?

Obviously, your child can't open a Roth IRA unless he or she has some earned income. Fortunately, most teenagers today do have at least part-time jobs that earn them at least a few thousand dollars a year.

Under the law, if your teenager earns $1,000 during the year, he or she is allowed to contribute $1,000 to a Roth IRA. Now, don't worry, I'm not crazy. I know that very few teenagers (if any) are going to want to take all their earnings and put them into a Roth IRA. So here's what I suggest. Show the chart on page 97 to your teenager and tell them that if they're willing to contribute to a Roth IRA, you'll match their deposits dollar for dollar. In other words, if they put in $200 over the course of the year, you'll add an additional $200.

The government doesn't care where the money used to fund a Roth IRA comes from. All it cares about is how much the account owner happens to have earned that year. I have some creative clients with their own companies who've put their minor children on the payroll with a salary of $2,000 a year, which they then use to fund a Roth IRA. They have to report the $2,000 as income for the child, but as of 1999 a child under age 18 could earn up to $4,300 without owing any federal income tax.

Needless to say, being able to start building a retirement nest egg at such a young age is a great thing. But to me, even more important than the money he or she is getting to sock away is the fact that the child is learning about the importance of saving and is getting into the habit of funding a retirement account. If you can get a teenager or a college student in the habit of saving now, you will have done something absolutely fundamental to help him or her Finish Rich! As a parent, it's a phenomenal gift to give to your children.

You Can't Buy an IRA!

By now, I hope you've recognized the importance of contributing to a retirement account—and figured out which type of account makes the most sense for you and your partner.

As I noted earlier, how the two of you invest the money in your retirement accounts may be the most important decision you make concerning your financial future. Unfortunately, many people don't really understand what they are doing when they make this decision.

All too often, here's what happens. A couple gets motivated to open an IRA, and so they head down to the local bank. There, they are introduced to the on-site financial advisor, who says, "Mr. and Mrs. Jones, do we have a great IRA opportunity for you! It pays 6 percent for 24 months."

"Is it safe?" Mr. and Mrs. Jones ask.

"Oh, yes," the advisor replies, "it's very safe. In fact, it's insured and guaranteed."

So Mr. and Mrs. Jones sign the papers, write a check, and leave the bank smiling, thinking they have "bought" an IRA account that pays 6 percent for two years.

Well, that's not really what happened. The fact is, you can't "buy" a retirement account! What Mr. and Mrs. Jones did was *open* an IRA account. Once that was done, the bank's representative put the money they gave him to fund the account into a 24-month certificate of deposit that pays 6 percent a year.

Remember, whether you're dealing with an IRA, a 401(k), or any other kind of qualified retirement plan, the process is always the same: you open the account and then you decide where to invest the money. That's what Mr. and Mrs. Jones were doing, even if they didn't realize it. You have to tell the bank or brokerage firm that's administering your account how you want your money invested! If you don't, the money could wind up literally just sitting there, earning little or no interest!

I always explain this in seminars, and virtually every time I do, there are people who are literally stunned to hear it. Sometimes they get mad. I recall one seminar where an older fellow named Peter stood up and told me flat out, "You are obviously new to the business, young man. My wife and I have been buying IRAs for years at our bank and the rates are great! We're getting 7 percent."

"Terrific," I said. "It sounds like you've invested your IRA contributions in a certificate of deposit with a 7 percent annual return."

Peter shook his head angrily. "You don't know what you're talking about. I would never invest in a CD for retirement."

"Really?" I said. "So what do you think you're invested in?"

"I told you," Peter replied. "A bank IRA account."

At this point, Peter's wife started looking concerned.

I went to the chalkboard and led Peter through the steps: you open an IRA account, your money goes into the account, you decide how it is to be invested.

Still, he wouldn't give up. "I really don't think that I invested in a CD," he insisted.

"Well," I said, "don't you think you should make sure you know how your IRA money is invested? If I were you, I'd call your bank tomorrow and find out."

The following day, Peter did just that. Needless to say, he found out that his bank had put his money in a certificate of deposit, just like I'd said. The good news for Peter was that he was in fact earning 7 percent. Often, people find out their money is sitting in an IRA earning nothing because they never instructed the bank or brokerage on what to do with it.

If you think this is dumb, you are correct—it's *really* dumb. Unfortunately, there are probably millions of Americans with retirement accounts who have no idea how their retirement money is invested. Since you are a Smart Couple who plans to finish rich, I know this will not happen to you.

WHAT IF I OWN MY OWN BUSINESS?

First, let me say congratulations! I say this because I admire entrepreneurs and because, as a business owner, you are eligible for the best retirement accounts around. Second, let me urge you to avoid a mistake that too many business owners make—deciding that setting up a retirement plan is too much of a bother.

Remember, you are in business to build a financially secure future for yourself and your family—and how can you do that unless you pay yourself first? As a business owner, the best way to pay yourself first is by setting up one of the three types of retirement plans meant for self-employed people:

- Simplified Employee Pension Plan (also known as a SEP-IRA)
- Defined Contribution Plan (also known as a Keough Plan)
- Savings Incentive Match Plan for Employees (known as a SIMPLE IRA)

Establishing one of these may take a little effort on your part, but, hey, you're an entrepreneur—you should be used to going the extra mile. In any case, it's more than worth it. While the regulations regarding distributions and early withdrawals are pretty much the same as the ones that govern IRAs and 401(k) plans, the rules on contributions to retirement plans for business owners are much, much better, allowing you to put away up to $40,000 a year, tax-deferred—possibly even more. That's huge! We're talking big money here!

SIMPLIFIED EMPLOYEE PENSION PLAN (SEPs)

SEP-IRAs are very attractive to small business owners because they are easy to set up and require the least paperwork. If you run a small business, are a sole proprietor, participate in a small partnership, or are a Subchapter S corporation, this is probably the type of retirement acount you'll want to set up.

Originally, with a SEP-IRA, you were allowed to make a tax-deductible contribution of up to 15 percent of your employees' annual compensation. (The annual percentage limit for self-employed individuals was 13.043 percent). In 2001, the maximum legal contribution was $25,500.

The 2001 tax-reform act changed the whole game. As of this writing, there was still a little confusion as to how the next tax law would affect SEP-IRAs, but most experts interpreted it as follows: Starting in 2002, you can contribute as much as 15 percent of your income (up to a maximum of $30,000 a year) to a SEP-IRA.

Certain obligations go along with establishing a SEP-IRA. If you have people working for you who are over 21 and have been on your payroll for at least three of the last five years, you also must include them in your SEP-IRA, contributing on their behalf the same percentage of their annual compensation that you do of your own. In other words, if you put in 10 percent of your compensation, you also must contribute an amount equal to 10 percent of theirs. (By the same token, if you decide not to put in any money for yourself one year, you don't have to put any money in for them.)

The one disadvantage of a SEP-IRA is that the contributions you make for your employees are immediately 100 percent vested (which means the money you put in for them is theirs to keep, even if they leave your employ the next day).

DEFINED CONTRIBUTION PLANS (Keough Plans)

If you run your own business and can afford to put away more than 25 percent of your income, a defined contribution plan may make the most sense for you. With certain defined contribution plans, starting in 2002, you can make a fully tax-deductible contribution of as much as 100 percent of your income, up to a maximum of $40,000 a year! (After 2002, the maximum you will be able to contribute to a defined contribution plan will be adjusted annually for inflation in increments of $1,000.)

Defined contribution plans are especially good for business owners who earn significantly more than their employees. As a result of a feature called Social Security integration, highly compensated employees (which generally means the business owner—that is, you) are allowed to contribute a bigger percentage of their compensation than other workers. This means that you can put in, say 25 percent of your compensation without having to make an equally large contribution on behalf of your employees.

There are three main types of defined contribution plans: money-purchase plans, profit-sharing plans, and defined-benefit plans.

Money-Purchase Plans Starting in 2002, you can put away as much as 25 percent of your annual income in a money-purchase plan, up to a maximum of $40,000 per participant per year. (Some experts say the new law actually allows you to contribute up to 100 percent of your self-employed earnings, but as of this writing there is still some disagreement about this. New tax laws always create some confusion in the beginning; by 2002, I am sure it will be crystal-clear. As always, I recommend that you consult a professional tax and/or financial advisor before making any critical investments or tax related decisions.)

As with a SEP-IRA, you are required to make equal-percentage contributions for your employees, but you may create a vesting schedule for these contributions (meaning the employees must remain with your company for a set period of time before they can claim the money you have put into the plan on their behalf). The only downside to a money-purchase plan is that the size of your annual contribution is fixed; once you decide on a percentage of your income, you're stuck with it. If you want to change it later (say, because you had an especially good year and can afford to contribute more—or because times suddenly got tough, and you want to put aside less), you have to amend the plan document. The required fixed contribution often makes profit-sharing plans more attractive to business owners.

Five-Star Tip: If you change the size of your contribution, make sure you amend your plan document. Otherwise, the IRS could subject the plan (and you) to penalties.

Profit-Sharing Plans These plans are wonderful retirement benefits that can be good for both owners and employees. As the name implies, a profit-sharing plan is meant to encourage business owners to share company profits with employees in a good year. Under this type of plan, starting in 2002 you can contribute up to 25 percent of your income (to a maximum of $40,000). But unlike a money-purchase plan, which requires you to contribute the same percentage of your income every year, profit-sharing plans are flexible, allowing owners to change the size of their annual contribution—and even skip a year entirely—as conditions dictate.

Like all the defined-contribution plans, profit-sharing plans also permit Social Security integration, meaning they can be structured so that the percentage you have to contribute for your employees might be less than you'd have to put in under a SEP-IRA. Another advantage to this type of a plan over a SEP-IRA is that it allows you to create a vesting schedule for your employee contributions.

Five-Star Tip: If you find all this confusing, you are not alone. This is why self-employed people who don't have employees normally go for SEP-IRAs, which are much easier to set up and monitor. So if you don't have any employees and want to get moving, start with a SEP-IRA. You can always upgrade later to a defined contribution plan.

Defined-Benefits Plans Business owners over the age of 50 who have no employees and enjoy a high level of dependable income should consider setting up one of these plans. The reason: Defined-benefits plans allow you to put away more money than any other plan around. If you can afford to contribute more than $40,000 a year and are confident that you can do this yearly until you reach 59$1/2$, this plan is for you. Starting in 2002, the maximum that could be contributed into this type of plan will be increased from $140,000 to $160,000 (depending on age, income, and retirement date). This is not, however, a do-it-yourself kind of retirement plan. To set one up, you will need to hire a financial advisor who specializes in defined-benefits plans as well as a third-party administrator to write the plan document for you. You also will want to work closely with an accountant to make sure your plan conforms to all IRS guidelines and that you are filing the yearly reporting forms correctly. But don't let this extra work scare you. If your income is sufficiently high, in just ten years you could put enough into a defined-benefits plan to be able to retire!

THE SIMPLE IRA

The biggest disadvantage of defined contribution plans is that they don't allow your employees to put their own money into the plan. That's not a problem with the new SIMPLE IRA. Introduced in 1997, this plan is meant for small companies (those with less than 100 employees) looking for an easy and affordable retirement program—in other words, something simpler and cheaper than a 401(k) plan.

As with a SEP-IRA, the employer must contribute to the plan on the employees' behalf, and these contributions vest immediately. Then again, they are relatively small—limited to between 1 and 3 percent of each employee's total compensation.

As of 2002, you and your employees can each put as much as

$7,000 a year into a SIMPLE IRA. Over the following five years, the maximum allowable contribution will increase steadily as follows.

Increase in SIMPLE IRA Contributions

YEAR	MAXIMUM CONTRIBUTION (IF AGE 49 OR YOUNGER)	MAXIMUM CONTRIBUTION (IF AGE 50 OR OLDER)
2002	$7,000	$7,500
2003	$8,000	$9,000
2004	$9,000	$10,500
2005	$10,000	$12,000
2006	$10,500 *	$12,500 *

*For those age 49 or younger, increases after 2005 will be adjusted for inflation in $500 increments. For those age 50 or older, increase after 2006 will be adjusted for inflation in $500 increments.

To help you digest all the tax-law changes I've covered above, here is a summary chart to make it easy for you to compare plans quickly.

Summary of New Retirement Account Provisions
Annual Contribution/Deferral Limits

YEAR	TRADITIONAL & ROTH IRA (UNDER 50)	TRADITIONAL & ROTH IRA (OVER 50)	401(K) & 403(B) PLAN (UNDER 50)	401(K) & 403(B) PLAN (OVER 50)	SIMPLE IRA (UNDER 50)	SIMPLE IRA (OVER 50)
OLD LAW	$2,000	N/A	$10,500	(N/A	$6,500	N/A
2002	$3,000	$3,500	$11,000	$12,000	$7,000	$7,500
2003	$3,000	$3,500	$12,000	$14,000	$8,000	$9,000
2004	$3,000	$3,500	$13,000	$16,000	$9,000	$10,500
2005	$4,000	$4,500	$14,000	$18,000	$10,000	$12,000
2006	$4,000	$5,000	$15,000	$20,000	$10,000 *	$12,500
2007	$4,000	$5,000	$15,000 *	$20,000 *	$10,000 *	$12,500 *
2008	$5,000	$6,000	$15,000 *	$20,000 *	$10,000 *	$12,500 *
2009	$5,000 *	$6,000	$15,000 *	$20,000 *	$10,000 *	$12,500 *
2010	$5,000 *	$6,000	$15,000 *	$20,000 *	$10,000 *	$12,500 *

*Indexed for inflation.

Source: Morgan Stanley.

Figuring Out Where All This Money Gets Invested

Now that we've covered *how* to save your retirement money, it's time to think about *where* you're going to invest it. Making investment decisions is really not that complicated. In fact, we can sum up everything you need to consider in what I call . . .

THE FINISHRICH RULES OF RETIREMENT INVESTING

> **RULE NO. 1**
> **Know what your money is doing.**

This may seem obvious, but I have to start with it. Don't ever put money in a retirement account and then forget about it. You have to know exactly what your retirement funds are invested in. Don't make the mistake of "thinking you know." Pull out your statements and get familiar with what you own. Whatever you do, don't keep your long-term retirement money sitting in a lazy investment like a certificate of deposit. In the financial-planning business, we call certificates of deposit "certificates of depreciation." That's because the return on CDs is usually so low that it doesn't even keep up with inflation.

CDs are great investments if all you're interested in is preserving capital—say, if you're already retired and can't afford to take any risk at all with your money. But if your goal is to build a retirement nest egg, investing in something that generates an annual return of only 5 percent or so is crazy. Actually, there's a technical term for that kind of retirement strategy: I call it *Going Broke Safely!*

> **RULE NO. 2**
> **Make sure your retirement money is invested for growth.**

You can't finish rich with fixed-return investments. It's that simple. Fixed-return investments such as certificates of deposit generally earn only 5, 6, or 7 percent a year—and if that's all you're making on your money, you may never be able to build substantial wealth.

The fact is, most people undercut their ability to Finish Rich by investing too conservatively. Because their retirement money is so important they don't want to take any chances with it. What they don't realize is that the biggest risk you run with a retirement nest egg is that it might not be substantial enough to live off of when you retire.

If your money is not growing at a rate at least 4 to 6 percentage points higher than inflation, you face the possibility of outliving your income. The bottom line here is that *you need to invest for growth*. In practical terms, this means that a portion of your retirement portfolio must be invested in equities. You can do this by purchasing individual stocks or shares in one or more equity-based mutual funds. But whatever form it takes, you've got to keep at least some of your money in equities.

> **RULE NO. 3**
> **Allocate your assets so that you maximize return while minimizing risk.**

The rule of thumb when it comes to investments is simple: the higher the return, the higher the risk. What this means is that a smart investor is always engaged in something of a balancing act. As I noted above, being overly conservative when it comes to your retirement nest egg can undermine your chances of finishing rich. On the other hand, you don't want to be too much of a gambler. The key to finding and maintaining the right balance between risk and reward is what is known as asset allocation.

Asset allocation is one of those terms that can sound more complicated than it really is. In fact, all we're talking about here is how much of your retirement money should go into relatively safe, relatively low-yielding investments (like fixed-return CDs) and how much should go into more risky, higher-yielding investments like growth stocks.

Figuring out how to allocate your assets doesn't need to be difficult. Obviously, as my grandmother liked to remind me, you don't want to keep all your eggs in one basket. But how do you know what proportion of your nest egg should be invested in equities vs. fixed-income securities? There are all sorts of ways to calculate this. For my part, I prefer the following simple rule of thumb.

Take your age and subtract it from 110. The number you get is the percentage of your assets that should go into equities; the remainder should go into bonds or other fixed-income investments.

Here's how this rule works. Say you're 40 years old. You subtract 40 from 110, and you get 70—which means you should put 70 percent of your retirement assets into stocks or stock-based mutual funds. The remaining 30 percent of your assets should go into safer investments such as certificates of deposit, money-market funds, or fixed-income securities such as bonds or bond funds.

If you'd prefer to keep things even simpler, forget about subtracting your age from anything—just put 60 percent of your retirement in stocks and the remaining 40 percent into bonds. Known as a "balanced account," this allocation typically delivers about 90 percent of the stock market's return with about 30 percent less risk. It's what I call a "sleep well at night" asset allocation, and it's especially good for people who are nearing retirement age.

While this may sound oversimplified, it's a great way of maximizing your return while minimizing your risk.

Once you've figured out how you want to allocate your assets, you'll need to choose the actual investments. Because this decision is more specific, I recommend you discuss it with a knowledgeable financial advisor. In any case, whether you plan to go it alone or just want to do your own research, there are plenty of useful Internet sites that can help you with retirement planning. (Check out some of the sites I listed on pages 114–116.) Personally, to help my clients, I use data and information from two sites (*www.ibbotson.com* and *www.allocationmaster.com*), both of which require expensive software, but they are the best and they are what the professional financial advisors use.

RULE NO. 4
Invest in your company's stock, but do your homework!

I mentioned earlier that if you work for a publicly traded company, one of your 401(k) options may be to invest all or part of your retirement nest egg in your employer's stock. As a loyal employee, you may feel this is definitely the way to go. But be careful. While it's certainly true that investing in your company's stock can make you very rich if the company does well (we've all heard about the employees of Microsoft, Dell, and Cisco who became millionaires), it can also make you poor if the company stumbles. And even great companies occasionally stumble. In 1987, for example, IBM's stock fell by more than 70 percent. There were people close to retirement age at IBM, heavily invested in company stock, who saw literally half their nest egg disappear in a matter of months.

Not only do great companies sometimes stumble but great economies sometimes slow, causing great stocks to crumble. So you want to be careful to limit how much of your retirement money you invest in one company's stock—even if that company happens to be the one you work for. Many experts recommend that you never invest more than 20 percent of your nest egg in your employer's stock. That's a bit conservative for me. If you work for a really terrific company and you know it's well run, don't be afraid to act on that knowledge. I currently have more than 50 percent of my 401(k) money invested in my company's stock. While that's a lot of eggs to keep in one basket, it has allowed me to grow my retirement account quickly, as our stock has gone up tenfold since the company went public six years ago.

What I recommend is that you do some research into your own company's stock. The simplest way to do this is to call your company's investor-relations department and ask for what they call an "investor kit." Virtually all publicly traded companies offer these kits. They include articles about the company, a copy of its latest annual report, and what is known as its 10-K. The 10-K is a report that all public companies are required to file annually with the Securities and Exchange Commission. It provides detailed information on the company and its finances. Whether or not you're planning to buy stock in your company, I suggest that you read its 10-K.

While the 10-K can look complicated, it's not really all that difficult to understand—and it can be incredibly informative. Indeed, reading through a 10-K will tell you everything from what your company does to how much its top executives are paid. It also details every possible thing the company thinks could go wrong that might adversely affect the price of its stock. This is really important information to know not just as a potential investor but also as a current employee.

Once you've absorbed all this, you can supplement your knowledge by going online and checking out one of the many Web sites that specialize in providing information about individual stocks.

There are too many to list here, but a useful roster would include the following:

www.nasdaq.com

www.edgaronline.com

www.marketguide.com

www.morningstar.com

www.quote.com

www.stockselector.com

www.valueline.com

www.valuestocks.net

www.ragingbull.com

www.quicken.com

www.smartmoney.com

www.thestreet.com

www.fool.com

RULE NO. 5
Make sure you read all of Step Eight.

In Step Eight, I'm going to list some of the biggest mistakes investors make. Make sure you read it all the way through, because committing just one of these errors could cost you a fortune in retirement income.

Well, that's it. The two of you should now have all the information you'll need to create your retirement basket and finish rich. You both should know why you need to max out your retirement contributions, and how to invest the money you've committed to put into your retirement plans.

Of course, none of this will matter if you're not totally motivated to *pay yourselves first.* I hope you both are. Remember, the one thing that can prevent you from finishing rich is you. If you don't do this stuff, it won't work. If you don't sign up for your 401(k) plan and max it out, or open and fund a SEP if you're self-employed, it's not going to happen. If you don't teach your children about Roth IRAs, they might not learn about them until it's too late.

The key is to act on this chapter *now.* If you set this book down and never come back to it but do what I discuss in just this one chapter, you've got a great chance of ending up in the top 10 percent of wealth in this country. But don't settle for just that. I want to get you to the top 5 percent. And with that in mind, let's look at how you are going to protect your wealth against the uncertainties of life by building a security basket.

BUILD YOUR

SECURITY BASKET

SO THE TWO OF YOU ARE putting aside a set percentage of your income, building a retirement basket that will enable you to finish rich. I'll bet you both feel a lot more secure about the future than you did when you first started this journey. You should, because you are. But that doesn't mean you can sit back and relax. Just the opposite—now is the time to start planning seriously for life's unexpected problems.

The Reality Is That Sometimes Life Is Messy

I'm a positive person and I'd like to be able to tell you that everything is always going to be just fine for all of us. Unfortunately, the reality is that sometimes things don't go that way. The reality is that sometimes things can go wrong—*really* wrong. People lose their jobs, marriages fall apart, businesses go bankrupt, breadwinners get sick and occasionally even die. *Stuff happens.*

There's no getting around it. Stuff has always happened, and it's not going to stop happening now just because you've decided to be smart about your finances.

But that's no reason for the two of you to get discouraged.

If you know that things can go wrong, then you can prepare yourselves, and being prepared puts you in a position of power. Having a "Plan B" in case things don't work out the way you want them to doesn't only make you *feel* secure, it actually *makes* you secure. That Plan B, of course, is your security basket, and building it is like building the foundation for your family's financial home. You could build a really great house (by doing a great job on your retirement basket), but if you don't put it on a solid foundation (a well-stocked security basket), that gorgeous home of yours (your financial well-being) could come crashing down on you and those you love.

Hope for the Best, but Prepare for the Worst

The point of a security basket is simple. It's meant to protect you and your partner and your children (if you have any) in the event you're hit by some unexpected financial hardship. This hardship could be something major, like the loss of a job or a death in the family. Or it could be something minor, like the car needing new brakes or the dishwasher going on the fritz. The point is that unanticipated problems are bound to arise, and while you may never be able to guess in advance where exactly they might come from, you can still be in a position to handle them.

In my seminars, I liken the security basket to what the automobile companies like to call their "passive restraint systems"—that is, the seat belt and air bag that are required in all new cars these days. When you get a new car, you pay for an air bag and you wear your seat belt as a matter of course. This doesn't mean you want or plan to get in an accident. You're simply being smart; you're making sure you'll be protected in the event of a crash. Well, that's exactly what we're going to do now. We're going to install a financial "air bag."

SIX THINGS TO DO RIGHT AWAY
TO PROTECT YOURSELVES

In order to be properly protected, you must fill your security basket
with the following six safeguards.

SAFEGUARD NO. 1
Set aside a cushion of cash.

When I was a little boy, my Grandma Bach used to tell me,
"David, always have some 'rainy day' money, because when the rain
comes, cash is king!"

It was good advice then, and it's good advice now. I know I feel better having a nice cushion of cash available in case of trouble. You will
too. So follow my grandma's advice and set up an emergency account
for yourselves. I want the two of you to think of this as your "air bag"
of cash, a cushion that will soften the blow in case you lose part or all of
your income for any reason (whether it's job loss, disability, a bad economy, or whatever).

The question, of course, is how much of a cushion is enough. How
much money do you need to set aside to feel protected—and, in fact, *be*
protected—against the "stuff" that "happens"?

The answer is simple. It depends on what you and your partner
spend each month. The key word here is "spend." It doesn't matter
what you earn. If you're making $5,000 a month, you don't really have
$5,000 passing through your hands each month, do you? After all,
you're putting at least 10 percent of it into your retirement basket (you
are, aren't you?) and you're paying a chunk of the rest to the government in taxes.

The two of you should have figured out how much you spend each
month in Step Four ("The Couples' Latté Factor"). If you didn't do it
then, definitely do it now. (You can use the form on page 273 called
"Where Does the Money *Really* Go?")

Once you know the figure, you can calculate how thick your cash
cushion should be. In my opinion, the bare minimum you should set
aside is an amount equal to three months of expenses. In other words, if

the two of you spend $2,000 a month, you need to keep at least $6,000 in cash in your security basket.

But that's just a minimum. In some cases, you might want to keep as much as 24 months of spending in reserve. I realize that's a huge spread. The reason it's so big is that the amount you should set aside depends on a lot of issues. For instance, if you suddenly lost your job, how long would it take you to replace your income? It used to be that the more money you made, the harder it was to find a new job. As a result, experts used to recommend that you should set aside a month's worth of expenses for every $10,000 a year in income you earned. (In other words, if the two of you had a combined annual income of $50,000 a year, the experts would suggest you set aside five months of spendable income.)

Is this sort of caution still necessary? In many sectors of the economy, things are so hot that you can lose your job—and have five offers for a new one in less than a week. But there are no guarantees, and hot economies can turn cold with breathtaking speed. As a result, it's hard to generalize. You and your partner should have a heart-to-heart talk about your spending, your ability to maintain your income stream if one or both of you was to lose your job, and what I call your "sleep at night" factor.

How Much Money Will It Take for Both of You to Be Able to Sleep Well at Night?

This "sleep at night" number is different for everyone—including partners. Almost invariably, one of you will require more of a financial security blanket than the other to be able to sleep well at night. While three months of expenses is the minimum I recommend to save, many couples choose to have as much as 24 months' worth of expenses saved. You need to decide *together* what makes sense for the two of you as a couple.

I will, however, offer one general rule: in my opinion, there is no reason to save more than 24 months of expenses in your security basket. Anything more than that is overkill. And one more thing: if you're in doubt about how much cash to keep in your security basket, err on the side of caution and save more, not less.

Don't Let the Banks Get Rich Off Your Cushion

It's not just how much you save in your security basket that matters. You also need to address *where* you save it. Most people put their emergency cash cushion in the wrong place—which is to say they keep the money in a checking or savings account at the local bank. That's too bad, because these kinds of accounts pay you almost no interest.

The fact is that the banks get rich off of ordinary checking and savings accounts. That's because while the money sitting in them (*your* money!) is out working for the bank, you're being paid barely any interest at all—and in many cases no interest whatsoever! Not too long ago, out of curiosity, I went to a local branch of one of the biggest banks in the country and asked how much interest they paid on checking-account deposits. The answer was 1 percent. As it happens, the national average is about 1 percent. Pardon me, but that's too low!

For your own good, please decide today that you will stop letting the banks pay you a low level of interest on your checking account. The fact is, you can go to virtually any brokerage firm in any city—or go on the Internet—and open what is known as a money-market checking account that will pay you between 3 and 4 percent in annual interest. In fact, many of the same banks that are now paying 1 percent interest on their checking accounts also offer money market checking accounts paying more than 4 percent. You just have to ask.

The rates that money markets pay are usually three to four times what a typical bank account is paying. The rate will vary depending on what federal interest rates are doing. That's a big difference. If you have $10,000 in security-basket money sitting in a bank checking account that pays 1 percent instead of 4 percent, you are losing out on $300 worth of interest a year. That's a lot of money to be just throwing away.

In most cases, money-market checking accounts also offer unlimited check writing, an ATM debit card that can also be used as a credit card (and in some cases also earn you frequent-flyer mileage), an annual summary statement that shows where your money was spent, and online bill payment! Think about that. You get a ton of great features and you earn more interest on your money.

Moreover, these money-market accounts are safe. In fact, they are probably the safest investment you can buy. And if you happen to be ultraconservative, you can even get an insured money-market account (though it will usually pay 1 to 2 percent less than an uninsured account). Again, many banks do offer these accounts, but you must ask for them.

Here's How to Find a Money Market Account

If all this about money-market checking accounts comes as news to you, don't worry—you're not alone. I can't tell you how many times I've talked about them during lectures and seminars and TV shows, and had people come up to me afterward asking me how they can get one. That's not surprising, since the banks don't want you to know about them.

The fact is, these accounts have been around for years. The key difference today is that you no longer have to be rich to open one. You used to need an initial deposit of $10,000 or more to be able to open a money-market checking account. These days, you can open one with as little as $2,000—and in some cases, with no minimum amount at all.

To save myself the trouble of having to answer all the e-mails I'm bound to get on this question, here is a sample list of several reputable institutions that offer these kinds of accounts. This list is not intended to be exhaustive, nor am I endorsing any of these brokerage firms. It's just meant to give you somewhere to start. In any case, there's no reason to go crazy researching where to open a money-market checking account. Whether you wind up getting 4.5 percent or 5.5 percent or even 6 percent, you'll still be doing a lot better than the 1 percent you may be getting now at your local bank.

E*TRADE ($1,000 minimum)
(800) ETBANK1
www.etrade.com

Fidelity Investments ($2,500 minimum)
(800) FIDELITY
www.fidelity.com

Merrill Lynch ($2,000 minimum)
(877) 653–4732
www.ml.com

Morgan Stanley Dean Witter ($2,000 minimum)
(800) 688–6896
www.msdw.com

Charles Schwab ($5,000 minimum)
(800) 225–8570
www.schwab.com

Edward Jones ($1,000 minimum)
www.edwardjones.com

Five-Star Tip: Interest rates change daily. To find the current rates on money market accounts, visit *www.bankrate.com.*

SAFEGUARD NO. 2
Both of you absolutely MUST write a will or set up a living trust.

People come up to me at seminars all the time and ask, "If I die, what type of will should I have?"

If you die?

I'm sorry, but we're all going to die. This is one fact of life that we simply can't avoid. People may be living longer these days, but sooner or later every one of us is going to wind up somewhere other than here. Sure, it's sad, but you know what the real tragedy is? The real tragedy is that two-thirds of us die intestate—that is, without having written a will or set up a living trust that specifies what should be done with our money and other property, to whom it should be distributed and how.

If you love anyone—*anyone*—you can't let that happen. You must set up a will or living trust!

This is not debatable. This is not couple-specific. If you are in a committed, long-term relationship, whether the two of you are married or not, you must arrange to have a qualified attorney draft a legal document that sets out what you want to happen in the event one or both of you becomes incapacitated or dies. Remember, stuff happens.

This legal document should address the following key issues:

What Should Be Done with Your Property When You Die?

Do you want all of your assets to go to your spouse or partner? Maybe you want to leave something to a sibling or a parent or a friend. What about your children? What about your partner's children? Perhaps there is a charity, church, or school you want to remember. If you don't prepare a legal document that spells all this out, you're going to leave a terrible mess for those you love. And I'm talking about a lot more than just a minor inconvenience. Families are torn apart by these sorts of issues all the time.

What Happens If Both of You Die at the Same Time?

You may think this is far-fetched, but it does happen and it's something you need to consider—especially if you have kids. What would you want done with your assets if the two of you were to die together? If you have kids, who would you want to raise them? Who should be responsible for managing their money? Unless you specify all this in advance, the government will step in and make these decisions in your place. Do you want the government deciding what to do with your kids? Smart Couples don't let the government decide anything this important. Smart Couples make sure they have a properly drafted will or trust.

What Happens If One of You Gets Sick (or Becomes Otherwise Incapacitated) and Can No Longer Make Decisions?

This thorny question is handled by a document known as a "living will." It's an attachment to your will or trust that spells out how each of you wants to be treated in the event either of you gets so sick or is so badly injured that you can't communicate your needs and desires. If, say, you are hit by a car and are brain dead, do you want the hospital to keep you alive by hooking you up to a respirator? Speaking personally, if it happened to me, I wouldn't. You may feel differently. The point is, if you don't specify this sort of thing in your will or trust, someone else is going to have to make this brutal decision for you. This is not the kind of issue you want your family fighting over in the midst of a tragedy. Among other things, your living will should contain a durable and health-care power of attorney. This gives a designated person (such as your partner) the legal right to make financial and medical decisions for you in the event you become incapacitated.

Wills and living trusts are not documents you should ever try to draft at home by yourself. Yes, it's true that you can buy a software program for $29.95 that supposedly provides you with all the forms and templates you need. But probate law is very tricky and complicated, and it varies from state to state. Moreover, one tiny mistake in a poorly drafted will or trust can invalidate the whole thing, or at the least open it up to being contested.

The point is, there's too much at stake here for you to take any chances. Spend the time and money to find a good attorney who specializes in wills and trusts, and have him or her draft the document for you. A decent will shouldn't cost you more than $1,000; setting up a trust is a bit more expensive—between $1,000 and $2,500. No, none of it is cheap . . . but believe me, it's worth it.

What Is a Living Trust?

Before we go any further, I should probably explain a little about living trusts. A living trust is basically a legal document that does two things. First, it allows you to transfer the ownership of any of your assets (your house, your car, your investment accounts, whatever you like) to a trust while you are still alive. Second, it designates who should be given those assets after you die. By naming yourself the trustee of your trust, you can continue to control your assets—which means that as long as you live, the transfer of ownership will have no practical impact on your ability to enjoy and manage your property.

The main advantage a living trust has over a simple will is that if you create a living trust properly and fund it correctly, your assets won't have to go through probate when you die. That is, your instructions regarding the distribution of your assets won't be reviewed by the courts. This is very, very important. By avoiding probate, you can save thousands of dollars in attorney's fees.

In addition, you will be able to maintain your estate's privacy. (Once an estate goes through probate, all the details become a matter of public record.) In a perfect world, this might not matter, but the world isn't perfect. Sadly, there are people out there who make their living reading probate records and trying to figure out how they can get their hands on your money. The fact is, anyone can say that they were promised a piece of your estate. They can show up in court and insist they were your best friend and that you promised to leave them $50,000 when you died. Even if it's a total fabrication, your family will still have to pay some attorney good money to fight the claim.

Another big advantage of a trust is that it can save your heirs a lot of money. If you have a large estate (that is, one worth more than $650,000), a well-written trust can reduce the estate-tax bill by tens— sometimes hundreds—of thousands of dollars.

There are too many different kinds of trusts for me to be able to list them all. The following five types are among the most common.

Marital and Bypass Trust This is the most popular trust I see. Often referred to as an "AB" trust, it is mainly used to reduce estate taxes. Done correctly, it can enable heirs to inherit as much as $1.3 million in assets without having to pay any estate taxes. (Normally, only the first $650,000 of an estate can be passed along tax-free.)

Revocable Living Trust This kind of trust is designed to protect your home and your brokerage accounts, and to help your estate avoid probate. It is extremely flexible and easy to set up, and can be changed whenever you like throughout your lifetime.

Qualified Terminable Interest Property Trust The QTIP trust is often used by rich people who've been married more than once. Say you've got a new spouse and want him or her to be provided for, but intend that your family fortune eventually go to your children by a previous marriage. A QTIP trust will provide income to your surviving spouse for the rest of his or her life, then pass to your children (or whomever you happen to name as the ultimate beneficiary).

Charitable Remainder Trust This trust allows you to continue to live off the proceeds of your estate even after you've donated it all to a charity (and presumably reaped some hefty tax advantages in the process). Typically set up by very wealthy families, it can provide you and your designated heirs with income for the rest of your lives, but once you are all gone, the estate will go to the charity.

Irrevocable Life Insurance Trust This is a great way to protect the real value of your life insurance from the brutal impact of estate taxes. Unfortunately, once you've set it up, it can't be changed, nor can you easily access your policy's cash value.

Because estate planning is so important and so complicated, I strongly recommend that you hire a qualified professional who specializes in this sort of thing. Don't hire the local attorney; hire an estate-planning expert who spends all his or her time drafting trusts.

What *Not* to Do with a Living Trust

The trick to making a living trust work for you is to fund it correctly. Many well-intentioned couples set up a living trust, but then they forget to switch their house title or their brokerage accounts from their own name to the trust's name. If you neglect to do this, instead of being protected, your most important assets could end up in probate when you die.

Changing the name in which an account or some other asset is held is called "replating." It's an easy process, but you have to remember to do it. Just call your brokerage firm or your real estate title company and explain to them that you've created a living trust and you need your account "replated." They handle this sort of thing all the time and will know exactly what to do.

You'll still need to double-check their work. A minor typo—a misspelled name or an incorrect account number—can create major problems later. Generally, the best way to protect yourself is to have your attorney add what's called a "spillover clause" to the trust. This is an addendum that lists what you intend to put in the trust; as a result, even if you forget to replate some assets, they'll still be covered.

Don't Put Your IRA in a Trust

Occasionally, a couple will take the advice of an inexperienced attorney who recommends that they put their IRA in their trust or make their trust the beneficiary of their retirement accounts. Or they will misunderstand their attorney and do this on their own. Leaving a retirement account to a trust is one of the biggest—and most common—mistakes people make with trusts. The fact is, on its own, a retirement account is not subject to probate or estate taxes. If your spouse has a qualified retirement account that names you as the beneficiary, you are eligible to inherit it free and clear. But if you put the IRA in the trust or if the beneficiary happens to be a trust—even if it's *your* trust—the retirement account can become subject to estate taxes. This is not a good thing, and I've seen it happen more than once. So if you set up a trust, leave your retirement accounts out of it.

Of course, this is hardly the only mistake people make concerning wills and trusts. Here are three other ones I come across all the time.

THE 3 MOST COMMON ERRORS PEOPLE MAKE
WITH WILLS AND TRUSTS

1. Not seeing it through

A couple meets with an attorney to discuss drafting a will or living trust. The attorney gives them a list of things to think about and decide—whereupon the couple goes home and never follows through. Or worse, they make the decisions but never get around to signing the trust documents. As a financial advisor, I see this constantly. In some cases, I've had clients take a full year to finish the process, mainly because they kept procrastinating. Don't procrastinate. Make an appointment with a lawyer, give yourselves a deadline, and get it done.

2. **Hiding the documents where no one can find them**

    People go to all the time and expense of drafting a will or living trust, and then what do they do? They hide the documents! Sometimes they hide the documents so well that they stay hidden, never to be found by those who need them.

    Either that or they put their will or trust documents in an obvious place—like a safety deposit box at the bank—and guess what they do with the key? That's right, they hide *it*.

    Pretty funny, right? Wrong. Your loved ones will have more than enough to deal with when you die without having to go on a scavenger hunt for your will or trust documents. To spare them this agony, I recommend that you put your will or trust documents (along with any other important papers, such as insurance policies, deeds, and the like) in an easy-to-find location—*and then tell your loved ones where it is!*

    You should also make sure your attorney has a copy of your will or trust documents on file. Most do this as a matter of routine, but double-check, just to be sure.

3. **Not keeping things up to date**

    I often meet couples whose wills or trusts were written 20 or 30 years ago and haven't been revised since. Indeed, I know plenty of couples whose wills still specify who should get custody of their children in the event both parents die—even though the children are now in their forties with children of their own. People at my seminars laugh when I tell them this, but it's more common than you might think.

    As the circumstances of your life change, your will or trust should change along with them. At the very least, make sure your will or trust is updated regularly. This means at least every five years . . . or anytime something material changes in your life.

One last suggestion: if you have elderly parents, make sure they've got a will or trust in place. You'd be surprised how many don't.

The reality is, if your parents don't get their act together, you will more than likely end up faced with a big mess. While the idea of initiating a conversation with your parents about wills and such may make you a bit uncomfortable, believe me—it will ultimately be more than worth the trouble.

SAFEGUARD NO. 3
Buy the best health coverage the two of you can afford.

The U.S. health-care industry is a mess, and it's probably going to get worse before it gets better. So there's no getting around it—with health-care costs continuing to skyrocket, you simply have to have medical insurance.

These days, you can easily spend $1,000 a day in a hospital, and that's not including surgery. I had a client who was never sick a day in his life suddenly discover he had cancer. He wound up spending $50,000 on chemotherapy in just a few months. Another otherwise healthy client of mine was involved in a car accident. In less than two weeks, he ran up medical bills totaling more than $100,000. In fact, a similar thing happened to me. When I was 15, I got hit by a car while I was riding my moped. It took six surgeries and three months in the hospital, followed by a year of physical therapy, before I was able to walk again. The bills totaled well into six figures.

Fortunately, both my clients and my parents had medical insurance that covered virtually all the costs.

Unfortunately, not everyone is so lucky. According to a recent study by the Kaiser Family Foundation, nearly one in five Americans under the age of 64 has no health-care coverage whatsoever. This is frightening.

So no debating here. You must have health insurance. The only questions in your mind should be how do you get it and what are your options.

Most couples fall into one of two categories. Either you're covered by an employer-provided health-care plan, or you're not—in which case the two of you will need to do some research and find a plan on your own. This may sound scary and difficult, but it doesn't need to be. If individual coverage turns out to be too expensive for you, you may be able to get a group rate through a professional organization or association. You might even check with your church or synagogue.

If you happen to have corporate medical coverage, don't think that lets you off the hook. In the end, every couple—even if they are covered by their employer—has to make some basic decisions about health-care insurance for themselves. With that in mind, let's take a little time to go over the basics of the most commonly available types of coverage.

What a Smart Couple Needs to Know About Health Insurance

There are basically two types of health-insurance programs to choose from these days—fee-for-service plans and managed care. Fee for service allows patients the kind of health care most of us grew up with. Unfortunately, because of the cost, fewer and fewer companies are offering it to their employees. Managed care is less expensive and, as a result, far more popular.

Fee-for-Service Plans

Once upon a time, most Americans had a family doctor whom they really knew and who really knew them. They went to this doctor whenever something was wrong with them, and if that something turned out to be especially complicated or obscure, the family doctor would refer them to a specialist.

Under a fee-for-service plan (also known as an indemnity plan), you can still be treated this way. You can continue to see your old family doctor, whether or not he or she is part of any program. You can switch physicians anytime you'd like, without needing anyone's permission. If you want to see a particular specialist, you go to that particular specialist. Once you've paid the deductible (which can range anywhere from $250 to $2,500 a year, depending on the particular policy), the plan typically pays 80 percent of your bill up to an annual cap.

There is, of course, a catch. The premiums for these sorts of policies are expensive—so expensive in fact that fewer than one out of every five companies is still willing to offer fee-for-service or indemnity coverage to their employees.

Despite the cost, if your employer happens to be one of the few who still offers the option of electing an indemnity or fee-for-service plan, I would urge you to consider it seriously. Yes, it will probably be the most expensive plan you can choose, but it's also bound to be the most flexible one, providing you with the most freedom and the most choices. Personally, when it comes to my health care, I like having the freedom to choose.

Managed Care

Because of their lower cost, most employers—not to mention most self-employed people—prefer managed-care plans these days. Managed care comes in three basic forms: through health maintenance organizations (HMOs), through preferred-provider organizations (PPOs), and through point-of-service (POS) plans.

HMO Coverage

A health maintenance organization is, in effect, a group of health-care providers who have joined together to provide comprehensive health-care coverage for subscribers. HMOs are generally the oldest managed-care systems around. They are also among the most restrictive.

When you sign up with an HMO, you are given a list of doctors from which you must select a "primary-care physician." Otherwise known as a "gatekeeper," this doctor is the one you must see whenever you have a medical problem, regardless of what the problem might be. In other words, if you wake up one morning and notice a spot on your leg, you can't go directly to your dermatologist. You have to make an appointment with your gatekeeper first. If it turns out you need to see a specialist, the gatekeeper will refer you to one within the HMO. If for some reason you want to see a specialist who's not part of your HMO, too bad. The visit will not be covered.

The good news about HMOs is that they are relatively inexpensive. Chances are they'll be the cheapest health-care option your employer offers. In most cases, you'll only have to make a $10 copayment when you visit your primary-care physician. The same is generally true for prescription drugs; indeed, some HMOs don't make you pay anything for drugs.

HMOs vary widely in cost and quality of service. Some people love their HMOs and will tell you they are the only way to go because they are so affordable and easy to use. Others will complain bitterly about not being able to see the doctors they want or get the treatment they feel they need. All things being equal, I'd spend more money and consider the next two options.

PPO Coverage

A preferred-provider organization usually consists of a group of individual physicians, medical practices, and hospitals that have joined together in a loose coalition to create a "group network." In some ways, PPOs look and feel a lot like HMOs, but there are some distinct differences that I think make the PPO approach much better. For one thing, PPOs don't require you to have a gatekeeper. You still have a primary-care physician, but if you want to see a specialist, you can go on your own without a referral. Also, you can use a specialist who's not a member of your PPO's group network and the PPO will still cover at least part of the bill.

Not surprisingly, all this flexibility comes at a price—literally. PPOs are more expensive than HMOs. Their premiums are slightly higher, the copayment may be $15 per visit instead of $10, and some PPOs require you to pay an annual out-of-pocket deductible of between $250 and $500 before their coverage kicks in.

POS Coverage

Point-of-service plans are becoming increasingly popular, probably because they offer subscribers the widest array of choices of any managed-care plan. Combining features from both HMOs and PPOs, the POS plan allows you either to stay within the plan's network of doctors (thus saving money) or to elect to go outside, in which case you have to pay a deductible (as with a PPO).

How Do We Choose Which Plan Is Best for Us?

This may sound crazy, but if you work for a company that offers a long list of health-care options, my suggestion is that you go with the most expensive choice. I say this because in almost every case the most expensive choice will provide you with the most options, and when it comes to your health care, I think it's crazy to cut corners.

You and your partner may be perfectly healthy now, but who knows what the future will bring? Tomorrow, you could find a lump on your chest or a spot on your back. Why sacrifice your freedom to see the doctor you want just to save $20 a month? It's simply not worth it. Eat out one less time a month or cancel those premium channels on your TV cable, and you've covered the cost of going with the most expensive health-care option that has the most flexibility.

If both of you happen to have corporate coverage, I'd suggest that you compare plans. One of them may be noticeably better than the other, in which case you may want to cancel the lesser plan and use the superior one to cover both of you. Over the long run, doubling up on one good plan may be cheaper than being on two separate ones. Don't do this, however, if the partner with the good coverage is at all likely to change jobs in the near future!

If You're Planning to Have Children . . .

Needless to say, couples who are thinking about having children should make sure they choose a medical plan that offers first-rate maternity coverage. If the two of you are planning to have a baby in the next year or two, call your company's benefits department and ask them which plan they recommend for prospective parents. If they won't give you any guidance, ask any coworkers you know who have had children.

In addition, it's always a good idea to contact the health-care providers directly. A really smart strategy is to select your medical plan *after* you select your doctor and your hospital. First, find the doctor and hospital you want. Then ask them which plans cover their services. Hopefully, you'll be able to sign up for one of these plans.

What About Self-Employed People?

Just because you're self-employed is no excuse not to have health-care coverage. These days, it's easier than ever to find affordable, quality medical insurance. Many entrepreneurs belong to professional organizations, and many of these offer group plans at reasonable rates. If you don't belong to such a group, why not consider joining one? Beyond that, you can always ask an independent insurance professional about getting coverage. Or you can go online and do your own research. The following Web sites are a good place to start.

AllBusiness
(415) 581–7600
www.allbusiness.com

e-Insure Services, Inc.
(312) 663–9663
www.einsurance.com

InsWeb Corp.
(916) 853–3300
www.insweb.com

MasterQuote of America Inc.
(800) 337–5433
www.masterquote.com

Quotesmith.com Inc.
(800) 556–9393
www.quotesmith.com

eHealthInsurance.com
(800) 977–8860
www.ehealthinsurance.com

Of course, if one of you works for a company that offers health-care coverage, your problem may be solved—simply go on your partner's plan. If the two of you aren't married, you'll obviously need to make sure the program covers domestic partnerships. Happily, an increasing number of companies are starting to do this.

SAFEGUARD NO. 4
Protect those who depend on you with life insurance.

Most people hate to talk about life insurance, but if you've got anyone in your life who counts on you for financial support, then you need to have some sort of protection plan in place in case something happens to you. And that's all life insurance is—a protection plan. When you die, the person (or people) whom you've designated as your beneficiary will get a lump-sum cash payment known as a death benefit. Certainly, there's no law that says when you die you have to leave someone else wealthy. But if there are people who depend on you—such as children or a nonworking significant other—you have a responsibility not to leave them in a world of financial pain.

Some Unfortunate Statistics

As a man, I hate to address this but the reality of life is that women tend to outlive us (on average, women live seven years longer than men). Combine this with the fact that women also tend to marry men older than they are and what results are some scary statistics. For one thing, the average age of widowhood in America is just 56. For another, nearly half the women over the age of 65 in the United States are widows.

All this is sad enough. Even worse, however, is to see a widow who thought her husband was insured—only to find out later (after it was too late) that he wasn't or that he didn't have enough coverage.

How Much Life Insurance Should We Buy?

What I said about health coverage applies here, too: life insurance is not a place to cut corners. Ideally, you want to purchase enough coverage to enable those you love to live comfortably should something happen to you. But how much is that?

Here's a list of questions the two of you need to ask yourselves in order to get a ballpark idea of how much life insurance you need.

1. Who relies on our income right now?

The first question you need to ask yourselves is who would get hurt financially in the event one of you were to die. If you have kids, could the surviving partner handle things financially on his or her own? What if both of you died at the same time? Don't assume that your parents or a sibling could or would shoulder the burden in your place. That's not fair to anyone. What if you're in a second marriage and have kids by a first? Could you depend on your ex to pay for your children's upbringing? If the two of you don't have children but live in a nice house and generally enjoy the good life, would the surviving partner be able to maintain that lifestyle if one of you passed away?

2. What does it cost those who depend on you to live for a year?

When you calculate this, make sure you include everything— taxes, mortgage payments, school costs, doctor bills, *everything*.

3. Are there any major debts that would need to be paid off or unexpected expenses you might incur?

If your spouse owes money (whether in the form of a mortgage, an auto loan, credit-card debt, back taxes, or whatever), you won't necessarily be let off the hook just because he or she has died. In fact, you could actually wind up inheriting the debt. Not much fun, which is another reason why you may need more insurance than you think. What about funeral expenses, probate costs, and estate taxes? These could run into tens of thousands of dollars, if not more. What if your partner owned a business? Could it continue to run without him or her? Are there business debts that would need to be paid off?

4. **Do either of you have a company policy?**

Many companies pay for a limited amount of life insurance for their employees. Find out if yours does, and if so, don't forget to factor in that death benefit when you calculate how much additional coverage you need. You should also find out if your policy at work is known as a "portable policy"—meaning you actually own it and can take it with you if you leave your job. If your company policy is not portable, you could find yourself in a very scary position, with no job and no life insurance coverage. So pull out your company policy and make sure you understand what kind of coverage you've got.

Finding the Right "Ballpark"

Now that you've gotten an idea of how big a financial "hole" your death might leave, you can calculate how much life insurance you should purchase. My ballpark recommendation is that you take out a policy with a death benefit that totals somewhere between 6 and 20 times your annual spending needs. For instance, if it takes $50,000 a year in spendable income to cover all your obligations, you may want to consider a death benefit of between $300,000 and $1 million.

Which end of that range should you lean toward? It depends on what your current assets are and how much of your debt you feel should be paid off. Needless to say, everyone is different. Some people want to assure that their dependents will never need to work again, while others feel a 10-year cushion is more than enough.

Make Sure You Insure a "Stay-at-Home" Parent

One of the biggest mistakes I see couples make with insurance is not insuring the parent who stays at home raising the kids. If you are married with children, or simply living together with children, don't make the mistake of insuring just the person who is "working" out of the house. Many men assume incorrectly that if their wife is a "stay-at-home mom," they are the only ones who need insurance, since they are the ones working. Really? What happens if "mom" or a stay-at-home "dad" dies? Someone is going to need to take care of the kids. That means either hiring a nanny or sending the kids to day-care full-time. Either way, this costs money! So be smart and insure both of you.

What Type of Life Insurance Should You Buy?

There are literally hundreds of different kinds of life-insurance policies. If you find yourself confused by all the variations, you are not alone. Indeed, when I ask people what type of life insurance they have, most don't really know. Fortunately, when you break it down, life insurance isn't really all that complicated.

There are basically two types of life insurance—term insurance, which builds no cash value, and permanent insurance, which does.

TERM INSURANCE

Term insurance is very simple. You pay an insurance company a premium, and in return the insurance company promises to pay your beneficiary a death benefit when you die. Specifically, term insurance provides you with a set amount of protection at a set price for a set period of time. As long as you pay the premium, you're covered. Stop paying, and your term policy will lapse—meaning, no one will get any death benefit when you die.

The main advantage of term life insurance is that it's relatively inexpensive. Indeed, term insurance is the most inexpensive type of life insurance around. It's also relatively easy to get. You can buy it on the Internet these days, where it's cheaper than ever.

The catch is that this type of policy builds no cash value. You can literally pay premiums into a term policy for 30 years, but if you then decide you no longer want or need it, you walk away with nothing. The point of term insurance is solely to provide your beneficiaries with a death benefit. That's it. It's a protection plan, pure and simple . . . and cheap.

Term insurance comes in two basic flavors—annual renewable term and level term.

Annual Renewable Term With annual renewable term insurance, your death benefit remains the same while your premiums get larger each year. That's because the older you get, the more likely it is that you will die within any given year. (Cheerful thought, isn't it?) More than likely, this is the type of policy you have if you work for a company and signed up for life insurance through the benefits department. The biggest advantage of an annual renewable term policy is that it is really inexpensive when you are young. Indeed, it is by far the cheapest way to buy insurance when you are just starting out. The problem is that as you get older (and the likelihood of death increases), the premiums can become prohibitively expensive.

Level Term Under a level term policy, both the death benefit and the premium remain the same for a period of time that you select when you first sign up. The period can range anywhere from 5 to 30 years. While this type of term insurance is initially more expensive than annual renewable term, it can actually turn out to be cheaper over the long run. For this reason, I usually recommend this type of term insurance to clients. If you choose a level term policy, I suggest you take it for a minimum of 15 to 20 years. If you are in your thirties or younger, a 20-year policy would at least protect your family in the years in which they are likely to have the greatest need for your income.

Who Should Consider Term Insurance?

This is actually an easy choice to make. Unless you are purchasing life insurance as an investment (which in most cases is *not* what you should be doing), I recommend you buy term insurance—specifically, a level term policy. The most sensible deal is probably to sign up for a 20-year policy. If rates come down, you can always "bust" the policy—that is, cancel it—and buy a new, cheaper one.

The Time to Shop for Cheaper Insurance Is Now!

Over the last 10 years, the cost of buying term insurance has been cut in half. What this means is that if you've currently got a policy that is more than five years old, you should either get on the Internet or call a good insurance agent to see if you can find a better deal.

In most cases, you should be able to save yourself hundreds of dollars a year in premium costs. Alternately, you can increase the size of your death benefit without having to pay an increased premium. I've had many clients actually double the size of their death benefits while continuing to pay the exact same premium.

As with so many other things we've discussed so far, this is not difficult to do—but it won't take care of itself. *You need to do it.* I remember a few years ago reviewing the finances of a couple in their early forties named Richard and Leslie. For the most part, they were in great shape, saving plenty of money and maxing out their 401(k) plans. But when I looked at their life insurance, I noticed that they were overpaying for the coverage they had. At the time, Richard was carrying a $250,000 policy, and I explained that for the exact same premium he could double the death benefit to $500,000. He and Leslie both nodded in agreement and said they would take care of it.

Unfortunately, this was one chore that never got done. A few years later, I heard some terrible news from Leslie. Richard had suffered a heart attack while they were on vacation and had passed away. Because they had neglected to change their policy, the death benefit Leslie received was half of what it might have been.

Leslie told me later that she and Richard really had intended to update their insurance policies. "We left your office really motivated to act," she said. "It's just that we got busy. I didn't expect Richard to die at 42. It wasn't planned."

The sad reality of life is that this sort of thing *never* is planned. So go check your policies now, and if they're more than a few years old, get yourself a better deal!

PERMANENT INSURANCE

Permanent life insurance is also known as "cash value" insurance. To put it simply, it's like taking a term policy and combining it with a forced savings plan that can help you build a nice nest egg. Eventually, you can either dip into these forced savings for income or use them to pay the annual premiums on your policy. The catch here is that permanent insurance is expensive. Indeed, it can cost as much as 5 to 10 times more than term insurance.

There are three main types of permanent life insurance: whole life, universal life, and variable universal life.

Whole Life Imagine paying for term insurance but adding a 50 percent surcharge to the cost of the annual premium and having some of that extra money put in a money-market account, where it can grow tax-deferred into a little nest egg for your old age. That's what whole life is. It's a term policy with a little cash-value basket added onto it. Insurance agents will tell you how great this cash-value basket is, and how safely and soundly the insurance company invests the proceeds. The problem is that the money is invested so conservatively that it seldom earns more than 4 or 5 percent a year—which is to say that the policy's cash value grows too slowly to really amount to anything.

Universal Life After decades of being sold on whole life insurance, people began to wake up and realize that it was not the great retirement vehicle they had been told it was. So the insurance industry came up with a new angle. "Instead of just putting your extra premium money in a money-market account," the industry told potential customers, "we will invest it more aggressively and pay you a great rate." Insurance agents sold these policies on the promise that policyholders could earn as much as 11 percent a year. They would flash fancy illustrations showing that if you earned 11 percent a year, your cash value would be just enormous in 20 years. These illustrations always looked really impressive. The problem was they were just illustrations, not guarantees. Universal life works great when the insurance company invests well, but it can be a disaster when the company doesn't. Many people who bought universal life policies back when rates were in the high teens have been shocked in recent years by annual returns of just 6 percent—and they still have to make premium payments.

Variable Universal Life Insurance If you feel strongly about purchasing permanent insurance—which is to say if you want life insurance that can also double as a retirement vehicle—I'd recommend variable universal life. With variable universal life you get a cash-value policy that allows you to control how the savings portion of your premium is invested. A good variable life policy may offer more than a dozen different high-quality mutual funds from which you can select. If you want to be conservative, you can choose a bond fund. If you want to be aggressive, you can choose growth funds. The point is, you are in charge. What makes this especially nice is that as with a 401(k) plan or IRA, the cash value of your policy can grow tax-deferred. That is, you can change investments, buying and selling funds as market conditions dictate, without having to pay taxes on any gains. Of course, as with any speculative investment, you can also lose money. There is no guarantee that your cash value will only go up.

Who Should Consider Variable Universal Life Insurance?

While I think that term life insurance makes the most sense for most people, there are certain circumstances under which you might want to consider buying a variable universal life policy. If the following five characteristics apply to you, variable universal life may actually be a good idea.

1) You want to build cash value for retirement.

2) You have at least 15 years to invest in the policy.

3) You earn a high income (at least $100,000 a year).

4) You are already maxing out contributions to a qualified retirement plan.

5) You understand the risks associated with mutual funds.

Keep in mind that variable universal life insurance is a complicated product that is currently being oversold to the wrong people. At the very least, you shouldn't even consider it if you're not already fully utilizing a 401(k) plan, deductible IRA, or other tax-deferred retirement account.

The reason insurance agents and some financial advisors are so motivated to sell you a permanent policy (whether in the form of whole life, universal, or variable) is that they make a lot of money off this kind of insurance. In some cases, the sales commission on a permanent insurance policy can be as much as 100 percent of the first year's premium. This is one of the reasons insurance agents are often so willing to come to your home for a meeting and will "follow up" by calling you again and again.

Where Should We Start?

If you are going to buy life insurance, the two of you should meet with a life-insurance professional—*not* a salesperson. Find someone who has been in the business for at least 10 years and really knows what he or she is doing. Make a point of asking friends and getting recommendations. Insurance is complicated and because of this I recommend getting professional guidance.

However, some people prefer not to buy through an agent or broker. If you're one of these people, do your research on the Internet. It's never been easier to buy life insurance on the Internet, and it's never been cheaper. Here are some great sources you can use:

Ameritas
(800) 552–3553
www.ameritas.com

e-INSURE Services, Inc.
(312) 663–9663
www.einsurance.com

InsWeb Corp.
(916) 853–3300
www.insweb.com

MasterQuote of America Inc.
(800) 337–5433
www.masterquote.com

Quotesmith.com, Inc.
(800) 556–9393
www.quotesmith.com

USAA Life Insurance Company
(800) 531–8000
www.usaa.com

SAFEGUARD NO. 5

Protect yourselves and your incomes with disability insurance.

I used to think disability insurance was a waste of money. Then I saw what happened to Christopher Reeve.

Here was a genuine movie star, a guy so fit and healthy that he literally embodied Superman. Then, in 1995, he fell off a horse and broke his neck. In an instant, everything he had done with his life up to that moment—and everything he was looking forward to doing in the future—all disappeared.

Today, though he still works in the movie business, Reeve is better known as a tireless advocate for the disabled. Through his Christopher Reeve Paralysis Foundation, he raises millions of dollars a year to support research aimed at finding more effective treatments and possible cures for spinal cord and other catastrophic injuries.

Reeve also endorses disability insurance. "I know all too well how quickly a person's life can change and the importance of ensuring a family's financial security," he says. "That's why I'm troubled by the fact that 60 percent of Americans lack any form of long-term disability insurance. That's far too many people at risk."

Reeve is right. Though far more people have life insurance than have disability insurance, the chances of your becoming sick or hurt are much greater than the chances of your dying prematurely. Without disability insurance you are playing Russian roulette with your income.

Consider the following statistics. In one year . . .

- One out of every 106 people will die.

- One out of every 88 homes will catch fire.

- One out of every 70 cars will be involved in a serious accident.

But . . .

One out of every 10 people will have to cope with a severe disability!

What this means is that the greatest threat to your ability to finish rich may be the risk the two of you face of serious injury or illness! And the younger you are, the greater your risk actually is.

Other than your health, your income is probably your most important asset. Lose it and you could be losing your primary means of financial security. That's why we all need disability insurance.

How Much Disability Insurance Do We Need?

Disability insurance is not designed to make you rich. Rather, like life insurance, it is a protection plan for your current earning power. Ideally, therefore, an adequate disability policy is one that would pay you the equivalent of the take-home pay you would lose in the event one or both of you were to suffer an incapacitating disability.

Most disability plans offer a benefit equal to about 60 percent of the policyholder's gross (or before-tax) income. That may not sound like much, but if you pay for the disability policy yourself, any income you receive from it will be tax-free, so 60 percent of your gross will probably be enough to maintain your standard of living. (After all, 60 percent of the gross is about what most of us actually take home.)

If your employer pays for your disability insurance, any benefits you receive from it will be taxed. This means that if the policy only pays 60 percent of your gross income, you're going to come up short. Indeed, once you've paid the taxes on your disability benefit, you're likely to find yourself with only a fraction of your normal take-home pay. To guard against this, you should consider purchasing what is known as a "gap policy" to make up the difference.

Don't Assume You Have Disability Insurance

Many people mistakenly assume they automatically get disability coverage from their employer. Don't assume anything of the kind. If one or both of you work for a company, first thing tomorrow check your benefits statements or phone your benefits departments to find out whether or not either of you has disability insurance. If you don't, find out if you can get it and start the application process immediately. If either of you is self-employed and doesn't currently have disability insurance, make getting it a top priority.

You should apply for disability insurance now while both of you are healthy. For some reason, people always seem to put this off, waiting until something is wrong with them before they start trying to get coverage. By then, of course, it is too late. And don't think you can fool the insurance company by fibbing on your policy application. Saying you're healthy when you know you're not, or that you don't smoke when in fact you do, is not only immoral, it's also pointless. Insurance companies will do just about anything they can to avoid having to pay out benefits—including hiring an investigator to check you out. Believe me, if you say anything on the application that's less than honest, they will find out, and your policy will be canceled. (And, no, you won't get your premiums back.)

Questions to Ask Before You Sign Up

1. **Is the disability plan portable and guaranteed renewable?**

   If you purchase your policy through your employer, you must make sure that you can take the policy with you if you leave the company. Also, you want a policy that is guaranteed renewable; there is no bigger rip-off than an insurance company that makes you "qualify" each and every year. This is how a bad insurance company gets out of having to pay you when you file a claim!

2. **Under what circumstances will the policy pay off?**

   Specifically, you want to know whether the policy will cover you in the event you're no longer able to do the work you currently do, or whether it pays off only if you are rendered unable to do work of any kind. In the insurance industry, this is known as "owner occupation" and "any occupation" coverage. Make sure you buy an owner-occupation policy. Why?

Well, take me, for example. I happen to make my living talking on the phone, meeting with clients, and speaking at seminars. Now, if I lost my voice and couldn't talk, I would for all intents and purposes be out of a job. But unless I had owner-occupation coverage, the insurance company could say to me, "So what if you can't talk on the phone or do speeches? There are plenty of other jobs you could do—like digging ditches. So we are not going to pay you any disability benefits." With owner-occupation coverage, they can't do that to me. This sort of coverage is more expensive, but it is much, much safer.

3. **How long does it take for the coverage to kick in?**

Most disability policies start paying benefits within three to six months after you've been declared disabled. The easiest way to reduce the cost of a disability policy is to lengthen that waiting period. The larger the cash cushion you have in your security basket, the longer you can stretch it out.

4. **How long will the policy cover me?**

Ideally, your disability policy should pay you benefits at least until you turn 65.

5. **Is the coverage limited to physical disability, or are mental and emotional disorders also covered?**

A major cause of disability these days is stress. Not all disability policies cover it, however. If you are in a high-stress occupation, make sure yours does.

As with all good and important things, there is a catch to disability insurance. It is expensive, as a result of which most people don't have it. (As Christopher Reeve noted, only about two out of five of us carry some form of disability insurance.) The reason it costs so much is that the insurance companies know there is a good chance they will have to pay off on the policies they write. (This alone should convince you that you need it.) In any case, my recommendation is that you first contact your company's benefits department and see if you can get it through them. Group policies tend to be less expensive and easier to get. If your employer won't cover you—or if you are self-employed—contact a disability insurer directly. Here is a list of some of the larger firms that provide disability insurance.

Aetna U.S. Healthcare
(800) 636–2386
www.aetna.com

Continental General Insurance Company
(402) 397–3200
www.continentalgeneral.com

Mutual of Omaha Insurance Company
(800) 775–6000
www.mutualofomaha.com

Northwestern Mutual Life Insurance Company
(414) 271–1444
www.northwesternmutual.com

State Farm Insurance Companies
(309) 766–2311
www.statefarm.com

Disability Insurance Services, Inc.
(619) 284–8444
www.diexpert.com

SAFEGUARD NO. 6

If either of you is in your sixties, it's time to consider long-term care coverage.

Once upon a time, individual families provided their own support systems to take care of sick or aged parents. Today, families are often spread out all over the country and as a result there is no support system. With average life expectancies climbing, more elderly people are finding themselves in need of either home care or a long-term care facility. Indeed, studies indicate that no fewer than one out of every three Americans over the age of 65 will eventually need this sort of help.

The cost of such care can be staggering—as much as $30,000 to $70,000 a year for residence in a long-term care facility. You may think that Medicare will cover your nursing-care needs. Unfortunately, the reality is that in most cases it won't.

Busting the Medicare Myth

According to a poll taken by the American Association of Retired Persons, four out of five of us assume that Medicare will pay for our basic nursing-care needs when we get old. As I noted above, we are in for an unpleasant surprise. The fact is, of the billions of dollars in nursing-home costs we incur every year, less than 10 percent are covered by Medicare.

The reason is simple. Most of the care that nursing homes provide to people with chronic, long-term illnesses or disabilities is custodial care, and Medicare does not pay for custodial care. Rather, Medicare is meant to take care of what are known as acute-care needs. For Medicare to cover a nursing-home stay, you must first spend three full days in an acute-care hospital and require skilled care or rehabilitation therapy at least five days a week. And even then, Medicare will cover you completely only for the first 20 days of your nursing-home stay. (After that, it may pay a portion of your care for the next 80 days, provided your health is actually improving as a result.)

And even if you turn out to be one of the lucky ones who meets the current qualification requirements, there's no guarantee that Medicare will still be around in 20 years. Many experts think that the government will not be able to continue the funding of Medicare in its current form for very much longer because there will be so many more elderly people who need it. What about Medicaid? Well, Medicaid is in essence welfare, and to qualify for it you must be virtually destitute. That's *not* how a Smart Couple wants to end up.

Long-Term Care

As valuable as it can be, LTC coverage isn't necessarily something you need to buy right away (especially if you are under the age of 50).

Most people start thinking about LTC coverage in their fifties and purchase it in their sixties. If you wait until your seventies or eighties, it can become prohibitively expensive. Unless you're in terrible shape, you can still get a pretty good deal in your mid-sixties.

When you're looking for LTC coverage, the first thing you need to understand is what it will not do. Long-term care insurance will not pay for acute care that you get in a hospital (say, in the immediate aftermath of a heart attack or a broken hip). This is typically the province of health insurance and Medicare. What LTC insurance will cover is the kind of care you get in a nursing home, a residential-care facility, a convalescent facility, an extended facility, a community hospice or adult-care center, or in some cases, care in your own home.

The type of LTC coverage you can buy varies from state to state. All things being equal, when you check out what's available in your state, I recommend that you consider a comprehensive policy. The reason is that right now both of you are probably healthy and as a result can't really predict what type of coverage the two of you will need in the future. A comprehensive policy will typically give you the most options. It will cost more, but should one or both of you eventually need the care, I'm confident it will more than justify the extra expense.

How to Keep Your LTC Premiums Down

The cost of LTC coverage depends on a number of variables. These include your age, the level of care you want, the amount of coverage ($100 a day, $200 a day, and so on), the length of waiting time before your policy kicks in, your state of health and age, and how long you want your policy to last should you need to use it.

Not counting short stays of less than three months, statistics show that most people spend an average of about three years in a nursing-care facility. Nonetheless, I recommend paying the extra 10 percent to 15 percent it costs to get lifetime coverage. If the extra cost is too much for you, you can reduce the premium price by requesting a higher deductible on your policy. What this means is that your policy will take longer to go into effect. Most LTC policies start paying off within 30 to 60 days after you enter a nursing facility or put in a claim for home care.

By stretching that out a bit, you can bring down your premium costs quite nicely.

Delaying the start of coverage may sound scary, but it's actually quite sensible, since you will probably be able to afford the first few months on your own. It's later on that you will need the most help. By taking a higher deductible and getting lifetime coverage you are covering the worst-case possibility, which is why you are buying this type of coverage in the first place. (By the way, the cost of this type of insurance can be tax deductible, so check with your accountant if you decide to purchase it.)

Questions to Ask Before You Sign Up

1. **What exactly does the policy cover?**

   Remember, there are several different types of coverage available and they vary from state to state. Make sure you know exactly what type of coverage you are being shown before you sign up.

2. **How much will the policy pay out in daily benefits? Will it be adjusted for inflation? At what point do my benefits kick in and how long will they last?**

   As I noted above, you can keep your premiums down by requesting a higher deductible. Also, it's probably worth paying a little more in order to get yourselves lifetime coverage.

3. **Does the policy contain a premium waiver or will I still have to pay the premiums after I start receiving benefits?**

   With this waiver, you won't have to worry about continuing to pay premiums while you are in the nursing-care facility.

4. **Is there a grace period for late payments?**

   Make sure there is. You would hate to find yourself in a situation where you accidentally missed a payment and then discovered that you'd lost your coverage.

5. Are there any diseases or injuries that are not covered?

The answer should be no.

Be Careful Whom You Buy From

Because LTC insurance is a relatively new insurance product, I recommend that you avoid purchasing an LTC policy from any company that hasn't been in the business for at least 10 years. And even then you should always check out the company's record. There are five major services that rate insurance companies (A. M. Best, Standard & Poor's, Moody's, Duff & Phelps, and Weiss), and you shouldn't buy a policy from any company that hasn't earned a top grade from at least three of them. You can find out what sort of ratings a company has received by asking it; if the company says it doesn't know or doesn't want to tell you, that's a good sign you should take your business elsewhere.

Here's how to contact two of the biggest providers of LTC insurance.

GE Financial Assurance
(800) 844–6543
www.gefn.com

John Hancock Life Insurance Co.
(800) 800–5523
www.jhancock.com

LTCinsurance.com
(401) 732–1879
www.ltcinsurance.com

In addition, make sure you find out what happens to your policy in the event the company is sold or goes out of business. Ideally, you want a guarantee that if your policy were to be transferred without your permission, the original terms on which you bought it would remain in effect.

You have now completed your security basket. In the process, you have done an amazing amount—far more than 95 percent of the population ever does—to safeguard the rich future together that the two of you deserve. Now it's time to turn from the security side of life to the fun part—building your dream basket.

STEP **7**

BUILD YOUR
DREAM BASKET

I'M AT THE AGE NOW WHERE everyone I know is having kids. When we visit our friends, their houses are filled with toys and children "playing." It's often hard to figure out exactly what the kids are doing—except that they're having the time of their life. They're not worried about bills, work, mortgage payments, or interest rates. They just want to have fun, play all day, and enjoy themselves. Their biggest concern is wanting to know when lunch is going to be. Most of all, they like to dream. For a kid, there's almost no difference between dreams and reality.

What makes kids' lives so special (and makes us so often wish that we were kids again ourselves) is that they dream all the time, and they dream big. Kids don't need to go to motivational seminars to be told they need to dream about what they want to do with their lives. Ask a bunch of kids what they want to do when they grow up, and they won't hold back. They'll tell you the most amazing things. When I was a kid, I told everyone I wanted to be race-car driver. That's what makes life so much fun for kids: they imagine being and doing anything and everything.

To my mind, one of the saddest things about getting older is that it becomes so easy to stop dreaming. It becomes so easy to stop "acting like a kid" and start being realistic. It becomes so easy to accept your life the way it is, to feel that what you have now and what you are doing today is as much as you can or should expect from the world.

Now I'm not suggesting that you shouldn't be grateful for what you have and how far you've progressed in your life. Quite the contrary—I believe it's critically important to be grateful for what the world has given you. What I'm suggesting is that deep in your hearts you and your partner have dreams that are going unfulfilled. There are things the two of you want to do and be that you have put in a "closet" somewhere and forgotten about. Or even worse, you haven't forgotten about these dreams—you've just given up on ever attaining them.

The number-one reason people let their dreams go unfulfilled—the reason they leave them in the closet of life, collecting dust—is money. That's the truth, plain and simple. People stop dreaming because they don't have the money it takes to transform their dreams into reality. In this chapter, I'm going to show you and your partner how to change that.

It's Time to Dream Again

Let's face it—just about everyone wants to have fun and be rich. The national pastime in this country is not baseball or football—it's playing the lottery. Literally millions of people buy lottery tickets every week, regularly spending a dollar or two (or five) in the hope of winning a jackpot. Why? Because, deep down, they believe that if their number comes up, they can be a kid again and start living their dreams.

Of course, the chances of this happening are so absurdly small that it's mind-boggling. You literally have a better chance of being hit by lightning than of winning the megajackpot or the powerball sweepstakes or whatever it's called in your state. But that doesn't matter. The reason so many of us play the lottery, watch those "millionaire" game shows on TV, or go to work for start-ups that pay in stock options instead of cash is because we all want to be able to dream big.

Dreaming big is the key to happiness. Dreaming big is energizing. Dreaming big is fun. Can you remember a time in your life when you used to dream big? When you had things you wanted to accomplish and you weren't afraid to talk about them? Do you remember what it felt like to not have to be so "responsible"? A time when you weren't consumed with income, career, family and bills and reality? When you were less boring?

Be honest. Many adults become boring as they get older. It's easy to get boring. We get into ruts and we stop "playing." Well, for the next few minutes, I want you to just "play along." Don't be realistic. Don't act like an adult. Pretend you're a child again and that you can do anything, be anyone, have fun. What would you do? Who would you become? What would you and your partner do together?

Learning How to Go for It

In Step Three, I talked about goal-setting. That's not what this step is about. We're not concerned here with how to earn more money, lose weight, or get organized. What we're concerned with here is how to really go for it. What do the two of you want to do that is totally fun, totally crazy, totally outrageous? Do you want to travel around the world? Go wine-tasting in Tuscany? Swim with the dolphins in Hawaii? Build your dream home with that dream kitchen? Or maybe it's a dream "cave" with a 50-inch television, a built-in bar, and a pool table?

I don't know what your dream is. But what I do know is that, as a couple, you deserve to dream together—and the time to start dreaming is now!

Understanding What It Takes

One of the greatest things I've learned in my life is that almost anything is possible if you just plan for it. As I explained earlier, the key to achieving your goals is to make them specific and measurable. You put them in writing and then you chart your progress toward them. This is as true for dreams as for anything else.

The fact is, some dreams don't even require money; they just take some planning. But most do take money, and with that in mind, we're going to learn how to create a dream basket that will enable the two of you to pay for your dreams.

Here's how I want you to start. Assuming that you and your partner are not literally reading this book at the same time, I want whichever one of you is reading it now to write up your own list of dreams first. Use the Dream Worksheet on the next page to list your top five dreams. Then get your partner to do the same thing.

Once you've each finished your individual lists, get together and make a "we dream" list. The "we dream" list is what you should focus on. Nothing will solidify a marriage or a partnership faster than having a "dream plan" that you work on together, as a team. To make sure this really happens, I suggest that the two of you set aside a specific amount of time to do this. Literally make an appointment with yourselves this week to spend at least half an hour writing out your top five dreams, first individually, then as a couple.

This is important. You can't just walk up to your partner at the end of the day, while you're getting dinner ready or putting the kids to sleep, and say, "What dreams do you have? Let's write them down." Your dreams are too important to treat so casually. Take them seriously. Make an appointment on your calendar to do this . . . and do it this week!

DREAM WORKSHEET
Designing and Implementing the Fun Factor!

The difference between this Dream Worksheet and the Purpose-Focused Financial Plan is that the Dream Worksheet is meant for you to focus on the "fun" stuff in life. In this exercise, write down the top five things that you want to do with your life that sound like "fun"—things you might not consider realistic but you would really like to do.

To do this, simply follow the six steps below and fill in the worksheet on the following page.

1. List your top five dreams. Remember . . . have fun with this. Be "kid-like," not adult-minded.

2. Make these dreams as specific and measurable as possible.

3. What action can you take in the next 48 hours to get the ball rolling? Remember . . . "I don't know" is not an answer.

4. Who are you going to share your dream with? No matter how crazy it may sound now, the sooner you share it with someone you love and respect the sooner that dream is going to feel real.

5. What value will this dream help you realize?

6. What will the dream cost? Even if you don't know the exact cost, make sure you write down an estimate.

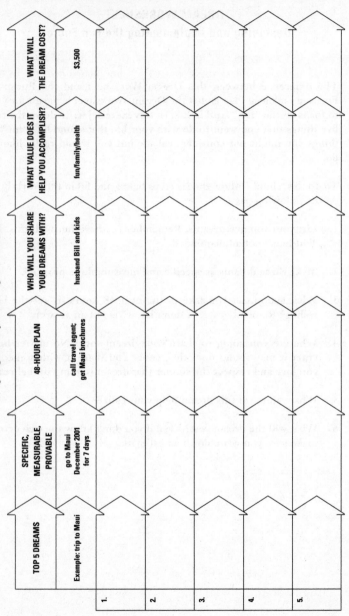

DREAMS
Designing and Implementing the Fun Factor™

TOP 5 DREAMS	SPECIFIC, MEASURABLE, PROVABLE	48-HOUR PLAN	WHO WILL YOU SHARE YOUR DREAMS WITH?	WHAT VALUE DOES IT HELP YOU ACCOMPLISH?	WHAT WILL THE DREAM COST?
Example: trip to Maui	go to Maui December 2001 for 7 days	call travel agent; get Maui brochures	husband Bill and kids	fun/family/health	$3,500
1.					
2.					
3.					
4.					
5.					

Don't Fall Into the "I Don't Have a Dream" Trap

I am constantly amazed at the way some people try to avoid improving their lives. For instance, I've actually had people (dozens of them over the years) ask me, "What if I don't have a dream?"

I'm sorry, but the only way you don't have a dream is if you're dead. Dead people don't dream. The rest of us have dreams. It's just that in many cases we've let our "dream muscle" atrophy because we haven't used it in so long.

If this is what's happened to you, build up your dream muscle the same way you'd work on any other muscle that's gotten out of shape. That is, don't start by trying to lift the heaviest weight in the gym. Start with a relatively small dream . . . like planning a romantic weekend get-away for the two of you—somewhere that's within driving distance and not too expensive. It doesn't have to be anything mind-blowing. The point here is simply that you and your partner are going to write down on a piece of paper a dream that the two of you want to make real, and then you are going to fund it. That's all there is to this dream-basket process.

By the way, even if you're not completely convinced you know what your dream is, start funding it anyway. The reason: sooner or later, you *will* know what it is, and when you do, you'll be glad you've already gotten a head start on putting aside the money you'll need to make it real.

Filling Your Dream Basket . . . the Importance of "Systematic Investing"

Now that you've put your dreams in writing, you have answered what I call the "why invest" question. Many people don't bother to change their spending habits or start saving simply because their future doesn't seem compelling enough to motivate them. But nothing creates leverage and motivation like a dream.

So now you know what your dreams are. Hopefully, the prospect of making them real has the two of you excited. The question now is, how are you going to pay for them? The answer is simple. You need to create a systematic investment plan devoted solely to funding your dreams.

I call this process filling your dream basket. Here's all there is to it. Just as you secured your future by deciding to pay yourself first a fixed percentage of your income for your retirement basket, now you're going to fund your dreams by committing to pay yourself an additional fixed percentage of your income that will go into your dream basket.

The key to making this work is to fund your dream basket on a regular basis. This is what is known in the investment industry as "systematic investing." With a systematic investment plan, you commit to putting a certain dollar amount into a specific investment on a monthly or weekly—or sometimes even daily—basis. These days, as a result of advances in technology, many mutual funds will allow you to make systematic investments of as little as $50 a month. I've provided a starter list of some of these mutual funds on pages 202–203. (Some mutual funds that require a minimum investment of $500 to $2,000 will waive the minimum if you commit to a systematic investment plan.)

Once you've set up a systematic investment plan, the brokerage firm or mutual-fund company will automatically deduct a predetermined amount of money from your checking or savings account on a predetermined date. The automatic aspect of the plan is what makes it work. Don't kid yourself into believing that you're going to be disciplined enough to sit down every two weeks and manually write a check and then mail it in. I've been helping people manage their money for years now, and I can tell you firsthand that even the most disciplined investors rarely stick to a systematic investment plan that isn't done automatically.

I've never been more excited about the concept of funding a dream basket than I am now because it has never been easier. Not only are most mutual funds now available to practically all investors through systematic investing, but the Internet has made the process of investing with small amounts of money unbelievably convenient. As you'll see, the great thing about funding a dream basket in this way is that as your investments increase in value, your dream will start to feel more real and more possible, and you'll find yourself becoming more excited and more motivated than ever.

How Much Is Enough?

The amount that you contribute to your dream basket is totally up to you. I suggest that you start by kicking in at least 3 percent of your after-tax income. That is, before you pay bills, sweep at least 3 percent of your take-home pay into your dream basket. Why 3 percent? Because most people—even those whom I call "dream challenged" (the ones who are going to fight this whole concept because they are afraid to dream)—will have a hard time arguing that they can't save an additional 3 percent of their income.

If you do this automatically before you pay the bills, you'll be amazed how quickly it becomes part of your routine—and how quickly the money starts to add up. If your partner happens to be a particularly dream-challenged individual, start by putting just 1 percent of your income into your dream basket, but make it a goal to increase the amount by another 1 percent within six months. Do this every six months, and at the end of two years you will be saving 4 percent of your income for your dreams—and you'll barely notice it!

How Exactly Should I Invest My Dream-Basket Money?

There are literally thousands of ways to invest. You can buy individual stocks and bonds. You can buy certificates of deposit. You can purchase commodities or preferred stocks. You can buy convertible bonds. You can acquire gold or silver, or art or stamps. You can buy shares in unit trusts. The list goes on and on.

Because there are so many investment choices, people often don't know what to do. As a result, they do nothing. When it comes to funding your dream basket, I don't want you to be so overwhelmed that you find yourself unable—or unwilling—to take immediate action. Nor do I want you to be held back by the amount of money you may be required to put up. So with these factors in mind, I'm going to suggest that you fund your dream basket by investing in mutual funds.

What Exactly Is a Mutual Fund?

One of the more interesting and scary discoveries I've made over the years is that there are a lot of people who invest in mutual funds without even knowing what they are. You wouldn't believe some of the answers I've gotten when I have asked people at my classes and seminars what they think a mutual fund is. People say things like "it's a big stock," "it's a safe investment," "it's a special stock," "it's a bank product used to help people buy stocks," "it's a holding tank where you put stocks," and on and on.

Well, for the record, here's the real definition of what a mutual fund is, according to Charles Schwab. In *Charles Schwab's Guide to Financial Independence*, he defines a mutual fund as an investment company that pools the money of many investors and buys various securities (such as stocks or bonds). Investors who own shares of the mutual fund thus automatically achieve the benefit of a diversified portfolio without having to buy individual investments themselves.

Why Investing in Mutual Funds Makes Sense

In my opinion, there are six key reasons why you should invest your dream-basket money in mutual funds.

1. **They are easy to invest in.** As I said before, many mutual funds today allow you to start a systematic investment program with as little as $50 a month. You can set this up, often at no cost, through a financial advisor or with the mutual-fund company directly.

2. **They offer instant diversification.** Even though you may be putting in as little as $50 a month, you immediately enjoy a stake in a portfolio that could include hundreds of stocks and bonds.

3. **They offer professional money management.** The people who run mutual funds are full-time professionals who bring incredible expertise and experience to the job. This includes professional research and trading execution.

4. **They are cost-efficient.** According to the Morningstar rating service, the average internal mutual-fund management fee is about 1.4 percent of the assets managed. You would probably wind up paying a lot more than this if you tried on your own to build and manage a portfolio of individual stocks and bonds.

5. **They are liquid and easy to monitor.** Most mutual funds are priced daily and are posted in the newspaper right next to the stock tables. Thus, you can easily find out how your investment is doing—every day, if you want to. And most mutual funds allow you to pull your money out with less than five days' notice.

6. **They are boring.** Because they are so diversified, mutual funds don't fluctuate in price as much as individual stocks or bonds. Many people consider this lack of volatility boring. As far as I'm concerned, in the investment world, boring is good.

Now that you understand why mutual funds are a good investment, it's time to consider which type makes the most sense for you. There are, after all, more than 13,000 mutual funds to choose from. To make things simple, I'm going to suggest exactly what type of mutual fund investment I personally would use to fund my dream basket. The only real variable is the time horizon—that is, how long you think it will take the two of you to accumulate all the money you'll need to fund your particular dream.

FOR SHORT-TERM DREAMS (LESS THAN TWO YEARS)

It doesn't get simpler than this. If you're saving for a short-term dream, such as going on a vacation or redoing the kitchen—anything you can achieve in two years or less—you need to invest conservatively and keep your money liquid (meaning easily accessible).

In my opinion, there is only one sensible investment that meets these criteria: your money should go into a money-market account. I discussed money-market checking accounts in Step Six as the smart alternative to regular bank checking accounts. In this case, you don't necessarily need the checking feature because you're not going to be using this money until you're ready to realize your dream. So what we call a "plain vanilla" money-market account—that is, one without any frills or features—may be all you need.

A money-market account is a mutual fund that typically invests in very liquid, very safe, very short-term government securities. As I noted earlier, money-market accounts can be opened at most brokerage firms with relatively small initial deposits. Indeed, in many cases, if you set up an automatic investment plan, you can fund them with as little as $50 a month.

These accounts are not only incredibly safe (to my knowledge, there has never been a money-market default), they are also quite stable. In recent years, they've generally offered an average annual interest rate of between 4.5 percent and 7 percent. In many cases, you can find money-market accounts that pay as much or more than a two-year certificate of deposit. What's more, money-market accounts are liquid, which means you can pull your funds out at any time without ever having to pay a penalty fee.

If you don't yet have a financial advisor, opening a money-market account can be a great way to begin a relationship with one. Get a referral from a friend or visit the local branch of a major brokerage company and ask to meet with an advisor. Explain that you're looking to open a money-market account and that you would like to set up a systematic investment plan to fund it. By the way, there are no commissions on money-market accounts, so you don't need to worry about the cost of setting one up. There isn't any.

FOR MID-TERM DREAMS (TWO TO FOUR YEARS)

In this time frame, things are a little trickier. If you happen to be ultra-conservative and don't want to risk your dream money, I'd recommend going with a short-term bond fund. However, if you're looking for more of a return—and can handle a little more risk—you should consider what's known as a balanced fund.

Short-term bond funds invest in really short-term government bonds, typically Treasury bills with maturities ranging from six months to four years. These types of bond fund are very safe, relatively stable (meaning the price won't fluctuate much), and generally offer an annual return roughly 1 percentage point higher than a money-market account typically pays. Because these funds offer such a small edge over money-market accounts, it's hard for me to get excited about them.

Balanced funds are mutual funds that invest both in stocks and bonds. A typical balanced fund will have about 60 to 70 percent of its assets in stocks and the remainder in bonds (usually Treasuries). Because it's so well diversified, this type of fund is less risky then a pure stock fund. And while it normally won't outperform the stock market, it should come close to matching it. Typically, a balanced fund will generate about 85 percent of the returns you would get from a similar-sized investment in the stock market. Indeed, over the last 30 years, balanced funds have generated annualized returns of about 11 percent.

Comparing balanced funds to straight stock funds is like comparing the tortoise to the hare. Balanced funds are slow and steady, but they will get you to where you want to go. These are by far my favorite "starter" investment.

FOR LONG-TERM DREAMS (FOUR TO TEN YEARS)

Once you get to dreams that are going to take you more than four years to save for, you should really consider putting your dream-basket money into growth-oriented investments. Because you've got more time, you can afford to take more risk to get a bigger return. To my mind, that means investing in stock-based mutual funds.

Where Do We Start?

As far as I'm concerned, the first place you should put your long-term dream-basket money is in an index fund. Index funds are simple, inexpensive, easy to set up, and they work. What more could you ask?

Index funds are stock mutual funds that mimic a specific index. In recent years, the most popular of these have been S&P 500 index funds. These funds invest in the 500 stocks that make up the Standard & Poor's index. Next to the Dow Jones Industrial Average (which consists of 30 or so "blue chip" stocks), the S&P 500 is one of the most commonly quoted stock-market indicators. That's because the performance of the S&P 500 pretty much matches the performance of the market as a whole.

The main reason index investing has become so popular is that it costs less than investing in other kinds of funds. What's more, index funds offer real tax advantages. Because index fund managers move in or out of particular stocks only when those stocks are added to or dropped from the index they're mimicking (something that happens relatively infrequently), there is barely any trading that results in taxable capital gains. In addition, while index funds may have lagged behind some actively managed funds in the go-go years of the late 1990s, historically they have tended to do better than most other funds. (Over the last 20 years or so, index funds have outperformed roughly 75 percent of the actively managed funds.)

If you want even broader exposure to the stock market than an S&P 500 index fund, you might consider a Wilshire 5000 Index Fund. As the number suggests, the Wilshire 5000 tracks the performance of 5,000 separate stocks, and as a result represents one of the most diversified market gauges you can find.

Here is a list of some popular index funds. Remember, they all represent investments in the stock market—meaning there is risk involved. So read their prospectuses before you invest any money.

S&P 500 Index Funds
Vanguard Index 500 (symbol: VFINX)
(800) 992–8327
www.vanguard.com
Minimum investment required for a regular account: $3,000/For
   IRA: $1,000
Systematic Investment Plan: Must first meet minimum invest-
   ment/$100 minimum for additional investments

Dreyfus S&P 500 (symbol: DSPIX)
(800) 782–6620
www.dreyfus.com
Minimum investment required for a regular account: $2,500/For
   IRA: $750
Systematic Investment Plan: Minimum requirement waived; plan
   can be started with $100 investment

Transamerica Premier Index (symbol: TPIIX)
(800) 89–ASK–US
www.transamericafunds.com
Minimum investment required for a regular account: $2,500/For
    IRA: $250
Systematic Investment Plan: Minimum requirement waived; plan
    can be started with $50 investment

Schwab S&P 500 Fund (symbol: SWPIX)
(800) 225–8570
www.schwab.com
Minimum investment required for a regular account: $2,500/For
    IRA: $1,000
Systematic Investment Plan: Must first meet minimum invest-
    ment/$100 minimum for additional investments

Wilshire 5000 Index Funds
Vanguard Total Stock Market (symbol: VTSMX)
(800) 992–8327
www.vanguard.com
Minimum investment required for a regular account: $3,000/For
    IRA: $1,000
Systematic Investment Plan: Must first meet minimum invest-
    ment/$100 minimum for additional investments

T. Rowe Price Total Equity (symbol: POMIX)
(800) 225–5132
www.troweprice.com
Minimum investment required for a regular account: $2,500/For
    IRA: $1,000
Systematic Investment Plan: Minimum requirement waived; plan
    can be started with $50 investment

Morgan Stanley Total Market Index Fund (symbol: TMIBX)
(877) 937–6739
www.msdwadvice.com

Minimum investment required for a regular account: $1,000/For
IRA: $1,000

Systematic Investment Plan: Minimum requirement waived; plan
can be started with $100 investment

Schwab Total Stock Market Index Fund (symbol: SWTIX)
(800) 225–8570
www.schwab.com
Minimum investment required for a regular account: $2,500/For
IRA: $1,000

Systematic Investment Plan: Must first meet minimum invest-
ment/$100 minimum for additional investments

A New Class of Index Funds

In the last few years, a new class of index funds has become
increasingly popular. Known as Exchange Traded Funds (or ETFs),
they are basically index mutual funds that trade like stocks on the
American Stock Exchange, meaning you can buy and sell them during
market hours just like you can buy and sell common stock. What
makes these funds so exciting to investors is that they are incredibly
liquid, incredibly tax efficient, and extremely low cost. The average
ETF has an expense ratio of about 0.2 percent—which happens to be
less than half the cost of an index fund and about one-sixth the cost of
an actively managed fund. And most of these funds sell for less than
$100 a share. How's that for ease of investing and diversification with
very little money?

As of this writing, the most popular ETFs are the S&P 500 Index
Depositary Receipts (known as Spiders, because their trading symbol is
SPY), the Dow Jones Industrial Average Model Depositary Shares (or
Diamonds; trading symbol: DIA), the NASDAQ 100 Trust (known as
Cubes, after its QQQ symbol), and the S&P MidCap 400 Depositary
Receipts (symbol MDY). There are also dozens of sector indexes and
world indexes known as WEBS.

ETFs can be purchased through virtually any brokerage firm or
online trading company. As time goes on, I expect to see more and more

investors and financial advisors (myself included) building portfolios with a combination of ETFs and actively managed funds. For more details on this exciting new investment vehicle, go to www.ishares.com or contact the American Stock Exchange at (800) 843–2639 (or online at *www.amex.com*) and ask for its free brochure on ETFs.

Moving Beyond the "Getting Started" Phase

Balanced funds and index funds are great places to start, but once your dream basket reaches a really large size—say, when it contains $50,000 or more—it's time for the two of you to consider building a diversified portfolio of mutual funds. To me, a diversified portfolio is one that contains shares in somewhere between 4 and 10 different funds.

One of the biggest mistakes that investors make these days is investing in too many different mutual funds. At The Bach Group, we sometimes see portfolios where people have accumulated shares in 20 or more funds. That's overkill. This usually happens when someone subscribes to an investment newsletter or magazine. Every time the magazine recommends a new fund, they invest in it. The result is what we call portfolio redundancy (meaning, you have too many investments that serve basically the same purpose). The problem with this is that it usually dilutes your returns.

BUILD YOUR PORTFOLIO AROUND "CORE" FUNDS

I'm a huge believer in building a portfolio that consists of what I call "core-type" mutual funds. I'm also of the philosophy that the key to successful investing is to keep the process relatively simple and straightforward. With this in mind, here are the six types of funds I believe you should consider when building a mutual fund portfolio. They are listed in the order of what I consider most conservative to most aggressive.

Large Capitalization Value Funds A large-cap value fund invests in companies with large market capitalizations—that is, companies whose outstanding stock has a total market value of $5 billion or more. Companies of this magnitude tend to be more secure and established than most, and as a rule, they pay quarterly dividends to shareholders. The "value" part of the name reflects the basic strategy these kinds of funds pursue. Generally speaking, the manager of a value fund looks for high-yielding large-cap stocks that sell at low price-earnings multiples. (That's a fancy way of saying that these funds like to invest in solid companies whose stock is selling at bargain prices.) By investing in these types of stocks, you can often get consistent returns with relatively low volatility. Although I'm a big fan of value investing, I have to admit that the last few years have been very hard on this approach. Indeed, many people consider the strategy to be old-fashioned, arguing that value stocks can't compete with the high-tech, "new economy" stocks. Personally, I think that's shortsighted. As far as I'm concerned, every portfolio should contain some value stocks.

Large Capitalization Growth Funds These types of funds invest in what are commonly referred to as "growth stocks." Large-cap funds typically look for stocks with a market value greater than $5 billion. Typically, growth stocks do not pay dividends because growth companies prefer to invest their profits in research, development, and expansion. Some great examples of large-cap growth companies are Microsoft, Oracle, Yahoo, Home Depot, Dell Computers, Intel, and Amazon.com. In the last few years, large-cap growth stocks have outperformed practically every other category of investing, producing great returns for the funds that invested in them.

Medium Capitalization Funds Otherwise known as "mid-caps," these funds invest in medium-sized companies—that is, those with a market capitalization of $1 billion to $7 billion. Such companies are usually newer enterprises that hope someday to grow to large-cap size. The potential for great returns here is high, but so is the risk. In recent years, mid-cap funds have performed off the charts, increasing in value at an average of more than 30 percent a year. As a result, even though you find a lot of volatility in this sector, I think most portfolios benefit from containing some exposure to mid-cap stocks.

Small Capitalization Funds It's getting harder to classify these funds because some small new company can go public these days with no earnings and overnight see its market capitalization suddenly spike to $1 billion or more. Typically, small-cap funds invest in companies with market caps that range from about $250 million to $3 billion. This reflects an ultra-aggressive approach, which can potentially produce great returns. Small-cap investing is a lot like betting on the hare instead of the tortoise. The younger you are—which is to say, the more time you have to recover from a potential downturn in the stock market—the more you can afford to invest in this way. Because of its aggressiveness I don't recommend putting more than 25 percent of your assets into this type of a fund.

International or Global Funds As the name implies, these funds invest in stocks from foreign countries. While an international stock fund invests solely in foreign stocks, a global fund will usually have only about 60 percent of its assets invested abroad; the remaining 40 percent will be in domestic stocks. Remember, as big as it is, the United States represents only about a third of the total world economy, and if you invest only in domestic stocks, you're missing out on a lot of opportunities. At The Bach Group, we usually recommend that investors keep about 10 to 15 percent of their portfolio in international or global mutual funds. If the European economy really starts to take off, you might want to increase this percentage, but for now I wouldn't put more than 15 percent of your assets into this type of fund.

Technology Funds I include this category because these days everyone wants to invest in technology, and that's what these funds do— they focus specifically on technology-oriented companies. While I'm a big believer in technology myself, the phenomenal run-up in high-tech stocks over the last few years makes me reluctant to recommend investing too heavily in this sector (no more than 30 percent of your portfolio). The fact is that most of the funds listed above will have at least 20 to 30 percent of their holdings in technology stocks anyway, so you don't necessarily need to invest in a technology fund in order to be invested in this sector.

AVERAGE FUND PERFORMANCE

For the Period:
12/31/84–5/31/01

PORTFOLIO INVESTMENTS	PERIOD'S AVERAGE ANNUAL RETURN
Dow Jones 30 Industrial Average w/ divs.	14.33%
S & P 500 Composite Index w/ divs.	13.07%
Mid-Cap Funds Average	17.40%
Growth Mutual Fund Index	12.79%
Small Company Growth Funds Average	13.18%
International Mutual Fund Index	13.96%
Growth & Income Fund Index	13.40%
Global Fund Average	12.55%
Balanced Mutual Fund Index	12.37%
High-Yield Bond Fund Index	10.62%
General U.S. Gov't Fund Index	8.33%
General Municipal Fund Index	8.64%
Money Market Fund Average	5.62%

Source: 2000 Lipper Analytical Services, Inc.

With 13,000 Funds to Choose From, How Do We Know Which One Is Right for Us?

Let's face it, even mutual-fund investing has become pretty complicated in recent years. There are so many different funds (upward of 13,000 at last count). So many ads screaming about performance. So many books, magazines, Web sites, television shows—all of them with their own suggestions on how to pick a mutual fund. It's enough to get a Smart Couple confused to the point of not taking action.

To help you get started on your dream basket, I've put together a list of mutual fund companies that allow you to invest as little as $50 a month. These companies can also assist you with building a retirement basket (they can help you fund a Roth IRA account). The list that follows includes both "no-load" mutual funds (meaning there are no sales commissions) and "load" mutual funds (which may impose either an up-front commission when you buy or a back-end sales charge if you sell early).

A lot of people say you should invest only in no-load funds. I don't believe that. What matters most when it comes to mutual funds isn't load vs. no-load, but which particular fund best suits your needs and how long you should hold on to it. There are times when it's definitely worth paying a small commission in order to get the professional advice that comes with a load fund. In any case, given that many financial advisors now work on a fee basis (something I'll explain on page 240), you can often get the commission on a load fund waived.

Mutual Funds That Allow You to Invest with as Little as $50 a Month!

There are many mutual funds that allow you to invest as little as $50 a month. The list that follows includes some really well-known mutual fund companies that provide systematic investment plans. Under a systematic investment plan, you arrange to have a specified amount of money (say, $50) automatically transferred from your checking account each month and invested in a mutual fund (or funds) of your choosing. Because it all happens automatically, you don't have to remember to write any checks or make any deadlines. In other words, it couldn't be easier. No discipline is required (except to make sure you have enough money in your checking account to cover the monthly debit). Indeed, you'll probably stop thinking about it after the first few months—and the next thing you know, your dream basket will be full of money!

Needless to say, you should never invest in any mutual fund without first reading its prospectus. And don't invest in any fund until any and all questions you may have about the risks involved have been fully answered by your advisor or the fund company itself.

"No-Load" Mutual Fund Companies
American Century
(800) 345–2021
www.americancentury.com
Automatic investment minimum: $50/month

Dreyfus
(800) 782–6620
www.dreyfus.com
Automatic investment minimum: $50/month

Fremont Funds
(800) 548–4539
www.fremontfunds.com
Automatic investment minimum: $50/month

INVESCO Funds
(800) 525–8085
www.invescofunds.com
Automatic investment minimum: $50/month

Strong Funds
(800) 368–1030
www.estrong.com
Automatic investment minimum: $50/month

Scudder Investments
(800) 728–3337
www.scudder.com
Automatic investment minimum: $50/month

T. Rowe Price
(800) 638–5660
www.troweprice.com
Automatic investment minimum: $50/month

"Load" Mutual Fund Companies
AIM Funds
(800) 959–4246

www.aimfunds.com
Automatic investment minimum: $50/month

American Funds
(800) 421–0180
www.americanfunds.com
Automatic investment minimum: $50/month

Franklin Templeton Investments
(800) 632–2301
www.franklintempleton.com
Automatic investment minimum: $50/month

Putnam Investments
(800) 225–1581
www.putnaminvestments.com
Automatic investment minimum: $25/month

Van Kampen Investments
(800) 341–2911
www.vankampen.com
Automatic investment minimum: $25/month

FOR REALLY LONG-TERM DREAMS
(TEN YEARS OR MORE)

There are long-term dreams and then there are *really* long-term dreams. Say your dream is to build a second home in Hawaii, but you know it won't be possible until your kids are out of college, which is at least ten years away. Where should you put your dream-basket money in the meantime?

Variable Annuities

Consider the variable annuity. Basically, variable annuities are mutual funds with an insurance policy wrapped around them. The insurance wrapper, as it's called, allows the money in the fund to grow tax-deferred. In this, variable annuities are like a nondeductible IRA—

with two big advantages: there are no income limitations on who can buy them, and you can put in as much money as you want.

You fund a variable annuity by contributing after-tax dollars, which are allowed to grow without Uncle Sam taking his annual bite. When you reach the age of 59^1/$_2$, you can elect to start taking money out. As with a regular IRA, you have to pay income taxes on your distributions, but only on the portion attributable to interest earnings. If you take money out early, before age 59^1/$_2$, you will pay a 10 percent penalty on your gains.

Sounds like a good deal, doesn't it? Well, it is. The closest thing to a catch here is the fact that you have to pay for the insurance wrapper. As a rule, the insurance fee runs about ^{1}/$_2$ to 1 percent of the annuity's asset value (i.e., if you've invested $100,000, the insurance will cost you between $500 and $1,000 a year). Some people regard this as a terrible disadvantage. I disagree. In most cases, the money you save by having your funds grow tax-deferred more than offsets the extra cost.

To my way of thinking, that's a no-brainer.

(Note: this is *not* a substitute for a retirement plan. You should make sure your retirement basket is fully funded before you start putting money into a variable annuity.)

The Downside of Variable Annuities

The biggest disadvantage of buying a variable annuity is that many variable annuities impose what is known as a seven-year deferred sales charge—a penalty fee you must pay if you sell your annuity or take any distributions from it within seven years of the purchase date. So make sure when buying an annuity to ask the sales person about "back end" sales charges. A good annuity shouldn't impose a premature sales charge of more than 7 percent or for longer than seven years. Since I'm suggesting that you consider annuities only if you are investing for 10 years or more, the deferred sales charge shouldn't be an issue for you.

What About Buying Individual Stocks?

Even though I strongly prefer systematic investing in mutual funds, it is possible now to do the same thing with individual stocks.

The disadvantage of this route is that you must decide which stocks to invest in, and you don't get the same immediate diversification and professional money management that mutual funds provide. Nonetheless, some people insist on including some individual stocks in their portfolios. If you're one of them, here's how to go about doing it.

DRIP Investing

A great way to invest systematically in individual stocks is to start what is known as a Dividend Reinvestment Program (or DRIP). Essentially, DRIP plans allow investors to purchase stocks directly from the companies that issue them. Once an account is set up, investors can continue to buy more stock systematically and have any stock dividends they earn reinvested automatically, often with no commission costs.

What makes DRIP programs so great in my opinion is that an investor who wants to build his or her dream basket can get started buying stocks with an investment of as little as $10 a month. As of this writing, there were 137 companies with minimums that low. And there were literally hundreds more that allowed minimum investments of $25 a month.

How Do We Set Up a DRIP Program?

Setting up a DRIP program is relatively easy. You first need to become a shareholder (that means owning at least one share of stock). This can be done through a full-service brokerage firm or a discount brokerage firm. Some companies now even allow you to purchase the first share directly through the company. This type of direct purchase is called a "direct purchase program." An example of a company that does this is McDonald's (the first company I ever invested in). For detailed information on DRIPs, I highly recommend going to *www.dripinvestor.com*. This is a great site that lists all the companies that currently offer DRIP programs. Another excellent site and service is *www.sharebuilder.com*.

We've covered a lot of ground in this chapter. Given all the recommendations I've made about how to invest your dream-basket funds,

I'm sure your head must be spinning. But remember—it really isn't that complicated. For the most part, smart investing is simply a matter of knowing what steps to take and in what order.

The fact is, becoming able to fund your dreams is a lot like opening a safe. Unless you know what numbers to turn to and how, you'll never get inside. With the right combination, however, the world's strongest safe can be opened with very little effort. The two of you now know the combination to your financial safe. Use the tools I have given you, in the right order, and your dreams can become a reality.

LEARN TO AVOID
THE TEN BIGGEST
FINANCIAL MISTAKES
COUPLES MAKE

IN THIS STEP, WE'RE GOING TO look at the 10 biggest mistakes couples make with their finances—and sometimes with their relationships. By learning what these mistakes are, you can save yourselves considerable heartache . . . and a lot of money. I'll warn you now that some of these mistakes will seem so obvious to you that you may find yourself saying, "Well, I knew *that* was dumb." But remember—knowing something is dumb and not doing it are two different things.

What I'd like the two of you to do with these 10 biggest mistakes is study them carefully and really discuss them with each other. If it turns out that you're making some of them yourselves, don't beat yourselves up over it. Rather, be happy you've learned something new that could conceivably save—or make—the two of you a fortune. In any case, the key is to take action. I don't want you just to nod in agreement and then do nothing. If you spot a mistake you've been making, correct it. If you come across a solution to a problem that hadn't occurred to you, start using it.

With that in mind, let's jump right in.

> **MISTAKE NO. 1**
> **Having a 30-year mortgage.**

Thirty-year mortgages are probably the most popular form of home financing around. They are also, in my opinion, the single biggest financial mistake people make in this country. In fact, I think 30-year mortgages are worse than a mistake. I think they are a scam—an outrageous scam pushed nationwide by both the banks and the government. And to make matters worse, this scam is about to get worse, because now the banks are starting to push 40-year mortgages.

What's my problem with 30-year mortgages? It's simple. Say you purchase a home with a $250,000 mortgage that you pay off over a 30-year period. Say the interest rate is 8 percent a year. When all is said and done, you will have actually given the bank $660,240. That's more than two and a half times the original loan amount. Why did you fork over all that extra money? The answer, of course, is that in addition to repaying the $250,000 principle, you were also obligated to pay the bank $410,240 in interest charges.

In all fairness, banks are in business to make money. They like to sell 30-year mortgages not because 30-year mortgages are necessarily a good deal for you, but because they are very, very profitable for them.

Now I also said that the government benefits when you buy a 30-year mortgage. How does that work? Well, to begin with, it was the government that had to decide to make mortgage interest tax-deductible, right? Do you think the government said, "Geez, let's make the lives of Americans easier by allowing them to deduct a good chunk of their mortgage payments"? Maybe . . . but, then again, maybe not.

Maybe the government's experts looked at the math and saw that encouraging people to take out 30-year mortgages would be a good thing for the government. After all, if you and your partner have a mortgage that you pay off over 30 years, guess when the two of you will most likely retire? You'll retire when you reach your sixties—which just happens to be precisely when the government *wants* you to retire.

Why doesn't the government want you to retire earlier than that— say, in your late forties or early fifties? Because when we retire, most of us sharply reduce the amount of income and Social Security taxes we pay. So if everyone started retiring early, the government might have a tax-revenue crisis on its hands.

Now don't get me wrong. I'm not antigovernment, nor am I suggesting that the banks and Washington are engaged in some sort of conspiracy. Their policy here makes good business sense for both of them. But here's the important thing: what's good for them is not always good for you or me.

Take Your 30-Year Mortgage and . . .

If you've already got a 30-year mortgage, what I suggest is that you . . . keep it. That's right. You can keep the 30-year mortgage you've got, and if you ever get a new mortgage, you should probably get one with a 30-year term as well. The fact is, 30-year mortgages give you a ton of flexibility.

By this point, I'm sure you're thinking that I've gone nuts or you accidentally skipped a page or two somewhere. Wasn't I just going on about how terrible 30-year mortgages are? And now I'm saying you should keep yours—and maybe even get a new one?

Well, here's the trick. By all means take out a 30-year mortgage, but under no circumstances should you take the full 30 years to repay it. If you do, you'll just be wasting all that time and money on interest. A much smarter decision is to pay off your 30-year mortgage early.

To do this, pull out your mortgage payment book and review what your last payment was. Now take that number and add 10 percent to it. That's how much you're going to send the bank next month, and every month thereafter. In other words, if you were paying $1,000 a month before, from now on you're going to be paying $1,100 a month. Inform the bank that you are doing this and that you want the extra $100 a month to be applied to the principal (not the interest).

If you keep this up, you'll wind up paying off your 30-year mortgage in about 22 years. Increase your monthly payment by 20 percent, and you'll have that mortgage retired in about 18 years (depending on the type of mortgage)! In short, this is a simple idea that can easily save you tens—if not hundreds—of thousands of dollars in interest over the lifetime of your mortgage.

If you're at all confused by this, call your bank or mortgage company and tell them you want to pay off your mortgage earlier than the schedule calls for. Ask them exactly how much extra a month you would have to send them in order to pay off your mortgage in 15, 20, and 25 years. Make sure to ask if there are any penalties for paying off your mortgage earlier (chances are the answer is no). Then ask them to send this information to you in writing. Most likely, they'll be happy to help you, and in any case, it shouldn't take them very long to do the calculations.

You can also get a pretty good idea on your own by using the mortgage calculators at the following Web sites.

Mortgage-calc.com
www.mortgage-calc.com

Mortgage-Net
www.mortgage-net.com

Mortgage 101
www.mortgage101.com

LendingTree.com
www.Lendingtree.com

E-Loan
www.eloan.com

One thing to keep in mind: when you make these extra mortgage payments, pay close attention to your monthly statements. Banks often don't credit mortgage accounts properly. I've had it happen twice with my own mortgage. In one case, we had been making extra payments for eight months—without a penny of it ever being credited against our principle. When we finally noticed, the bank said it thought the extra payments were meant to cover future interest we might owe. Can you believe that? It took us three months to sort things out. The moral: even if you're not making extra payments, watch your mortgage statement like a hawk!

The Big Tax Write-Off Myth

I know some of you are probably thinking that I've ignored one of the most important aspects of paying off a mortgage—the fact that mortgage interest is tax deductible.

You probably think 30-year mortgages are great write-offs because some accountant or financial advisor or well-meaning friend told you they were. And that's not totally crazy. On average, for every $100,000 in mortgage interest you pay, your tax bill will be reduced by $28,500 (28.5 percent being the federal tax bracket of the average citizen). But so what? Since when is it worth spending $100,000 in interest extra over the life of your mortgage in order to save $28,500 in tax payments?

Anyway, did you really purchase your house to be a tax write-off? I doubt it. Chances are you purchased your house to have a place to live, love, grow, and feel at home.

Furthermore, what do the two of you spend most of your time worrying about? If you're like most couples, it's paying the bills. And what's your biggest bill? If you are homeowners, it's most likely your mortgage payment. Now imagine not having to make one. People always tell me that one of their most important values is security. Imagine the security you would feel knowing your mortgage was paid off, that you owned your home "free and clear." No matter what happened at work or with the economy, you would know you were safe.

Believe me, debt-free home ownership is a goal worth striving for—and all it takes is an extra 10 to 15 percent on your monthly payment to make it a reality a decade or more early. And you know what else happens when you pay your home off in 15 years instead of 30? You retire earlier—on average, seven to ten years earlier. As your financial coach, that's an option I would like you and your partner to have.

With this in mind, beware of the brokerage or insurance salesperson who suggests you should pull equity out of your home and "reposition" it in some mutual funds or insurance products where it supposedly can grow faster. Don't fall for this. The only reason these salespeople suggest this sort of thing is because of the commissions they can earn off your gullibility. Remember . . . you can't park your car or sleep inside a mutual fund. That's what your home is for, so don't risk it.

What About Paying Off Your Mortgage Right Away?

If you're fortunate enough to enjoy some huge windfall—say, a lump sum inheritance or a big bonus at work—you may be tempted to take the money and pay off your mortgage in one fell swoop. But before you do anything like that, first get some professional financial advice. While I believe in paying off your mortgage more quickly than the bank would like, it doesn't always make sense to pay it off all at once. There are a lot of variables involved—such as the interest rate on your mortgage, how long you intend to stay in your house, how much money you have, and when you were planning on retiring—and the right course of action isn't always obvious.

MISTAKE NO. 2
Not taking credit-card debt seriously.

Credit-card debt can destroy a marriage. I don't care how much two people may love each other, if one of them is constantly spending the couple into debt, I can promise you that eventually the relationship will fall apart. If both parties are running up debts, it will simply end that much sooner.

Why do I say this? First of all, carrying credit-card debt is stressful. Knowing that you owe a company money and that you're being charged as much as 20 percent interest on the outstanding balance will make even the most laid-back person anxious. Second, the anxiety never goes away; it's there—all day, every day—until the debt is paid off. And not only does it hang over your relationship, it hits you smack dab in the face every month when the bill shows up. A stressful relationship is not a happy relationship—and unhappy relationships usually don't last.

Don't Wait to Find Out About Your Credit Record!

Nothing is worse than finding out that your partner has credit problems just when you're about to make a major purchase—say, when you're ready to buy your first home together. It's an exciting time. You decide you're ready for the responsibility that goes along with home-ownership, and it looks like you've finally got the money to swing it. So the two of you go to a mortgage company to get preapproved and—wham!—they run a credit check on you and out comes all this informa-tion about your own credit and your partner's credit that you never knew.

This happened to one of my closest friends, a guy named Alan, who makes a good living as a computer executive. When he and his new wife, Renee, started to look for a house in San Francisco a few years ago, he called a mortgage broker to get preapproved for a loan. This, he fig-ured, was a no-brainer. He'd already asked Renee if her credit was clean and she'd said of course it was.

So imagine his surprise a few days later when the broker called him back and asked if he was sitting down.

"What's wrong?" Alan asked the broker.

"Well," he said, "Renee has some credit problems. In fact, her credit rating is so bad that there's no way the two of you can qualify for a loan together."

Alan was stunned. "How can that be? My credit is perfect, isn't it?"

"Sure," the broker said, "but hers isn't."

The problem was those nice companies that give away the free T-shirts and make it so easy to get a credit card when you're a student. With their encouragement, Renee had opened a couple of those accounts when she was in college, charged a few items, and then had forgotten about them. Unfortunately, those nice credit-card companies don't forget. Instead, they had placed nasty little "no payment" flags on her record. And even though the amounts in question were relatively small (less than $200 on two accounts), that was enough to ruin her credit rating—and along with it, any chance she and Alan had of getting a mortgage together.

Fortunately for them, Alan's credit rating was strong enough to qualify him for a home loan on his own, and so they were still able to buy a house. Anyway, the point here is not to single out Renee, but to demonstrate how easy it is to be blindsided by a bad credit report. Even when you think you have your act together, you may not. The moral . . .

Find Out Your Credit Rating Now!

Don't wait to be surprised. This week go and get yourself a copy of your credit reports. It's actually quite simple. There are three main credit-reporting companies—Equifax, Experian, and Trans Union—and on request they will each provide you with a copy of your personal credit report for a charge of no more than $8.50. (In some cases, they'll give you your report for free.)*

Here's how to contact the companies:

Equifax
P.O. Box 740241
Atlanta, GA 30374
(800) 685–1111, (770) 612–3200
(800) 548–4548 (residents of Georgia, Vermont, and Massachusetts)
(800) 233–7654 (residents of Maryland)
Or online at *www.equifax.com*

Experian
P.O. Box 2002
Allen, TX 75013
(888) 567–8688
Or online at *www.experian.com*

Trans Union Corporation
Consumer Disclosure Center
P.O. Box 390
Chester, PA 19022
(800) 916–8800
(800) 888–4213 (if you have been declined credit)
Or online at *www.transunion.com*

---

*Residents of Colorado, Maryland, Massachusetts, New Jersey, and Vermont are entitled to one free credit report each year. So are welfare recipients, unemployed people who plan to seek employment within 60 days, anyone who believes their report is inaccurate due to fraud, and anyone who has been denied credit, employment, insurance, or rental housing within the last 60 days based on information in a credit report. Residents of Georgia are entitled to two free reports each year.

If you discover any inaccuracies or mistakes in any of your credit reports, get them fixed immediately. The procedures for doing so are relatively simple, and the individual companies will tell you exactly what's required. Basically, if you tell a credit-reporting company that your file contains inaccurate information, the company must look into your claim (usually within 30 days) and present all the relevant evidence you submit to whomever provided the information you're disputing. If this does not resolve the dispute, you may add a brief statement to your credit file, a summary of which will be included in all future reports.

If you discover that you've got some legitimate black marks on your credit reports (for example, some old unpaid bills that you've forgotten about), do whatever you can to correct the situation. In general, that means pay off those old debts and don't let any new bills go past due.

Beware of companies that say they can "fix" a bad credit report or give you a new, "clean" one overnight. There is nothing that will "fix" a bad credit report except the passage of time, a consistent record of responsible bill-paying, and contacting the credit-report companies and working with them to get your credit record clean.

There are a number of reputable nonprofit groups that can advise you on how to clear up a bad credit report or straighten out an inaccurate one. Two of the best are Consumer Credit Counseling Services, reachable online at *www.cccsf.org*, or toll-free at (800) 388–2227, and Myvesta (formerly known as Debt Counselors of America), reachable online at *myvesta.org*, or toll-free at (800) 680–3328.

MISTAKE NO. 3
Trying to get rich quick by day-trading.

The late 1990s were a very strange time. There was so much media attention on overnight millionaires—even billionaires—that it felt like everyone and his brother was hitting the jackpot, and that anyone who took more than a few months to amass a fortune was obviously doing something wrong.

Let's face it, if there were an easy way to get rich quick, we'd all be rolling in dough. The reality is that getting rich quick is not easy and it doesn't normally happen overnight. The truth is—and it's something you should never forget . . .

Accumulating Real Wealth Takes More Than Months or Years, It Takes Decades

It took my Grandma Bach 40 years of investing to become a millionaire. I'm not suggesting that it has to take you that long. I know I don't want to have to wait 40 years to get rich. But I do accept the fact that it will take me more than 40 minutes, or 40 days, or even 40 months. It takes time to build real wealth.

Sadly, a lot of people these days think they can shorten this process by actively trading stocks. Impressed by the new technology that allows them to buy and sell securities online—and enticed by the frankly misleading come-ons of some online brokerage firms—hundreds of thousands of people have become what are known as "day traders." They sit at their computers all day, buying and selling stocks at a frantic pace. They don't make their decisions on the basis of whether they think the underlying companies represent a good investment. Rather, they are guided by their sense of which way they believe the market's "momentum" is pointing.

To me, this is sad because actively trading stocks like this is the fastest way I know to lose a lot of money.

Day-trading is like going to Las Vegas. You might win once and be able to brag to all your buddies about it, but ultimately you will go home a loser. Please, please, please listen to me on this. The likelihood that you will get rich actively trading stocks is somewhere between slim and none. It's even worse if you do it yourself at home with an Internet hookup and a new online brokerage account. People who do this eventually lose.

Trading stocks for a living is a brutal occupation. Most experienced professionals consider themselves lucky if they get it right more than 50 percent of the time. If a professional trader is right barely 50 percent of the time, what's the likelihood of you doing any better? The likelihood is that you will do far worse.

For obvious reasons, the online brokerage firms want to encourage you to buy and sell stocks on your own at home. They want you to think that it's easy to trade like an expert. To that end, online brokerage firms spent more than $1 billion in 1998 and 1999 soliciting new business from people just like you.

Now don't misunderstand me. I'm not against online brokerage firms or online trading. I love being able to invest online. But I am worried about how easy it's become for otherwise sensible people to devastate themselves financially with a click of a mouse. I'm not exaggerating. You can literally wipe yourself out with a wrong click on the wrong stock at the wrong time. And that's scary.

According to a recent U.S. Senate investigation, not only do more than 75 percent of day traders lose money but over the long run they have "almost no chance of success." Here's why that's so.

Three Key Reasons Why Day-Trading Doesn't Work

1. **Commissions.** If you trade often enough, even small commissions can add up to a lot of money. If you buy a $10 stock and sell it for $11, commission charges can reduce your $1 profit by as much as 20 cents. If you sell your $10 stock for $9, your loss will be increased by that amount.

2. **Taxes.** If you buy a stock at $10 and sell it for $11, your $1 profit will also be reduced by the taxes you'll have to pay on it. As a day trader, your profit will almost certainly be what's called a short-term capital gain—meaning it came from the sale of an investment you held for less than 12 months. (Most day traders rarely hold a stock for 12 hours, let alone 12 months.) Since short-term gains are taxed as ordinary income, roughly 40 cents of your $1 profit could be claimed by the tax man.

3. **Poor Odds.** Okay, you've paid 20 cents in commissions and 40 cents in taxes on your $1 profit. All of a sudden, your 10 percent gain isn't looking so good. But wait a minute, you might say, you're still up 40 cents. True enough, but remember we assumed a trade in which everything went right—which is to say, you bought low and sold high. The fact is that everything doesn't always go right. Even in 1999, a record-breaking year for the stock market, more individual stocks were down for the

year than up. The people who made money in that market (aside from the professionals) weren't the day traders but the ones who invested in the market as a whole through mutual funds. And in the spring of 2000, when the market stumbled, the day traders got killed. Don't take my word for it, look at the numbers below. The chart shows that it's virtually impossible to time the market, because you have to be right almost all the time or you'll miss the best day of the year when the market goes up.

Missing the 20 Best Days Could Cut Your Return in Half

If you had invested a hypothetical $10,000 in the S&P 500 on March 31, 1995, by March 31, 2000, your $10,000 would have grown to $32,718, an average annual total return of 26.75%.

But suppose during that five-year period there were times when you decided to get out of the market and, as a result, you missed the market's 10 best single-day performances. In that case, your 26.75% return would have fallen to 17.42%. If you had missed the market's 20 best days, that 26.75% return would have dropped to 11.46%. Of course, past performance cannot guarantee comparable future results.

The Penalty for Missing the Market

Trying to time the market can be an inexact—and costly—exercise.
S&P 500 Index: March 31, 1995–March 31, 2000

PERIOD OF INVESTMENT	AVERAGE ANNUAL TOTAL RETURN	GROWTH OF $10,000
Fully Invested	26.75%	$32,718
Miss the 10 Best Days	17.42	22,316
Miss the 20 Best Days	11.46	17,201
Miss the 30 Best Days	6.48	13,688
Miss the 40 Best Days	2.15	11,123
Miss the 60 Best Days	-5.13	7,687

Source: Aim Distributors, Inc.

MISTAKE NO. 4
Buying stocks on margin.

Brokerage firms like to make investing as easy as possible for their customers. Among other reasons, this is why they are incredibly nice about lending you the money to buy more stock than you have the cash to purchase. As a rule, they will lend you up to 50 percent of the value of your account in cash or 100 percent in stock. In other words, if you currently own $10,000 worth of stocks, your brokerage firm will probably be happy to let you borrow $5,000 in cash or purchase up to another $10,000 worth of stocks "on margin"—that is, without your having to put up any additional cash. They'll simply advance you the money to buy the extra stocks.

Let's say Microsoft stock is trading at $80, and you want to buy as many shares as you can because you think at that price Microsoft is a steal. If you can come up with $10,000 in cash, your broker will let you buy $20,000 worth of Microsoft—meaning instead of just 125 shares, you can get 250. That's definitely a good deal if the stock goes up, because owning more shares means you'll make a lot more money.

But what happens if the stock falls in price? Let's say Microsoft suddenly collapses by roughly 50 percent, from $80 a share to $40 a share. All of a sudden, your $20,000 investment is worth only $10,000. From the brokerage's point of view, the $10,000 loan it granted you is now a lot riskier. Brokerage firms don't like being in this kind of position. Each firm has its own policy, but the general rule is that once the equity-to-margin ratio on your account begins to approach 50 percent, the brokerage firm will start getting concerned—and you will more than likely get what is known as a "margin call." All of this will be stated in the brokerage's margin agreement.

Again, the specifics vary from firm to firm, but typically you will be given approximately 72 hours to pay off—in cash—enough of your margin debt to lower your equity-to-margin ratio to a level the brokerage firm finds more comfortable. If you can't come up with the money, the brokerage will "sell you out"—meaning it will sell off as much of your Microsoft stock as it takes to meet the margin call.

"But wait," you say. "I don't want to sell Microsoft at $40. That's way too cheap. I'm a long-term investor. I bought to hold."

Well, not on borrowed money you didn't.

The moment you borrow money from a brokerage firm to finance a stock purchase, you give up control over your account. Brokerage firms have the right to "sell out" margined positions in all sorts of circumstances, and they are not shy about exercising those rights. In the volatile markets of 2000, countless investors were sold out of their positions without even the courtesy of a telephone call. For many of them, April 14, 2000, will forever be remembered as "margined-to-death day." On that particular day, both the Dow Jones Industrial Average and the NASDAQ set new records for one-day drops. Good stocks saw their prices cut in half, and all sorts of unsuspecting people discovered the hard way how dangerous investing on margin can be.

My rule of thumb when it comes to this sort of thing is simple: never buy stocks you can't afford to pay cash for. If for some reason, you simply have to margin your account, never let your margin debt exceed 10 percent of your account's value.

One more thing: if your broker is constantly urging you to buy on margin, you've got a broker who is willing to take too much risk with your financial future. Find yourself a new one.

MISTAKE NO. 5
Not starting a college-savings plan soon enough.

You can't talk about financial planning for couples and not address the issue of college costs. But before I get into the details, there is an important point I need to stress. You shouldn't even consider putting aside money for your kids' college costs unless you are already putting at least 10 percent of your income into a pretax retirement account.

Your security basket comes first. College funding comes second. I see too many parents sacrificing their financial security for the sake of their children's college education, and that's a mistake. The greatest gift you can give your children is to ensure that you won't be a financial burden to them. If worst comes to worst, your kids can always get a part-time job when they're in high school and start putting aside their own money for college. There are also countless scholarships and loan programs for deserving students.

Now that I've let you off the hook emotionally about what you owe your children in terms of paying for their college education, let's consider something all of us already know.

COLLEGE IS EXPENSIVE . . . AND GETTING MORE SO EVERY YEAR

According to the College Board, the average cost (including tuition, room and board, books, and transportation) of attending a state college in the 2001–2002 academic year was $11,770. For private colleges and universities, the figure was $26,481. And that was just the average. The most expensive institutions—a group that includes most of the best schools—cost upward of $40,000 a year.

Any way you look at it, that's a lot of money. And it's getting worse every year. According to the experts, college costs are expected to continue rising at a 4 percent annual rate for the foreseeable future. So advance planning is important.

Fortunately, saving for college does not need to be overly difficult or complicated. There are currently four basic types of college-savings plans.

UGMA and UTMA Accounts

The oldest type of college-funding mechanism is not designed specifically for college costs. Established in some states under what's known as the Uniform Gifts to Minors Act (UGMA) and in others under the Uniform Transfers to Minors Act (UTMA), these are simple trusts that are set up by parents for the benefit of their minor children. Typically, the account name will be something like "Jim Smith as custodian for Jim Smith, Jr."

What UGMA and UTMA accounts do is allow parents to transfer assets to a child without having to hire an attorney to set up a special trust. Normally, minors are not allowed to own assets like stocks or mutual funds or even bank accounts without a trust being established on their behalf. What makes these accounts popular is that they are easy to set up and manage. (Any bank or brokerage firm will happily take care of it.)

There is no limit on how much you can contribute to an UGMA or UTMA account, though anything over $10,000 a year may subject the child to federal gift taxes. While the assets in the account legally belong to the child, they are managed by whoever was named as the account's custodian (usually one of the parents). Assuming the child has no other income and is under age 14, the first $1,400 of any investment income earned by the account is tax-free.

The bad thing about UGMA and UTMA accounts is that when the child reaches the age of majority (either 18 or 21, depending on what you elect when you fill out the paperwork on the account), control of the account shifts from the custodian to the child. In other words, you can spend the better part of two decades saving for college for your adorable little boy, but if he grows up to be a monster who decides on his eighteenth birthday that he wants to use the money to buy a new Porsche and go to Europe with his girlfriend, there's nothing you can do about it. (Don't laugh; I've seen this happen.)

529 Plans

Section 529 plans are the future of college-savings accounts. What the 401(k) plan has become to retirement planning, the 529 plan will likely be to college savings. Named for the section of the Internal Revenue Code that created them in 1996, these plans are so new that not many parents know about them. Neither do many financial advisors.

What Section 529 of the tax code does is authorize states to establish two types of college-savings plans. The first type is what is called a prepaid tuition program; the second is a college-saving plan. The prepaid tuition program is ideal for a parent who knows way in advance that she wants to send her child to a specific school in a specific state. Not very likely, is it? This is why I prefer the college-saving plan. The proceeds from a college-saving plan can be used to pay for expenses at any accredited institution of higher education (even foreign universities).

Here is what a 529 college-savings plan does for you.

- It allows you to put away over $100,000 in tax-deferred savings for each of your children's college educations. As long as the money you put in the plan stays in the plan, you don't pay taxes on its growth, dividends, or capital gains.

- Starting in 2002, you can withdraw savings from a 529 plan tax-free. (Before 2002, withdrawals were taxed at the child's rate.)

- You keep control of the money. Unlike UGMA and UTMA accounts, 529 plans don't hand control over to the kids when they turn 18 or 21. If you fund the account and then decide your kids don't deserve the money, you can take back the cash, no matter how old they are. (You will be hit with a 10 percent penalty on the profits, but that's it.)

- It permits others to help you fund your kids' college costs. The government allows a contribution of $50,000 per child in a single year—the gift tax is then credited over five years. For kids with wealthy grandparents, this can make great sense from an estate-planning standpoint.

Forty-eight states have already enacted Section 529 plans. The best place to start your research on these plans is *www.savingforcollege. com*, which offers an incredible library of relevant material. Also check out *www.tiaa-cref.org* (one of the largest investment managers of 529 plans) and *www.scholarshare.com* (with its long list of links, a great resource for college planning in general).

Educational IRAs

Known as EIRAs, these plans starting in 2002 allow you to contribute $2,000 a year per child. The money grows tax-deferred, and when it is distributed for college expenses (which must be done by the time the child reaches age 30), it comes out tax-free. While these plans are better now that you can save more than the original $500 a year maximum contribution, they still are not in my opinion as good as the

529 plans. The $2,000 limit is still low and you give up control of the money. If your child doesn't go to school, the money is ultimately refunded to them, not you!

Variable Annuities and Mutual Funds

Variable Annuities If your child is more than 10 years away from college, open a variable annuity in your name and make your child the beneficiary. It won't be difficult to find a good variable annuity that offers dozens of excellent mutual fund investment options. Basically, what the annuity does for you is allow you to invest your money in mutual funds and then watch it grow tax-deferred. True, if you withdraw the profit on the money before you reach the age of 59$^1/_2$—whether to pay for your kids' college education or anything else—you'll get hit with an income-tax bill plus a 10 percent penalty. But, remember, that money has been enjoying tax-deferred growth for more than a decade. So chances are you'll still come out ahead.

What's more, you never have to surrender control of the money—either to the state or to your child. You make the investment decisions, not some committee of government bureaucrats. And if your kid decides he'd rather join a punk-rock band than go to college, you can keep the money you've saved for him and let it continue to grow tax-deferred for Mommy and Daddy's retirement.

Mutual Funds If your child is headed to college in less than 10 years, then open a separate brokerage account in your name and invest as much as you can in a good solid growth fund. If you use an index fund or one of the Exchange Traded Funds I discussed in Step Seven, taxes won't be much of an issue, since there really won't be any capital gains to speak of until you liquidate the account when the tuition bills come due. And, again, because the money is in your name, you remain in control of it.

Web sites for College Planning
www.collegeboard.com
www.finaid.org

www.petersons.com
www.NASFAA.org

MISTAKE NO. 6
Not teaching your kids about money.

According to the National Council on Economic Education, 66 percent of high school students polled on basic economic principles flunked the test. Adults didn't do much better. Some 57 percent of them failed. Two-thirds of those tested didn't know that in times of inflation, money does not hold its value. Two-thirds of the kids didn't know that the stock market brings people who want to buy stocks together with those who want to sell them.

I find these results frightening, and hopefully you do, too. But being concerned isn't enough. Unless we do something, the situation is not going to change.

When you went to primary and secondary school, how many classes on investing did you have? Did your junior high and high school teachers ever tell you about retirement accounts, how to pay for a mortgage, the ins and outs of stocks and bonds, and the miracle of compound interest? When I ask these questions in my seminars, invariably less than one person out of 20 answers in the affirmative. Often, the response is so poor that I'll tap the microphone and ask, "Is this thing working? Can you people hear me?" This usually gets a laugh . . . but no additional yeses.

How can this be? How is it that our schools, which are supposed to prepare us for the real world, don't teach us anything about money?

One of the basic purposes of education is to prepare students to be productive adults in our society. By this standard, our educational system is failing us. Education about money should be a mandatory part of our national curriculum. Starting in the first grade, we should begin teaching our kids the basics about finance. This should continue every year, right through the end of high school.

When I was growing up in the 1970s, a big thing in elementary and junior high school was the Presidential Physical Fitness Test. For years, I wanted to win the presidential patch that proved I was physically fit. I remember the first time I took the test. I was in the third grade and I couldn't do one pull-up. I was totally embarrassed and ashamed, but I was motivated. It took me five years, but finally in the eighth grade (the last year you could take the test) I achieved my goal. I was able to do so many sit-ups and push-ups that the PE instructor stopped counting when I reached 50 and simply said, "Done."

I'll never forget what it felt like to cross the finish line having run a mile in less than the six-minute qualifying time. I had done it. I had reached my goal of being a Presidential Physical Fitness "winner." Some twenty-odd years later, I remember that moment as if it happened yesterday.

Why am I droning on about this? It's because I have an idea. Just like we had a Presidential Physical Fitness program, we should institute a Presidential Financial Fitness program. We should create a mandatory education program, starting in the first grade, with special accounts that motivate kids to learn about personal finance by offering them the chance to win symbolic awards. Let's make learning how to be smart about money something that everyone does, not just the children of the rich (who are generally very good about teaching their kids how to become richer).

Education has always been the great American equalizer. We've always preached that anyone can become anything they want if they get a good education. Well, let's stop tying our kids' hands behind their backs and pushing them into the real world without an education about money. Let's teach them now how to live and finish rich!

If you agree with me, go to *www.gov.com.* and let your representatives in the House and the Senate know. This site tells you how to reach your representative. If a hundred thousand of us do this, they'll have to listen!

Until the Government Wakes Up . . .

In the meantime, if you don't start teaching your kids about money, no one else is going to. The question is, how do you start?

I was lucky growing up because my grandma Rose Bach and my father, Marty Bach, started teaching me about money when I was just seven years old. Together, they helped me to make my first investment in the stock market (one share in McDonald's Corp.). My dad, who taught investment classes for almost 30 years, often took me with him to his seminars, and he talked to me about investing, the economy, and managing money just like he would talk to his adult clients.

Equally important, my father always shared with me and my sister, Emily, what was happening to our family financially. When business was good, he would explain why and how he was investing the family's money. When things went awry financially (and sometimes they did), he shared with Emily and me just what had gone wrong and how it might affect us.

In short, money was something that we all talked about at the dinner table. It was a normal topic of conversation, as it should be. It's hardly surprising, therefore, that Emily and I both grew up to become investors, and at most only a little surprising that we later both became financial advisors. The point is, we both grew up knowing how to handle money, and as a result we're both in solid financial shape.

Unfortunately, most parents don't teach their kids about money the way my grandmother and father taught Emily and me. I say "unfortunately" because the less your kids learn about money, the more likely it is that they will one day fail financially.

You don't have to be a financial professional to be able to teach your kids about money. You can still talk to them about how you are saving for retirement and why. You can discuss with them how you handle your credit-card debt, what sort of investments you are making, and how you make sure your financial practices reflect your values.

A good way to begin the process is by showing your kids the chart on page 94 that illustrates the miracle of compound interest. Explain to them about how a little saving every month can go an awfully long way. Kids are interested in being rich. And they love learning about money.

You should also take advantage of all the free information you can find these days on the Internet. There are a ton of great Web sites where kids and parents can learn about money together. According to a recent survey, the average child spends four and a half hours a day playing video games, surfing aimlessly on the Internet, or watching television.

Get your kids to spend just 10 minutes of that time each day at one of the following sites and they'll be learning, just as you are now, how to live and finish rich.

FIVE GREAT FINANCIAL WEB SITES FOR KIDS

www.kidsenseonline.com This site is all about teaching kids about money. There are sections here for kids, parents, and teachers. The site makes learning about money fun. It has a "Facts of Money Quiz" you can take to see quickly what you know about money . . . or don't know. It has a place for teachers to go to learn about a preapproved school curriculum to help kids learn more about money. The site recently surveyed 1,000 kids for a study about their money sense. The results of this survey are very interesting (and posted on the site).

www.bigchange.com Ever wonder how to motivate your child to start saving some of his or her allowance? This Web site teaches kids and parents how to set up and manage an allowance program that both of you can get excited about. Among other things, it includes an interactive calculator that children can use to see how much of their allowance they need to put aside for how long in order to reach whatever happens to be their goal. Most importantly, it teaches kids the value of money, how to set up a business, and how to become a smarter consumer.

www.finishrich.com. This is my company's site. If you click into its resource center, you will find a section called Kids & Money. Among other things, this section contains a sample letter that you can cut and paste to send to your congressman and senators urging them to support mandatory financial education in schools. We also have a long list of links to the best sites on kids and money, which we'll do our best to keep as current as possible. (If you find a site that you think deserves to be on our list, please let us know and we will add it.)

www.strongkids.com Aimed at a slightly younger demographic than msdw's "nextgeneration," this interactive site, created by a mutual-fund company, teaches children how to invest.

www.kidsmoney.org This is a home-grown portal, meant more for parents than for kids. It includes links to books, articles, and games—all focused on teaching kids about money.

Additional sites to visit:

www.kidsbank.com
www.moneymentors.com
www.coolbank.com
www.kiplinger.com/kids
www.kidsource.com
www.richdad.com
www.nyse.com
www.federalreserve.com
www.bankrate.com

MISTAKE NO. 7
Neglecting to sign a prenuptial agreement.

The bottom line is that you need to make your kids a part of the family's financial planning process. Remember, you can't ultimately protect your kids from the "real world" if you don't teach them about money.

Prenuptial agreements are a touchy subject, but that doesn't mean we should ignore them. Increasingly popular but hardly routine, they can take many forms. Typically, a "prenup," as it's usually called, is a legal document drafted by an attorney that you and your partner negotiate and sign before you get married. Basically, it sets out the terms of the marriage and specifies who is to get what in the event the two of you wind up getting divorced. Some prenups simply list all the assets each partner is bringing to the union, while others are filled with detailed clauses setting out exactly what each party's marital responsibilities are going to be.

Who Doesn't Need a Prenuptial Agreement . . . and Who Does

If neither you nor your prospective spouse has any assets to speak of, I've got great news: you can skip this section. You don't need a legal document to tell you how to divide what you don't have. But if one of you owns a lot more stuff or earns a lot more money than the other one, or if both of you have substantial assets (like stock options), then a prenuptial agreement is definitely called for. In fact, if there is anything significantly unequal about your respective stations in life—say, one of you has kids from a previous marriage or stands to come into a major inheritance one day—you probably should protect yourself with a prenup.

As I noted earlier, more than half of all marriages end in divorce. It's sad, but true. What's more, divorces tend to be messy. They hurt emotionally and they can cost a lot financially. A prenuptial agreement won't make the process of divorce easy, but because it settles in advance all those arguments over "what's yours and what's mine," it can make it easier.

But Prenuptial Agreements Aren't Romantic

There's no sugar-coating it. Asking the love of your life to sign a prenuptial agreement while the two of you are planning your wedding does not make for great romance. Then again, handing over 50 percent of a fortune that you or your parents spent the better part of a lifetime building isn't much fun either.

Even though it may be a pretty difficult subject to bring up, I suggest you address it early on in your engagement (or even before you become engaged). Don't wait until the week of the wedding to let your beloved know you'd like him or her to sign a prenup. Each of you needs to have your own attorney review the document and make suggestions. That takes time. And don't think you can rush the process. If your estranged spouse can later plausibly claim that he or she signed the agreement either under duress or without fully understanding what it meant, the entire thing can be declared null and void.

So start the process early, and make sure you are both represented by your own attorneys. If you can't get your attorneys to agree—and it's true, most lawyers live to argue—there are now specialists called prenuptial arbitrators who will listen to both sides and then recommend a compromise. Lastly, don't assume that doing a prenuptial agreement says something bad about your relationship. The truth is that a prenuptial agreement can have a very positive impact on your future. It can force you to start dealing with your financial values and goals right at the beginning of the marriage. Many couples have found that this process actually brought them closer and made them more serious about their financial future.

Prenuptials Are No One Else's Business

One final word on the subject: you have a right to keep this private. If you and your partner agree to sign a prenup, it's no one else's business— not your best friend's or your parents' or anyone else's except the two of yours. Don't feel you have to explain it or justify it. As long as the two of you are comfortable with the agreement, that's all that matters.

> **MISTAKE NO. 8**
> **Not having a greater purpose beyond the two of you.**

So far in this chapter, we've talked about educating your kids about money and saving for college. Earlier in this book, we talked about investing and buying insurance and how to build a million-dollar retirement account. All this is important—essential even. But as important as it is, there are things more powerful than money when it comes to ensuring your long-term success as a couple.

Most successful long-term relationships share similar traits. Having worked closely with hundreds of couples, I've noticed over the years what the really strong ones have in common. They recognize the vital importance of patience and compromise. They possess common values and goals. But perhaps most striking of all, the really solid couples, the ones who seem happiest and most fulfilled, all seem to have dedicated their lives together to some greater purpose. This greater purpose can be many things. For some couples, it's a religious calling. For others, it's a charity or some community project.

I think we all have an urge to give our life some greater purpose. Unfortunately, it's all too easy to get so busy working and trying to get ahead that we convince ourselves this greater purpose is something that can wait until we have time. Maybe next year, we say, or the year after that, or when we retire.

I'd like to suggest that you and your partner stop putting this off. Sometime in the next 12 months pick a greater purpose together and dedicate a little time (and maybe even some money) to following through on it. Find something that is not for the family directly but *involves* the family. Recently, Michelle and I rode our bikes 575 miles in seven days across the state of Montana on an AIDS ride. The ride was created by Pallotta TeamWorks to bring awareness to the world about AIDS and the need for an AIDS vaccine. We raised thousands of dollars for this great cause, trained for four months, and had the experience of our lives as we rode with 1,000 other riders. The week changed our lives, and it is something we plan to do again in 2002. For more details on this ride and events like it, visit *www.bethepeople.com*. In 2002, we will be creating a team of riders called Team HumanKind to ride from Paris to Amsterdam. If you would like to join us, visit our website at *www. finishrich.com* for details.

Many people say they don't give their time to some cause or charity because they don't know how (or where) to get started. If that's your challenge, try one of these Web sites. All are run by non-profit organizations devoted to matching up willing people with worthy causes.

www.give.org

www.helping.org

www.idealist.org

www.independentsector.org

www.nvoad.org

www.volunteermatch.org

www.charities.org

You can also call your local chamber of commerce or town council. You'll be amazed how many organizations need your time and help locally.

MISTAKE NO. 9
Not figuring out who's responsible for what.

I can't tell you how often couples at my seminars ask me for advice about how to divide the financial responsibilities: Should they have joint accounts or individual ones? Who should pay which bills? Should their paychecks be pooled or kept separately?

When Michelle and I got married, we thought the answers to these kinds of questions were obvious.

"Honey," I said, "you keep your money in your account and I'll keep my money in my account, and I'll pay most of the bills and you pay some of the bills, and then eventually we'll open a joint account and start a savings plan for 'our' money, and then if we go on a vacation . . ."

"No, honey," Michelle said, "we should put all our money in one account. After all, we're married now and everything should be together because we love each other and that's what couples who love each other do, plus it will be great to really know how all our money is being spent."

Oops, maybe it wasn't so obvious.

In fact, as I told you at the beginning of this book, Michelle and I had our first fight over this issue. The point is that you shouldn't assume that both you and your partner are somehow automatically on the same page when it comes to the question of how you are going to organize your finances and who is going to be responsible for what. If you haven't already done so, the two of you need to sit down together and specifically work all this out. The alternative is chaos and potentially major strife.

Now, there is no one "right answer" as to how a couple should organize their finances. But having worked as a financial advisor to hundreds of couples (not to mention being married myself), I feel safe in offering the following general guidelines.

1. **Each partner needs his or her own money.** Regardless of whether or not you both work, each of you should maintain your own checking and credit-card accounts. If Michelle buys me a gift for my birthday, I don't want to know what she paid for it. I also don't need (or want) to know every detail of where she spends her money. It's not my business. By the same token, I want my own space when it comes to how I spend money. It's not a matter of hiding anything; it's that we all need a certain amount of privacy. Having our own accounts gives us a very necessary sense of personal space.

2. **Each partnership should have an "our money" account.**
   While each partner should have his or her own separate bank
   account, if the partnership is long-term and committed, there
   should be a pooled or joint account as well. This account can
   provide the funds for all the household bills. It can also be
   where your security-basket money ultimately gets saved.
   Michelle and I actually have **two** "our money" accounts: one
   for our security basket and one for our dream basket. We pay
   our bills from our "security basket," making sure we always
   have at least three months of expense money saved (after the
   bills are paid).

3. **Spell out who's responsible for paying which bills.** I personally hate paying bills. Writing checks puts me in a bad
   mood. On the other hand, I also don't like worrying about
   whether the bills were paid. When Michelle and I first got
   married I paid some bills and she paid others. Often, a bill
   would fall through the cracks, ending up in what I call "I-
   thought-you-paid-it land." This is not a good place to be,
   since it leads to many arguments and quite a few late fees. In
   the end, Michelle and I decided that I'd pay all the bills. (I still
   hate doing it, but at least I don't have to worry about whether
   or not it's getting done.) Needless to say, we could have as easily decided that Michelle would pay them all, or that I would
   pay one month and she the next, or some other system. The
   point is that we sat down and worked things out. We didn't
   leave our bill-paying to chance. Neither should you.

4. **Keep in mind that there are no hard and fast rules.** If pool-
   ing all your money works for the two of you, that's great. If
   keeping it all separate works, that's great, too. Ultimately, you
   need to do what works for you as a couple. But it does need to
   work for *both of you.* In many marriages this single issue of how
   to handle the checking accounts and pay the bills is a monthly
   battle. You can't have a great marriage or long-term relationship if every month you find yourselves fighting about who's
   responsible for what when it comes to your finances.

MISTAKE NO. 10
Not getting professional financial advice.

The fact that you have read this far into the book tells me you're truly someone who is serious about money. As I mentioned earlier, very few people who buy personal-finance books actually get past more than a few chapters.

By now, I would hope that you are very excited about your future and what you'll be able to do with it. It's also possible, however, that your head is spinning with all the information I've given you. Financial planning is not something you master in a day or a week or even a month. It's a lifelong journey, and as is the case with many long journeys, it's often best to hire yourself a guide.

That's how I think of financial advisors. They are like professional coaches or guides. You and your partner decide together where you want to end up, and then you go out and hire a professional to guide you along your path to living and finishing rich.

Now, some people are born "do-it-yourselfers." They simply have to do everything themselves—including managing their money. If you're one of them, I salute you. Hopefully, this book will make it easier to make smart decisions about your money. On the other hand, if you are the type of person who appreciates getting advice and enjoys working with professionals, then hiring a financial coach makes a lot of sense.

The Rich Hire Financial Advisors

The rich almost always use financial advisors. This is not my opinion; this is a fact. According to a recent study by Dalbar, which surveys investors, 89 percent of investors with portfolios worth more than $100,000 prefer to hire a financial advisor. That's something to think about if you are not yet as rich as you want to be.

Hiring a financial professional to assist you is not a sign that you are weak or lazy. Smart, successful people hire coaches all the time. Tiger Woods, who is arguably the greatest golfer ever, still works with a golf coach. He doesn't say, "Oh, I know everything there is to know about golf, I'm done learning." He uses a golf coach to keep getting better. Michael Jordan, the greatest basketball player of all time, was devoted to his coach, the Bulls' Phil Jackson. Academy Award–winning actress Helen Hunt still works with an acting coach. Some of the world's most successful CEOs now have business coaches.

Why do successful people like these hire coaches? Because they know that to achieve extraordinary results you've got to keep learning, and a good coach makes learning a lot easier. A good coach gives you honest feedback and objective criticism, and can often see things about you that you can't. In my own practice, my greatest value to some clients is simply in being honest and providing a wall off which they can bounce ideas.

So how do you find a good financial advisor? It's not always easy, and I can't offer you any magic formulas. What I do have are Eight Golden Rules for hiring a financial advisor that should make the process easier and, in the end, help you hire the perfect coach.

EIGHT GOLDEN RULES FOR HIRING
A FINANCIAL ADVISOR

RULE NO. 1
Hire locally.

I get requests from people all over the world asking me to manage their money. What I generally tell them is to try to find an advisor in their own backyard. You should consider doing the same. Why? Because if you're going to put your wealth in the hands of a financial coach, you want someone you can work with face-to-face. In my opinion, it's crucial that your advisor be a person with whom you can form a really strong relationship—and ideally meet with at least twice a year. As the years go by, we may all find ourselves routinely communicating via the Internet or video conferencing, but in terms of building both confidence and understanding, there is no substitute for meeting personally with the individual or team that is handling your money.

With this in mind, all the suggestions I am going to provide are intended to help you find a financial advisor in the general vicinity of where you live. This doesn't mean he or she should be literally down the block. Depending on where you live, hiring someone "locally" could translate into driving a few hours to a nearby city. But, ideally, you shouldn't have to go any farther than that to find someone really good.

RULE NO. 2
Get a referral.

It may sound like a cliché, but the best way to find a top-notch financial advisor is to ask the wealthiest person you know whom he or she uses as a financial advisor. This wealthy person doesn't have to be a friend; he or she may be just an acquaintance, or even your boss. Most people are flattered to be asked for advice, and in most cases they'll be happy to refer you to their advisor. What this means is that they will call their advisor on your behalf and introduce you. Generally speaking, unless you have a lot of money, you'll have a hard time getting in to see the best advisors without this type of introduction.

The truth is that really good advisors usually have account minimums—that is, they don't take on a new client unless that client has some sizable amount of money to invest. But if you get a referral, the door that might have been otherwise closed gets opened. For example, if one of my top clients refers a friend or family member to The Bach Group, that friend or family member is going to get red-carpet treatment at our office. We want to keep our top clients happy, and that means taking care of those they refer to us, even if the account is below our standard minimums. That's the power of a good referral from the right person.

RULE NO. 3
Check out the advisor's background.

Nothing else matters if you don't follow this rule. I don't care how successful someone looks, how highly recommended the advisor comes, even whether his or her name is on the building—if you don't check out your advisor's background, you are setting yourself up for trouble.

There are many advisors who appear to be successful, but who, in fact, are really nothing more than good salespeople. Some sincere-sounding advisors stretch the truth, embellishing their experience and educational background. Some very charming advisors have had formal ethics complaints filed against them. Some even have criminal records.

There's only one way to protect yourself against this sort of thing. In order to become licensed to sell securities, brokers and financial advisors have to pass tests and register with the National Association of Securities Dealers. So before you hire a financial advisor—in fact, before you even meet with one—visit the NASD Web site at www.nasdr.com and run a search on the advisor you're considering. (If you don't have Internet access, you can telephone the NASD at 800–289–9999.) It will tell you everything you'll ever need to know about a registered advisor's background: educational, work, and business history; licenses held and in what states. Everything.

Perhaps most important, the NASD will let you know if an advisor has any "disclosure events" on his or her record. A disclosure event is an ethics complaint or a criminal prosecution, and you probably don't want to hire a financial advisor who has one. The NASD Web site won't reveal the nature of any particular disclosure event that may be on your advisor's record, but it does permit you to request additional information by mail.

RULE NO. 4
Be prepared.

Being prepared means that you have with you all of your pertinent financial documents. In the Appendix on page 279, you'll find a copy of my FinishRich Inventory Planner™, a document organizer that will help you figure out what papers you'll need to bring to that first meeting.

If you are uncomfortable sharing your personal financial information with an advisor, you're not ready to hire one. Showing your financial records to an advisor is like exposing your body to a doctor. In order to be able to help you, the professional has to be able to conduct an examination. And don't worry about being embarrassed. Just like a doctor, a financial advisor sees countless "patients"—and lots of them are probably much worse off than you.

> ### RULE NO. 5
> **Always ask about the advisor's philosophy.**

When you go to your first meeting, make sure to ask the advisor about his or her philosophy of money management. A serious professional should have no trouble explaining his or her approach to investing simply and coherently. If yours can't do this, take your business elsewhere.

What you definitely don't want is a salesperson. A salesperson won't lay out a philosophy. A salesperson will spend most of the time telling you what you want to hear. "Oh, Mr. Jones," he or she will say, "you like stock trading, do you? Well, I'm a specialist in stock trading." "Oh, you're getting stock options? Well, I'm a specialist in stock options." "Oh, you're interested in buying a variable annuity? Well, variable annuities are all I do."

You probably think I'm exaggerating. I'm not. These kinds of responses are actually taught by sales trainers. Someone who uses them is not the kind of advisor you want. You want someone who will spend most of the first meeting with you reviewing your financial and personal situation. Someone who will ask a lot of questions, not do a lot of talking (i.e., selling). Someone who doesn't brag about performance. If an advisor starts promising you high returns (say, anything higher than 7 to 12 percent a year), leave the office immediately and don't look back. Too many advisors these days use the remarkable returns of the recent bull market to position themselves as investing wizards.

Repeat after me . . .

Past performance is no guarantee of future performance!

An advisor you can trust talks about "reality investing." Although stocks have generated an average annual return of close to 18 percent over the last 10 years, that doesn't mean that the stock market will continue at that pace. In fact, if anything, it means it won't. In our office, we don't just show how well the stock market has done in the last 5 or 10 years. Doing that makes things seem "too good." Instead, we regularly show prospective clients the historical rates of return the stock market has averaged over the last 75 years. Over that extended span, the market has produced an average return of about 11 percent a year. And there have been plenty of years—even decades—in which stocks didn't make money.

RULE NO. 6
Go with your gut.

Your first meeting with a financial advisor is like a date. And much as with dating, you typically know right away if there is a connection. There will be a little voice inside you that says, "I trust this person, it feels right," or "I'm not sure," or "No way, José."

Go with your initial gut feeling. I usually know in the first 10 minutes whether or not I want to work with someone. In fact, I can usually tell over the phone when they call to make the appointment whether this is someone with whom I'd enjoy having a long-term relationship. Every time I've gone against this gut feeling, I ended up with a problem client.

Remember, when you hire a financial advisor, you're looking for a long-term relationship. Ideally, he or she will be helping you with your money for decades. If you start off with someone you don't have a good feeling about, the moment something goes wrong (like the market dropping), you'll be looking to bail out and find a new advisor.

RULE NO. 7
Be prepared to pay for the advice you get.

Professional financial advisors do not give you free advice. You'd think this would be obvious, but in this Internet world where we've gotten so used to everything being given away (or at least offered at steep discounts), many people actually think they can go into a financial professional's office and get the benefit of his or her experience and knowledge for nothing. Sorry, but it doesn't work that way.

So how do you pay for your advice? The financial-services industry has been going through massive changes in recent years, but there are two basic fee structures used by most professional financial advisors.

Commission-Based Advice

A commission-based advisor earns a fee each time he or she buys or sells an investment for you. For the past hundred years or so, this is how the majority of stockbrokers have worked, and it's very popular among financial advisors.

The good thing about commission-based advice is that if your advisor is an ethical person who doesn't trade the account much, it can turn out to be very inexpensive. Say you invest in 10 stocks or a half-dozen mutual funds and hold them all for years. Chances are you're not going to have to pay very many commissions. Unfortunately, some commission-based advisors will yield to the temptation to keep moving your money—that is, to create transactions that might not be really necessary in order to generate fees. This practice is called "churning," and it's illegal.

If you ever suspect that your account is being churned, stop approving all those trades and get a second opinion. I'm constantly stunned when I meet with prospective clients whose accounts have been churned. One lady I met a few years back handed me a brokerage statement that contained eight solid pages of trade confirmations. Her account totaled just $50,000 in assets—and yet it had generated $10,000 in brokerage commissions. It was sickening. The broker must have been calling her virtually every day to get her to okay this ridiculous level of trading.

When I asked her how this had happened, she said she thought this was how it worked. "I didn't know any better," she told me.

Make no mistake about it—an ethical advisor will never trade your account like this. The annual commissions on your account should not come to more than 2 to 3 percent of the account's total value. In other words, that poor woman's $50,000 account should have generated maybe $1,500 in commissions for the year . . . max! In fact, the industry standard for a commission-based account is less than 1 percent.

Don't get me wrong. There are a lot of fantastic advisors out there who charge commissions. (Indeed, in some cases, we still do this at our group.) But if you hire a commission-based advisor, make sure it's someone you trust, and keep an eye on the level of trading.

Fee-Based Advice

With fee-based advice, you pay an annual fee for all the services your financial advisor provides, including all your trades, meetings, proposals, performance reports, etc. Generally speaking, the fee is a set proportion—normally between 1 and 2.5 percent—of the amount of money the advisor is managing for you. So if you have $100,000 to invest, the advisor will charge you $1,000 to $2,500 a year.

Just a few years ago, fee-based advisors were relatively rare. Now virtually every major brokerage firm in the country is embracing this kind of payment structure. And because of the competition, the price of fee-based advice is quickly coming down. It's now possible to get a professional advisor to manage a professionally structured portfolio of mutual funds for just 1 percent annually.

Most of my new clients are fee-based. As far as I'm concerned, this structure has a lot of advantages. For one thing, there is now no possible conflict of interest. Since the advisor's pay depends on the value of your assets, it's in the advisor's interest to see your assets grow. Moreover, fee-based advisors get paid only if their clients are serviced well and kept happy. If they invest their clients' money and then forget about them, the clients will leave and the fees will stop coming. For this reason, fee-based advisors tend to be more service-oriented. To fee-based advisors, new clients represent more than a one-time sale; their businesses are based on long-term relationships. (By the way, if you hire a fee-based advisor, make sure you tell your tax accountant, because under some circumstances the fees you pay may be tax-deductible.)

RULE NO. 8
If you can't get a referral, do your own research.

There are now many great services to help you find a financial advisor. Below is a list to help you get your search started.

The Financial Planning Association
(800) 322–4237
www.fpanet.com
This site allows you to search by zip codes for the names of certified financial planners.

National Association of Personal Financial Advisors
www.napfa.org
This site allows you to search by zip codes and offers links to fee-only advisors.

Dalbar Inc.
(800) 296–7256
www.dalbar.com
This respected financial ratings service has partnered with Microsoft to act as a referral source for financial advisors with five years or more of experience and clean records. Although advisors pay to be on Dalbar's list, the fact that they submitted to a record check tells you they are serious about their business.

Checking Out an Advisor's Background

National Association of Security Dealers
(800) 289–9999
www.nasdr.com
This is the DMV of financial advisors. Always start here.

Certified Financial Planner Board of Standards
(888) 237–6275
www.cfp-board.org
This group sets and enforces the standards advisors must meet in order to call themselves certified financial planners. Its site allows you to check the status of a CFP certificant.

National Association of Insurance Commissioners
(816) 842–3600
wwwnaic.org
This group is an organization of state insurance regulators.
Through its online National Insurance Producer Registry
(NIPR), you can find information on more than 2.5 million
insurance agents and brokers, including their licensing status and
disciplinary history.

Become an "A" Client

It is not enough simply to hire a good financial advisor. You want
whomever you hire to pay attention to you—ideally, to consider you
one of his or her most important clients. Most people think that in
order to be important to a financial advisor, you need to have lots of
money. Nothing could be further from the truth. I have clients with
assets that range from $25,000 to $100 million, and I can assure you that
some of the smaller ones are just as important to me as the biggest ones.

The fact is, it's not just money that determines how much your
financial advisor cares about you. It's how you treat your financial advisor that matters. As an example, I have a client, Francine, who opened
an account with me with just $1,000. I put Francine's money into a stock
that tripled in value, so all of a sudden she had $3,000. I also bought this
stock for more than a half-dozen other clients. Most of them made significantly more money than Francine because they had more invested.
Unlike any of them, however, after the stock took off, Francine showed
up at my office one day with four bottles of wine as a gift for me and
each of my assistants. Now, I don't know what the wine cost Francine. I
don't even remember whether it was red or white. What I do remember
is that this small gesture of hers was talked about in our office for weeks.
We couldn't believe how special it was. I'm still talking (and now writing) about it six years later.

So when your financial advisor makes you some money, take a
moment to say "thank you." Sure, it's his or her job to make you money.
But that's no reason not to show your appreciation. No matter how

small your portfolio, a small gesture like a simple thank-you note or a bottle of wine can transform you to an "A" client.

Another great way to say "thank you" to your advisor—and become as a result an "A" client—is to refer the advisor some new business (that is, to recommend that a friend hire your advisor). Not only will this show your advisor how much you appreciate what he or she has done for you, it may turn out to be just what your friend needs to get her financial life together.

And it's not just financial advisors who should get this sort of consideration. When Francine gave me that little gift, it made me realize that I had never once expressed my appreciation to any of the professionals on whom I depend: my attorney, my CPA, my doctor, my haircutter, the mechanic who looks after my car—the list goes on and on. So three years ago I started sending them all thank-you notes and in some cases a gift basket at Christmas. The first time I did this, my doctor called me personally to say "thank you." Guess what? Even though my doctor is routinely booked up three months in advance, I never have to wait for an appointment anymore. I just seem to get right in. My car mechanic framed my thank-you letter and posted it on the wall of his waiting room. My CPA seemed to find more deductions the next year.

I'm not kidding. Because of my small gifts and notes, my relationship with all these professionals is now different. They remember me because I made a small gesture to say "thank you." Try it. Our parents were right: Saying "thank you" goes a long way.

Whatever You Do . . . Don't Give Up!

There's one other big mistake that investors often make—and it may be the biggest one of all. They give up.

Back at the beginning of this book, I told you the story of how my grandmother lost all the money she had saved her first year of investing. That experience could have easily convinced her that she should just stop trying. She could have decided that it just wasn't worth it. After all, she had made some huge mistakes. She had invested on tips, used a mediocre broker, failed to do her own research.

When she told me the story, I asked her what had kept her going after that disastrous first year. She smiled and said, "David, I looked at my life and said, 'Rose Bach, if you want to be rich, don't you dare quit now.' "

Imagine the strength it took to make that decision not to quit. Her friends teased her constantly. "Oh, Rose," they'd say, "come to lunch with us." "Oh, Rose, you don't need to worry about retirement—you'll have Social Security." "Oh, Rose, why do you worry so much? The future will take care of itself." Why were her friends so unsupportive? Maybe because they were afraid of what she might accomplish—that she would become rich and they wouldn't.

Remember, you have a choice in life: you can accept what you have or you can decide to live life with a plan and a purpose—which is to say, to its full potential. Following through on that decision to go for it isn't always easy. You're going to make mistakes—hopefully not the ones I listed above, but there are bound to be some. And that's okay. In fact, it's perfectly normal. The important thing is to learn from your mistakes, to get back up again and to keep moving forward. Like everything else that's worthwhile, living and finishing rich takes real commitment. But if you and your partner want it badly enough, I know in my heart that, working together, you can make it happen.

INCREASE YOUR
INCOME BY 10 PERCENT
IN NINE WEEKS

OVER THE LAST EIGHT CHAPTERS, we've been talking about all sorts of practices and techniques designed to help you and your partner live smart and finish rich. As I've said repeatedly, if the two of you follow only a few of them, you'll be better off than 90 percent of the population. If you do *all* of them, you've got a great chance to be in the top 1 percent.

Now, however, I want to let you in on a little secret. As important and useful as the previous eight steps have been, none of them are likely to have the immediate, powerful impact of what I am going to show you in this final step of our journey together—namely, how the two of you can increase your incomes by 10 percent or more in just nine weeks.

But wait a minute. Haven't I been saying throughout this book that the size of your paycheck doesn't matter, that if the two of you just do the right things (like "paying yourselves first" 10 percent of your income), you already make enough money to be wealthy?

Absolutely. I have been saying that. And I believe in my heart that most people do make enough money to build wealth if they use their wealth and invest their money wisely. But here's another truth I know. If I can show the two of you how each of you can grow your income by 10 percent over the next nine weeks, and then you do everything else I've shared with you in this book, your chances of living and finishing rich not only dramatically increase, but you will also get rich faster. That's because there is nothing that will grow your wealth more massively and quickly than increasing your income.

You Deserve a Raise!

So let me ask the two of you a question. Do either or both of you deserve a raise?

Over the years, I've asked this question in my seminars hundreds of times. The interesting thing is that when I ask a room of a hundred people how many of them think they are underpaid, the majority of the people in the room—in some cases, *all* of the people in the room—raise their hands. The fact is that most people think they are being underpaid. And that includes people who are self-employed. (How can self-employed people be underpaid? Very easily. Self-employed people can work too many hours for what they earn, possibly because they are not charging enough for their goods and services.)

Anyway, back to my question. Are you and your partner being paid what you are worth? Chances are the answer is no. Chances are you are overdue for a raise and you know it. But here's the problem. Raises don't just fall into our laps. We have to go out and get them.

With that in mind, I want you both to really focus on two things: (1) that you do deserve to make more money than you're currently making; and (2) that it is in your power to do something about it.

This simple idea—that whether you are an employee or an employer, you are actually in charge of how much you earn and how soon you get your next raise—is the basis of a powerful concept I call ProActive Income™. I created this principle a few years ago to help my students and clients see their incomes as a part of their overall financial plans. The goal of the ProActive Income approach is simple . . . and exciting—the idea is that by taking matters into your own hands, you can proactively increase your income each year by 10 percent or more.

Important Note

The job market has changed drastically in just the last year since *Smart Couples Finish Rich* was released in hardcover. We've gone from the "dot-com" boom to the "dot-com" bust." Companies have laid off thousands upon thousands of workers. As a result, it's really easy in this slowing economy to be told you are just "lucky" to have a job. Don't fall for it. The single hardest part of any business is finding good people. Good people who work their tails off and add real value get job raises in bad economies. In fact, employees that survived the layoffs of 2001 are now finding themselves in many cases with better jobs and more pay in 2002. What about you? Don't let this economy or a recession slow down your progress.

At Work We Don't Get What We Deserve . . . We Get What We Go For!

Many people manage their careers, but they forget to manage their income. Imagine this scenario: you've been working your tail off at work for the past six months and you're exhausted. You've been putting in 50-hour weeks, working weekends and late nights to help the company grow. Then one day you show up at work to find your office set up for a party. There are balloons and cake, and as you walk to your desk, all your colleagues jump out from their cubicles and scream, "Surprise!" Your boss comes up, claps you on the back, and says, "Because of your hard work, this company is doing better than ever. As a result, we want you to take an extra week of vacation, and with your permission, we'd like to give you a 20 percent pay raise."

Can you imagine this taking place? Probably not. That's just as well, because this wonderful fantasy is not going to happen. Nor is anything similar likely to happen if you're self-employed. Most likely, your customers aren't going to show up one day and announce, "You've done such a great job that we think we should be paying more for your services. Please raise your prices by 10 percent on your next invoice."

The reality is that there is only one real way to make more money, and that's for the two of you to decide that from now on that you are going to manage your careers and your incomes proactively.

The Power of ProActive Income™

One of the great things about growing your income and getting a raise is that you see the financial result of your actions immediately. Many of the skills and strategies I've coached you on in this book take a while to produce visible results. For example, the power of compound interest is an amazing thing, but it takes years to see it work. Getting a raise can take 48 hours. If you are self-employed and you decide to raise your rates by 10 percent and your next customer agrees to your higher rate, the result is immediate.

But there's even more to it than that. Perhaps most important, by succeeding in this way, you and your partner will experience firsthand the power of proactive management. You won't believe what the impact of this simple concept can be. I promise you—it will change your outlook as nothing else has ever done. Simply proving to yourselves that you can both raise your incomes by 10 percent in just nine weeks will make the two of you realize that you really are in control of your financial future. You really are in charge.

What It Means in Dollars and Cents

If you both increase how much you make by 10 percent every 12 months, you will just about double your joint income in seven years.

Now think about the impact on your lives if you were to do this.

Most working people these days get annual pay increases in the 3 to 4 percent range. So what I'm suggesting you go after doesn't represent all that much of a leap. In fact, my 10 percent suggestion is really a bare minimum. Either or both of you can certainly shoot for more. Why not try to grow your incomes by 30 percent this year? People do it all the time. In fact, one of the biggest morale issues at large companies today is that new employees often get paid 30 percent more than existing employees who have been at the company for 10 years.

What does this tell you? It tells you that life is not fair. Loyalty is often not rewarded. But rather than complaining about it, why not take advantage of this state of affairs by being the kind of employee who goes out and gets the raise? Instead of watching it happen for others, you can decide to make it happen for you. Remember, raises don't just fall into your lap; you have to go out and get them.

Why on Earth Would My Employer Be Willing to Give Me a 10 Percent Raise?

If you are good at your job and add real value to your employer's business, the chances that you will be able to get a raise sometime in the next nine weeks are really high. On the other hand, if you're not good at your job and you don't add real value at work, the chances of your getting a raise are low. This is incredibly simple stuff. Many of the same companies that are offering new employees 30 percent more than current employees are also making it a proactive goal to get rid of the bottom 25 percent of their workforce. That's because they are realizing that it is cheaper to pay more for a top employee who can produce results quickly and consistently than to try and raise the skill level of a mediocre employee who's been on the job for years.

So before you go out and confidently ask for that raise, ask yourself honestly, are you worth it? If the answer is yes, chances are your boss would much rather give you a raise than have to find a replacement for you. Most professional openings in today's job market are filled by agencies or headhunters whose fees are based on the salaries of the positions they're filling. The standard commission starts at 30 percent, which means it can cost more than $15,000 in agency fees just to replace a $50,000-a-year employee. And that doesn't include training and lost productivity. When all is said and done, it may cost your boss as much as $150,000 to find someone who can take your place and then get him or her up to speed (and even then there's no guarantee that he or she will be as good as you).

All of a sudden, your request for a 10 percent raise is starting to seem pretty reasonable, isn't it? Good. That's how you want to be thinking.

You Don't Know My Company . . . It Simply Doesn't Give 10 Percent Raises

People often challenge my ProActive Income concept on the grounds that in some workplaces, no one gets 10 percent raises—ever. As a woman at one of my seminars once put it: "At my company, they have a policy of never giving more than a 4 percent annual raise. That's the way it is and that's the way it will always be." At another seminar, another woman made a similar point. "We're all members of a union where I work," she said. "Our wages are set by contract for the next three years."

My response to both of these women was the same. "Ladies," I said, "this is America. No one is forcing you to work where you work. You've *decided* to work there. If you stay at a job where you get a fixed annual increase in pay each year without *any possibility* of getting more, you're not only losing out on additional income you may deserve, but even worse, you may be losing out on your passion for living."

I asked the woman who worked for the company with the 4 percent pay-raise ceiling whether she was at all passionate about her job. "Isn't it hard to be motivated when you know that no matter how well you do, you're never going to be rewarded for the effort?"

She looked at me angrily and said, "Yes, it frustrates me to no end. There's simply no motivation to do good work."

"In other words," I replied, "you're being motivated to do mediocre work. Which really means that you are being motivated to be a mediocre person, which is about the worst possible way to go through life."

Now the woman was really upset. "Well, I don't consider myself mediocre," she protested, "but would *you* put in an outstanding effort if you were me?"

"Definitely not," I said. "What I'd do is ask for a bigger raise and if I didn't get it, I'd start looking for a new career opportunity."

Sometimes You Don't Even Have to Threaten to Quit

People in management are paid to say, "Sorry, but this is the way it is." In fact, companies make exceptions to their policies all the time. Employees who approach management with ideas on how the company can operate more efficiently or make more money—or who can show their bosses specifically how they are able to add more to the bottom line—often discover that the policy of fixed annual raises isn't as rigid as they thought.

It's also important not to give up in the event your first request for a raise (or your first suggestion about how the company can make more money) doesn't go anywhere. Just because you're turned down once doesn't mean you'll be turned down the second time you ask. Or the third time. Remember, this is your income we are talking about. It's worth fighting for. That's what being proactive is all about. Don't be embarrassed to ask for more money. You deserve it.

How Do I Get a Raise If I'm Self-Employed?

Self-employed people can give themselves raises by increasing what they charge for the goods and services they provide. If you bill $40 an hour, then you need to raise your rates by 10 percent to $44 an hour. A landscaper I use raises his rates by 5 percent every six months like clockwork. Sometimes he cites a reason, like the cost of gas has gone up or fertilizer has become more expensive. Generally, though, the increases are so gradual that I barely notice them.

It wasn't until I was thinking about this subject that I realized that his rates had literally doubled in less than five years. No wonder he's able to buy himself a brand-new sports car every year. He's been proactively giving himself a raise of better than 10 percent a year for as long as I've known him. Pretty smart. But you know what? You can do the same thing. So whatever you charge right now, I want YOU to raise your rates by at least 10 percent. If you can't fathom doing this, then start charging 5 percent more and make it a goal to raise your rates by another 5 percent in less than 12 months. Within a year, you'll have given yourself a 10 percent raise.

All right, we've covered most of the basic questions. Now let's get down to specifics. Here's how to go about increasing your income by at least 10 percent over the next nine weeks.

THE PROACTIVE INCOME NINE-WEEK PLAN

WEEK ONE:
Get real.

I call Week One "reality time," for our plan begins with a brutally honest discussion in which you and your partner discuss how you are each doing in your respective careers.

The point here is not to put each other down or harp on what either of you should have done last year or the year before. The past is the past. You can't go back and get a raise for the last five years. You have to focus on today and what you can do tomorrow. The best way I know to do this is to step back and take a really hard look at your situation.

Here's what you should be focusing on.

How Much Do You Earn on an Hourly Basis?

If you are paid a regular salary, this should be relatively easy to figure out—but you have to do it correctly. That is, you have to figure out how many hours a week you really work. These days, most people are paid for a 40-hour work week, yet many of them are actually working 45 to 60 or more hours a week. In many cases, people leave the office and then put in an extra few hours at their home computers doing work over the Internet. Or they always carry a cell phone or beeper with them, which allows them to stay in constant touch with the office—meaning that no matter where they are or what they're doing, they are almost always really working. Knowing what you really earn an hour is critical to valuing your self-worth and time. So be honest. What's your real hourly wage?

The power of knowing what you earn an hour hit me recently when I received a bill for $95 from a plumber who had come out to my house to fix a problem and had spent all of seven minutes on the job.

I was shocked by the amount. "But you were here only seven minutes," I said.

He shrugged. "It doesn't matter if I'm here 7 minutes or 59 minutes and 30 seconds. I bill $95 an hour with a one-hour minimum."

I couldn't help but smile. This guy knew what his time was worth. You need to know the same thing. When many people work this out, they find they are actually earning a lot less than they thought. Usually, this is because they are working 60 hours a week while being paid for 40. (On the other hand, some people who spend a lot of time at the office just fooling around may discover—if they are really honest about how much time they actually spend working—that they're being paid very well indeed.)

Are You Working for a Good Company?

You should know by now whether or not you're working for a good company—that is, one with a bright future that offers you an opportunity to grow. Be honest here. Unless you're independently wealthy, you work in order to earn money. In other words, you are trading your free time in exchange for income. If you work for a poor company—or even just an average one—you've got a problem.

It's even worse if you work in a declining industry. I've had friends who were employed in dying industries, and I watched them have to work harder and harder each year just to stay even. On the other hand, other friends of mine have put themselves in growing industries, and by being in the right place at the right time, they doubled, tripled, and even quadrupled their incomes in a remarkably short amount of time.

If you are currently working for a "sinking ship," you should still go after that 10 percent raise, but you should also find yourself another line of work as soon as you can. When it comes to your career, there's no honor in going down with the ship.

Are You Currently in Complaint Mode or Action Mode?

The first two questions may start you thinking about a lot of things that may be wrong in your career. Or they might do the opposite and make you realize you've got a really great job. Either way, the main thing you're supposed to be doing in this first week is simply assessing your situation.

Once you're done thinking about things, however, you are going to have to act. The simple truth is that in order to grow your income, you need to be in what I call "action mode." Unfortunately, many of us aren't there. Rather, many people spend their time in "complaint mode."

Complaint mode is a dangerous state to be in. Not only is it annoying to friends and family, complaining actively prevents you from making any real progress.

People in complaint mode typically say things like:

- The project I'm working on is pointless.

- My skills (or contributions) are never appreciated.

- My commute is too long.

- My company's management doesn't know what it is doing.

- My coworkers don't pitch in.

- My boss is a jerk.

- My job stinks.

You get the idea.

Complainers make complaining a regular pastime. When you ask how they are, the response is invariably a litany of complaints. The worst part is that this can be contagious. If you're in a relationship with one of these complainers, you may find yourself responding to their complaints with a list of your own, just so you won't feel left out. Often, kids feed on this, and they start complaining about school at the dinner table. Many couples even "group complain" on the weekends: they get together over dinner and share what a terrible time they all had during the previous week and how much they all wish the weekend was longer.

It's actually pretty funny if you step back and look at it.

I'm not pointing fingers here. I've done this myself. The point is that sooner or later you have to face up to the fact that complaining gets you nowhere fast. So if you are in a relationship with a complainer—or happen to be one yourself—starting this week here's your new watchword: "No more complaining!" Or as my wife, Michelle, says to me,

"Let it go!" (She actually says this in such a long, drawn-out way that I can't help but smile. And then I usually shut up.)

So here's the deal: you've got a one-week grace period. For the first seven days of our nine-week plan, it's okay to list, look at, and complain about your problems at work. After Week One, however, 110 percent of your time and effort must go into action.

WEEK TWO:
Write down exactly what you want.

Getting your 10 percent raise is like achieving any other goal. The first step to making it real is to write it down. And that written description shouldn't be some vague hope. It must be specific, detailed, and include a deadline date.

So what I want you to do in Week Two is write down the following on a piece of paper: how much you currently earn, how much of a raise you are seeking, how much you will be earning when you get your raise, when you plan to begin your efforts, and when you expect to achieve your goal (i.e., get your raise). This last part is especially crucial. If you don't set yourself a deadline, the process won't work. Without a deadline, it's wishing, not doing.

When you've filled in all the information, sign and date the paper and have your partner witness it. That way you'll be even more committed.

The paper should look like something like this:

NAME: Julie King
SALARY NOW: $50,000
PERCENTAGE INCREASE I'M SEEKING: 10 percent
DOLLAR AMOUNT OF INCREASE: $5,000
NEW ANNUAL SALARY: $55,000
STARTING DATE: 8/1/2001
DEADLINE DATE: 10/1/2001

SIGNED: _____

PARTNER'S SIGNATURE: _____

Once it's complete, make several copies of the paper and put them where you will constantly be coming across them: post one on your bathroom mirror, put another on the nightstand next to your bed, stick a third to the refrigerator door, keep a fourth in your wallet or purse.

Obviously, it shouldn't take you a full week to do this simple exercise. In fact, it shouldn't take you more than a few minutes. But if it takes you a week to get around to it, that's fine. The point is that by the end of the week you need to have put your goal down on paper and posted that paper where you can see it.

It may seem silly, but if you don't do this simple exercise, the rest of the process isn't going to work. That's because your subconscious isn't going to believe you are serious. Trust me on this. Just keep playing full out. If you finish this exercise the first day of Week Two and want to jump ahead to Week Three, by all means do so. But don't skip this part just because it seems so easy. There is a blank ProActive Income form in the Appendix (page 284) you can fill out and use.

WEEK THREE:
Clean up the mess.

Nothing will change your attitude about your life and work faster than cleaning up your messes. If you're at all normal, your life—both at home and at work—is probably messier than you would like it to be. Having a cluttered home may be nobody's business, but if you have a cluttered office or cubicle or desk at work it's going to cost you money—and possibly a raise.

I'm not kidding. If your work space is a mess, everyone else in your office is going to see it and pass judgment on you. And they'll be right to do so, because a disorganized office means you're probably wasting time—and losing money—looking for stuff. That's a fact. According to the American Demographics Society, Americans waste a total of 9 million hours a day searching for misplaced items. What that works out to, says efficiency expert Jeff Mayer, the author of *Time Management for Dummies*, is that the average person spends an hour a day looking for papers *on the top of his or her desk!* In a similar vein, the *Wall Street Jour-*

nal reported that the average U.S. executive wastes fully six weeks a year searching for missing information.

In short, nothing gets in the way of making new money like an old mess. Unfortunately, being organized is generally not part of the curriculum at school, and it's rarely taught at work. As a result, most of us are basically winging it. To be sure, entire books have been written on the subject of how to get organized, and there are classes you can take to learn how to be neat. But here's a simple way to jump-start the process. Just go into your office this weekend and spend one full day cleaning it out. I promise you—the change will turbocharge your attitude and your productivity at work. In fact, other than changing jobs or careers, there is hardly anything you can do that will have as much impact on your work life as cleaning out your office. And this applies even to those of us who are fairly neat.

I learned the power of cleaning out my office the "right way" about three years ago. Up until then, I was a total packrat. I had research reports and old copies of the *Wall Street Journal* sitting in stacks three feet deep. Every inch of flat space had something on it. As a result, I would start my workday feeling overwhelmed, and I would finish it feeling exhausted.

Not anymore. Today my office is spotless and my file drawers are close to empty. When I come into my office, I literally feel relieved. This alone makes me feel more positive and be more productive, which I know has enabled me to earn a higher income.

Here's how I did it.

Six Hours to a Clean Office

Unless your office is a world-class disaster area, this entire exercise should not take you more than half a day. And if it is a world-class disaster area, then you really need to be doing this, no matter how long it winds up taking.

The first thing to keep in mind when it comes to cleaning your office is that you should always do it on a weekend, not during office hours. Show up in jeans and T-shirt. Bring some music and some lunch and a box or two of large garbage bags, and plan on making it an all-day deal. You should be able to get it all done in half a day. But even if it takes you until well into the evening, make it a goal to finish the whole project in a single day. That way you know you will be going in one way and coming out another—namely, finished and neat. That's important for your morale.

Now open up those garbage bags and get started tossing.

Start with the top of your desk. Take every paper, memo, and file folder that is sitting on top of your desk and put it into a file box (or multiple boxes, if need be). Everything. When you're done, the top of your desk—which you've probably not seen in a year or so—should be empty. Once it is, I want you to polish the top of your desk. Don't worry about all the stuff in the boxes. We'll get to those. Just polish the top of your desk. You'll be amazed how invigorating it is to see your office suddenly looking clean.

1. Take the boxes you just filled into a conference room (or some other open area). Go through all the papers you took off your desk, stack by stack, piece by piece. Any unread memo, report, or whatever that is more than 30 days old gets tossed. If it wasn't important enough to read when you first got it, it's even less important now. Also toss anything that you're not legally required to keep or that isn't critical to your career. I'll bet you find that 75 percent of what was on your desk can be thrown away. Take the stuff you have to keep and put it in file folders that you label appropriately and then *put it all in a file cabinet.*

2. Next attack the drawers in your desk. Open every single file and ask yourself, "How long has it been since I looked at this file?" If the answer is more than a year and you don't legally need to keep the file, throw it away. If it turns out you do need to keep the file, ask yourself if you need to keep every paper that's in it. Most likely, you don't. Be ruthless about this, and dump everything you don't absolutely need. Just a few hours of this should free up over half of your file space.

3. Take home any personal mementos that you don't absolutely love. By removing old stuff from your office, you'll be motivated to bring in more current things. Freshen up the plants, bring in new pictures. If you have to spend 40 to 50 hours a week in your office—and most of us do—make it an environment you love, and not simply tolerate.

4. Commit to keeping your new clean office . . . clean. Let's face it, unless you radically change your habits, you are going to mess up your new clean office in way less than nine weeks. Don't let this happen. Sure, we all know messy workers who say, "That's just how I am. I'm too busy to be neat." Well, that's no excuse. The fact is that a clean office can help you make more money. It happens to be a fact that the higher you look in the corporate power structure, the cleaner the offices get. I don't think it's a coincidence. Clients and coworkers take you more seriously and will respect you more when your workplace is neat and professional looking.

Throw It Away and See If It Comes Back . . .

A successful executive once told me he tosses out literally all of his internal mail. When I asked what happens if something important gets lost in the process, he replied, "David, 95 percent of the stuff corporations send around is unnecessary. Someone is getting paid to create this stuff, print this stuff, stuff this stuff, and distribute this stuff. It's almost all stuff that no one ever asked for and it's almost all stuff that I certainly don't need. If it is really important and I throw it away, it will come back. Someone will always let me know if I've missed something important."

"Anyway," he added, "if that happens five times a year, it's a lot."

At the time, I thought he was crazy. In the years since then, however, I've learned that he was right. These days I now toss almost everything. I also rarely open any mail (electronic or regular) that I didn't ask for. If you're not disciplined, you can waste hours each day at a typical company reading pointless communications. It's crazy.

When You're Done With the Office, Clean Out the House

After you've finished with your office, your next job is to tackle your house. Make a date with Goodwill or the Salvation Army for a pickup (that's now your deadline date), and get started cleaning. Use three criteria to decide what to keep and what to throw away: 1) Do you love it? 2) Do you use it? 3) Is it of either real or sentimental value? If you can't answer yes to at least one of these questions, out it goes.

Most people have closets that are half full of clothes they haven't worn in years. If you've got an item in your house that you haven't used or worn in a year, you probably don't need it anymore. Give it to someone else to enjoy, get yourself a tax deduction, and reduce the clutter in your life. Cleaning out your house with your partner is not only truly empowering, it also costs virtually nothing to do. In fact, if you have a garage sale, you can actually make money. (My suggestion, however, is that you give away your stuff to a charitable organization. You'll have a cleaner home and you'll feel good about helping others. It's a double win.)

WEEK FOUR:
Get clear on how *you* add value.

The only reason a boss will give an employee a raise is because that employee is worth it—in other words, because he or she adds value to the enterprise. So before you ask your boss to give you a raise, you need to make sure you understand exactly how you add value.

Don't assume you know because you might be dead wrong. Often, people spend the better part of their workday focused on trivia that doesn't really matter rather than the important things that really add value. How do you make sure you know which is which? It's simple. You ask.

What I suggest is that you make an appointment with your boss to discuss how you might be able to add more value on the job. Tell him or her that you're on a mission to improve the quality of what you do, and that you'd like five minutes of his or her time to discuss how you might best accomplish this. Bring a pad and a pen to the appointment, and explain to your boss that your goal is to find out two things: 1) what you currently do that adds the most value to the company, and 2) what else you might do that would add more value.

That's all you need to do. Once you've posed these questions, your job is simply to listen to (and take notes on) what your boss has to say. When your boss has finished answering, you should restate what you understood the message to be. Then tell your boss that you would like to meet again in a few days after you've had a chance to work out an action plan based on his or her suggestions.

Take your notes of the conversation home with you and type them up. Then work out a simple agenda of things you can do to accomplish what the boss wants and type that up, too. When you have your second meeting with your boss, hand her or him your typed summary and agenda. Explain that you are committed to doing what it takes to add more value. I promise you—your boss will be impressed. No one does this sort of thing. It may be simple, but it's the most effective way imaginable to lay the groundwork for your raise.

If you're self-employed, you can do essentially the same thing with your customers. Ask them what it is that you do that they feel adds value to their lives. What else could you be doing to add value? Your customers may have the key to how you could increase your income. You just have to ask.

You can even do this with your significant other. Many of us often lose sight of what it is we bring to the relationships we're in. The more you know, the easier it is to add more value to the relationship—and get more joy out of it. This may have nothing to do with income, but it has everything to do with your happiness. If you have children, try it with them. Ask them what you do as a parent that they think adds value to your relationship, and ask them what else you could do to add more value. You might find them turning the tables and asking you the same question.

WEEK FIVE:
Focus on the 80/20 rule.

If you've spent any time in the business world, you may be familiar with the idea that in sales and commerce, 80 percent of your revenue tends to come from 20 percent of your customers. This notion is based on an idea that was first articulated more than a century ago by an Italian sociologist named Pareto. What became known as the Pareto Principle basically says that 20 percent of what you do accounts for 80 percent of your results. In other words, 80 percent of your effort really doesn't matter all that much.

What's Your Top 20 Percent?

Understanding the implications of this principle can transform your effectiveness both as an employee and as an employer. If you can figure out which of your efforts account for most of the value you add on the job and then increase this proportion from 20 percent of your day to, say, just 30 percent, you can conceivably increase your productivity by 50 percent! And you can do this with what really is a very small amount of additional effort.

Smart companies have been taking advantage of this fact of business life for many years now. They realize that the key to growth and future success lies in being able to "wow" their top clients. This is why most major corporations today offer their best customers special rewards programs like Platinum Clubs or Gold Level Memberships.

What about *your* career or business? Where does the lion's share of *your* income come from? What did your boss say when you asked how you could add the most value? If you're self-employed, do you know who your best customers really are? Can you list the ones who make up your top 20 percent right now? If, in the next 36 months, you can bring in a new group of customers just like your current top 20 percent, you'll probably double the size of your business. The bottom line with the 80/20 rule is that the more you're able to identify—and focus on—the 20 percent of effort that produces the 80 percent of results, the more successful you are going to be.

Remember, you may be paid for your time, but you are rewarded for your results. During this week, focus on and figure out what it is that you do that comprises your top 20 percent. How do you spend the time at work that really produces the results that are responsible for the bulk of your income? From now on, you must focus more on these activities—and less on the stuff that takes up 80 percent of your time but doesn't really produce anything worthwhile. In simple terms, it's all about focusing on what gets results, and cutting out everything else that wastes your time and energy.

WEEK SIX:
Put yourself in play.

A big part of being able to get a raise is having the confidence to ask for one. Many people lack this confidence because they've been working with their head down for so long and have so little idea what else is "out there" that they don't realize just how valuable they and their skills are.

If you don't really know what other companies are paying people to do jobs similar to yours, you can't possibly know what you should be earning. It used to be considered rude to ask others what they made. Not anymore. This isn't about keeping up with the Joneses. It's about maintaining your professional respect. If you are being paid $40,000 a year for doing a job that commands $65,000 a year at some other company, you are being cheated. And it's not necessarily your employer's fault. After all, it's your employer's job to keep costs down. It's your job to grow your income and build your wealth.

So how do you find out if you are being compensated fairly? The trick is to put yourself in play. One of my favorite examples of how this works involves a young woman named Lauren who took one of my classes and later became a client. When we first met, she was 27 and was doing very well in her career, earning $55,000 a year as a consultant. Unfortunately, three years later, when she was 30, her salary had only increased to $65,000. Lauren was frustrated. Her company just wasn't coming through with pay raises, even though she was still working as hard as ever.

After hearing her complain about this for the fifth time, I told her to stop grumbling and do something about it. "Pick up the phone," I said, "and call your company's number-one competitor. Tell them what you do, that you work your tail off, that you're really good at your job, and that you're frustrated with your situation. Tell them you may be looking for a new opportunity and ask if they would be interested in speaking with you."

Lauren followed my advice. Within a month, she had been invited to three interviews and was offered a new job at $95,000 a year plus a $20,000 signing bonus—in other words, practically double her current income! Needless to say, her old company begged her to stay, offering to increase her annual salary to $85,000 and promising to give her a salary review every six months instead of just once a year.

Unfortunately for them, it was too little too late. Lauren left. Before long, her base salary had jumped to more than $125,000 a year. The additional money she now earns has allowed her to save enough to buy her first home, and at age 33 she is building both wealth and career responsibility. Had she not put herself in play, she never would have known what else was out there, and she'd still be toiling away, underappreciated and undercompensated.

Keep in mind that the time to look for a new job is now. You may have no interest in leaving your current employer, and you may be totally happy, but how can you really know what's best for you if you have no idea what else is out there?

Here are three quick things you can do to put yourself in play.

1. **Attend a job fair.** Job fairs are now a big-time recruitment tool. No longer aimed at inexperienced recent graduates and desperate people looking for low-end jobs, they take place in every major city almost every single month. To find one in your area, simply look in the careers or business section of your daily newspaper. You can also look online at *www.jobfind.com*. The great thing about job fairs is that in one day you can be exposed to dozens and dozens of companies. Some job fairs feature hundreds of major companies recruiting and presenting. The key to making a job fair work for you is to come prepared. Create a professional-looking resume and dress for success. When you spot a company you might be interested in, approach its booth the same way you would approach a job interview. Introduce yourself and hand a copy of your resume to the recruiter. Keep in mind that many of these recruiters have a quota to meet. They are not just there to collect resumes. Rather, they are expected to identify a certain number of real potential hires. In other words, they may be even more eager than you to make connections and schedule interviews. At technology-oriented job fairs, it's not uncommon for a company's top executives (sometimes even its founder) to be working the booth

and for job offers to be made literally on the spot. These companies often need workers more than workers need jobs.

2. **Look online.** The future of job hunting is on the Internet. If you don't have Internet access at home, visit your local public library. But don't do your online job searching at work. Not only is that unethical, but many companies now monitor their employees' online activity. In other words, surfing the Web for a new job on company time could lead to your getting fired. Here are some places you might want to begin.

www.yahoo.com The largest and most popular portal on the World Wide Web, Yahoo currently offers more than 100 different job-site listings. Go to *http://careers.yahoo.com*.

www.jobsearch.org This is America's Job Bank, a government-run site with over 1.5 million job listings.

After you've checked out these two sites, you might look at commercial job-placement sites. Among the biggest and most popular.

www.monster.com

www.hotjobs.com

www.headhunter.net

www.jobtrak.com

www.careerbuilder.com

Most of these sites allow job-seekers to post their resumes. This is a wonderful service, but if you work for a large corporation, be careful as an increasing number of large companies now scan these sites for the resumes of employees who may be thinking about moving on. Some sites let you post a "blind resume" that doesn't include your name or postal address. (Interested employers contact you through a private e-mail address.) This is the safest way to put yourself in play.

You should also look at local portals. Most cities now have great local Web sites that often list the best jobs. In San Francisco, where I live, one of the most popular such job sites is *www.craigslist.com*.

3. **Talk to friends.** The best jobs are often filled through word of mouth. Many companies today offer their employees cash bonuses worth thousands of dollars if they refer someone who winds up getting hired. So let your friends know that you're looking. But be specific about what you're looking for—what type of work environment, what type of job, pay, etc. The more specific you can be, the better. It may sound like a long shot, but your new dream job could be waiting for you at a good friend's company.

> **WEEK SEVEN:**
> **Practice asking for the raise.**

It's now time to stop thinking about how much of a raise you want—and to start diagramming it. This week write down on a summary page exactly how much of a raise you want and why you believe you are worth it. List what you've done to add value to the company this year, and how you see yourself adding value in the future. You can use this summary page as a reference sheet when you actually sit down to ask your boss for the raise. It's also often a good idea to back up your verbal request with a written one. Putting most anything in writing makes it more real. At the very least, it will make your request impossible to ignore. As a matter of policy, many companies require their executives to respond to requests for pay increases when they are made in writing.

Now that you have a clear, written summary of what you're going to be asking for and why, it's time to start practicing. Ask your partner to play the part of your boss, and see how your pitch sounds to him or her. If you're uncomfortable practicing this with your partner, sit in a room by yourself and practice it. But whether you're alone or doing it with someone else, you really should rehearse your presentation aloud.

I can't emphasize enough the importance of hearing yourself asking for the raise and stating your case out loud a half-dozen times. For one thing, it will make your subconscious believe it. For another, you need to hear what you sound like. Indeed, you might even want to tape-record yourself. If you're at all "practical," this may sound silly, but trust me on it. You need to hear your voice asking for the raise. You don't want to hear it for the first time when you're actually doing it. After all, you don't want to look surprised when you ask; you want to look self-assured. So listen to yourself and keep practicing until you sound cool, collected, and confident. Try to anticipate the kind of objections your boss might make, and rehearse how you will respond to them.

Obviously, no matter how good you are at your job, your boss is not going to jump up and hug you when you ask for a raise. It's his or her job to keep costs down. The key to achieving your goal is to make your boss realize that it makes more economic sense for the company to grant your request than to try to replace you. The same can be said if you're self-employed. Practice asking for your rate increase, before you do it.

> **WEEK EIGHT:**
> **Ask for the raise.**

You can prepare all you want, but none of it will do you any good if you don't actually approach your boss and ask for the raise. Without direct action on your part, nothing is going to happen.

By now, you should know the right way to ask for a raise, and you should be prepared to make your pitch. You've had your informational meeting with your boss. You've learned how you add value (and are hopefully already adding even more). You've put yourself in play (and hopefully seen what else is out there). Your office is spotless and you are focusing on your top 20 percent of critical value-added activities. You know what you deserve (which may well be more than a 10 percent raise) and you are ready to ask for it.

Hopefully, you are feeling confident. But even if you're not, you should still go ahead and ask for the raise. The fact is, even if you've ignored my advice so far, and the only thing you've done over the previous seven weeks is make an appointment with your boss, you still have an excellent chance of getting your raise. *But you've got to ask.* So ignore any friends or family members who may be telling you that what you're doing is crazy. Just make an appointment with your boss and state your case. The worst thing that could happen is that your boss says no—in which case you've learned something important (namely, that it may be time to start looking for a new job or perhaps a new career, or maybe that you need to focus harder on how to add more value).

If you're self-employed, this is the week you raise your prices. Specifically, you should charge your next new customer at least 5 percent more for your goods or services than you've been charging your old customers. If you're not adding new customers, you should inform your existing clients that you now have a new pricing structure.

One final tip: when asking for a raise—whether of your boss or your customers—remember to present your request in percentage terms, not a dollar amount. "I'm looking for a 10 percent increase" generally goes down a lot easier than "I want you to pay me $5,000 more this year."

WEEK NINE:
Celebrate your success.

Even if you don't get your raise immediately, you should celebrate. The fact is that it takes courage to ask for a raise, and anyone who does it deserves a pat on the back. So plan in advance what you and your partner will do to celebrate your having taken action!

Too often in life, we get so focused on the result that we lose sight of the process. The basic point of my ProActive Income concept is not simply to help you win some specific raise, but to encourage you to think about your income in a new and different way. Whether you earn it as an employee or as a business owner, you should regard your income as something that you actively manage and work on. The idea isn't to go after some particular number, but to make sure you're always pro-actively focused on making progress.

I've suggested that you ask for a 10 percent annual pay increase because that happens to be a specific, easily measurable goal. Other, equally significant job-related goals may involve promotions, transfers, or being given more responsibility. Whatever the case may be, it's important to remember that you cannot make progress passively. You have to be bold and take action.

You also need to remember that while taking action will sometimes bring you exciting victories (in which you get exactly what you wanted, or more), you are also bound to encounter the occasional roadblock (which will stop you dead in your tracks). These sorts of ups and downs are perfectly normal over the course of a career. As a result, you should never miss a chance to celebrate a victory (even if it's a small one, like getting your office cleaned out). The more you get in the habit of rewarding yourself for taking action, the more willing you'll be to take risks and accept challenges.

The number-one reason people stop trying at work and in life is that they have set themselves up for failure by deciding that nothing less than perfection is acceptable. The truth is that perfection does not exist. The key to living smart and finishing rich is to regard the pursuit of progress as a journey—a journey that you enjoy along the way by making sure to celebrate the small victories as well as the big ones.

Take Time to Appreciate Each Other

This has been the final step of our nine-step journey to learning how to live and finish rich. I'm honored to have had the opportunity to be your personal financial coach and motivator. I hope you've enjoyed this journey we've taken and that you and your partner are now looking at your lives, both together and individually, in a bright and exciting new light.

THREE WORDS THAT
MAKE A DIFFERENCE

IT'S NOW TIME for the two of you to continue your journey together by living in line with your values and making your dreams and financial goals a reality. But I want to leave you with a thought that I think is critical. Money may be important, but it is not the be-all and end-all. The greatest gifts we human beings can receive are life and love. You and your partner right now have both, and that's something no amount of clever purchasing or investing can get anyone.

Often, in our pursuit of goals and wealth, we lose sight of what matters most. Life is short, and sometimes it gets taken away from us before we realize how special it is. Insurance merely provides money to the people we love; it doesn't bring us back. If you are in a relationship with someone right now—if you've found that special person with whom to share your life and love—then you are truly blessed, because you've overcome one of the hardest challenges there is. Compared to that, this money stuff is actually pretty easy—especially now that you have the knowledge to do it right.

So take some time to relax. *Smart Couples Finish Rich* is not about the two of you changing each other and learning how to sacrifice. It's about growing with each other and loving life together. You don't have to stop having fun to live and finish rich. In fact, the more fun you have on this journey we call life, the more you are guaranteed to live and finish rich.

With that in mind, take a few moments to stop and think about why it is you love your partner so much. Remember why and how you fell in love and what it is that made this person so special to you. You might consider taking 15 minutes to put this in writing. But whether you do or not, take a few minutes and let your partner know how much you really love him or her and why. The three words "I love you" can never be heard enough. We've got a serious "I love you" deficiency in this country and the best place to start fixing it is at home. So give out a dose right now of "I love you" to your partner, to your parents, to your friends, and especially to your kids, if you have any. You'll feel better and you might just change the life of someone you care about forever.

Finally, remember that this journey we call life is a gift. It shouldn't have to take losing someone you love, or becoming deathly ill yourself, to appreciate it. My hope for you is that you start living with all the passion you have deep down inside of you. You know, in five years, you can either be five years older or five years older living with more passion, living more richly, and being closer to finishing rich. Ultimately, the choice is yours, and it will be determined by what you do, not what you want. I hope in some small way this book and our time together has helped the two of you to look at your lives and get excited about your future again. Really going for your dreams takes strength, and I know deep in my heart that you both have that strength.

Until we meet again along the journey . . . have fun and live rich!

WHERE DOES THE

MONEY *REALLY* GO?

One of the most important parts of getting your financial life to-gether is having a solid grasp on exactly what your current cash flow is. To do this, use the worksheet below.

First, determine how much you earn . . .

Your Income

Wages, salary, tips, commissions, self-employment
income $_____

Dividends from stocks, bonds, mutual funds, savings
accounts, CDs, etc. $_____

Income from rental property $_____

Income from trust accounts (usually death benefits
from an estate) $_____

Alimony, child support, Social Security widows benefits	$_____
Social Security benefits	$_____
Other income	$_____
TOTAL MONTHLY INCOME	**$_____**

Second, determine what you spend

Your Expenses

Taxes

Federal income taxes	$_____
State income taxes	$_____
FICA (Social Security taxes)	$_____
Property taxes	$_____
TOTAL TAXES	**$_____**

Housing

Mortgage payments or rent on primary residence	$_____
Mortgage payment on rental or income property	$_____
Utilities	$_____
Homeowners or renters insurance	$_____
Repairs or home maintenance	$_____
Cleaning service	$_____
Television cable	$_____
Home phone	$_____
Landscaping and pool service	$_____
Monthly Internet service	$_____
Condo or association dues	$_____
TOTAL HOUSING	**$_____**

Auto

Car loan or lease $_____

Gas $_____

Car insurance $_____

Car phone $_____

Repairs or service $_____

Parking $_____

Bridge tolls $_____

TOTAL AUTO $_____

Insurance

Life insurance $_____

Disability insurance $_____

Long-term-care insurance $_____

Liability insurance (umbrella policy) $_____

TOTAL INSURANCE $_____

Food

Groceries $_____

Food outside of home $_____

TOTAL FOOD $_____

Personal Care

Clothing $_____

Cleaning/drycleaning $_____

Cosmetics $_____

Health club dues and/or personal trainer $_____

Entertainment $_____

Country club dues	$_____
Association memberships	$_____
Vacations	$_____
Hobbies	$_____
Education	$_____
Magazines	$_____
Gifts	$_____
TOTAL PERSONAL CARE	**$**_____

Medical

Health-care insurance	$_____
Prescriptions and monthly medicines	$_____
Doctor or dentist expenses	$_____
TOTAL MEDICAL	**$**_____

Miscellaneous

Credit-card expenses	$_____
Loan payments	$_____
Alimony or child support	$_____
Anything you can think of that I missed!	$_____
TOTAL MISCELLANEOUS EXPENSES	**$**_____
TOTAL MONTHLY EXPENSES	**$**_____

Murphy's Law Factor

Take the total expenses and increase by 10 percent	$_____
TOTAL INCOME	**$**_____
Minus total monthly expenses	$_____
Net cash flow (available for savings or investments)	$_____

FINISHRICH INVENTORY
PLANNER™

DETERMINING YOUR NET WORTH

STEP ONE: FAMILY INFORMATION

Client Name_____

Date of Birth_____ Age_____ Nickname_____

Spouse's Name _____

Date of Birth_____ Age_____ Nickname_____

Mailing Address_____

City_____State___Zip_____Home Phone _____

Work Phone _____Fax _____ E-mail _____

Spouse's Work Phone _____Fax _____E-mail _____

SS#_____ Spouse's SS#_____

Employer_____

Job Title_____

Spouse's Employer_____

Spouse's Job Title_____

Are you retired? Yes ____Date Retired_____No____Planned Retirement Date_____

Is your spouse retired? Yes____Date Retired_____No___Planned Retirement Date_____

Marital Status: Single____Married___Divorced____Separated____ Widowed_____

Children

Name	Date of Birth	SS#
1.		
2.		
3.		
4.		
5.		

Dependents

Do you have any family members that are financially dependent upon you or could be in the future?

(i.e. parents, grandparents, adult children, etc.) Yes ___ No___

Name   1. _____ Age _____

Relationship_____

Name   2. _____ Age _____

Relationship_____

Name   3. _____ Age _____

Relationship_____

Name   4. _____ Age _____

Relationship_____

Name   5. _____ Age _____

Relationship_____

STEP TWO: PERSONAL INVESTMENTS (DO NOT INCLUDE RETIREMENT ACCOUNTS HERE)

Cash Reserves

List amount in banks, savings & loans, and credit unions

Name of Bank Institution	Type of Account	Current Balance	Interest Rate
Example: Bank of America	Checking/Savings/Money Market	$10,000.00	2%
1.			
2.			
3.			
4.			
5.			

Fixed Income

List fixed-income investments

Example: C.D., Treasury Bills, Notes, Bonds, Tax-Free Bonds, Series EE Savings Bonds	Dollar Amount	Current %	Maturity Date
1.			
2.			
3.			
4.			
5.			

Stocks

Name of Company	No. of Shares	Price Purchased	Approx. Market Value	Date Purchased
1.				
2.				
3.				
4.				
5.				

Do you have stock certificates in a security deposit box? Yes _____ No _____

Mutual Funds and/or Brokerage Accounts

Name of Brokerage Firm/ Mutual Fund	No. of Shares	Cost Basis	Approx. Market Value	Date Purchased
1.				
2.				
3.				
4.				
5.				
6.				

Annuities

Company	Annuitant/Owner	Interest Rate	Approx. Market Value	Date Purchased
1.				
2.				
3.				

Other Assets (i.e., business ownership, etc.)	Approximate Market Value
1.	$
2.	$
3.	$

STEP THREE: RETIREMENT ACCOUNTS

Are you participating in an Employer Sponsored Retirement Plan?
(These include Tax-Deferred Retirement Plans such as 401(k) Plans and 457 Plans) Yes _____ No _____

Company where your money is	Type of Plan	Approximate Value	% You Contribute

You:

1.			
2.			
3.			

Spouse:

1.			
2.			
3.			

Do you have money sitting in a company plan you no longer work for?

Yes _____ No _____ Balance _____ When did you leave the company?_____

Spouse:

Yes _____ No _____ Balance _____ When did you leave the company?_____

Self-Directed Retirement Plans

Are you participating in a retirement plan? (These include IRAs, Roth IRAs, SEP-IRAs, SAR-SEP IRAs, and SIMPLE plans)

Name of institution where your money is   Type of Plan   Approximate Value

You:

1._____
2._____
3._____
4._____
5._____

Spouse:

1._____
2._____
3._____
4._____
5._____

STEP FOUR: REAL ESTATE

Do you rent or own your own home?

Own _____ / Monthly mortgage is _____ Rent _____ / Monthly rent is _____

Approximate value of primary home $ _____Mortgage balance $ _____=

Equity in home_____Length of loan ___Interest rate of loan ___Is loan fixed or variable?____

Do you own a second home?

Approximate value of second home $ _____Mortgage balance $ _____=

Equity in home_____Length of loan ___Interest rate of loan ___Is loan fixed or variable?____

Any other real estate owned?

Approximate value $ _____Mortgage balance $ _____= Equity in

home_____Length of loan ___Interest rate of loan ___Is loan fixed or variable?____

STEP FIVE: ESTATE PLANNING

Do you have a will or living trust in place? Yes _____ No ___ Date it was last reviewed_____

Who helped you create it? Attorney's name_____

Address_____

Phone _____ Fax _____

Is your home held in the trust or is it held in joint or community property? _____

Risk Management/Insurance

Do you have a protection plan in place for your family? Yes _____ No _____

Life Insurance Company	Type of Insurance (i.e., Whole Life, Term, Variable, etc.)	Death Benefit	Cash Value	Annual Premium
1.				
2.				
3.				

Tax Planning

Do you have your taxes professionally prepared? Yes _____ No _____

Name of accountant/CPA _____

Address _____

Phone _____ Fax _____

What was your last year's taxable income?_____Estimated tax bracket?_____%

STEP SIX: CASH FLOW

Income

Your Est. Monthly Income _____Estimated Annual Income _____

Spouse's Est. Monthly Income _____Estimated Annual Income _____

Rental Property Income: Monthly _____ Annually_____

Other Income (i.e., partnerships, Social Security, pensions, dividend checks, etc.)

Type of Income	Monthly

Annually

1._____

2._____

3._____

Expenses

Monthly Estimated Expenses $_____Annual Estimated Expenses $_____

What do you earn a month after taxes? $ _____

What do you estimate you spend?   - $ _____

Net Cash Flow   = $ _____

STEP SEVEN: NET WORTH

Total Assets $ _____

Total Liabilities   - $ _____

Estimated Net Worth   = $ _____

PROACTIVE INCOME™

Name: _____

Salary Now: _____

Percentage Increase I'm Seeking: _____

Dollar Amount of Increase: _____

New Annual Salary: _____

Starting Date: _____

Deadline Date: _____

Signed: _____

Partner's Signature: _____

PURPOSE-FOCUSED
FINANCIAL PLAN™

The additional Purpose-Focused Financial Plan worksheets that follow are for your partner to fill out and for the two of you to fill out as a couple. The guidelines on pages 83–84 will help you both think about five key goals that you each want to accomplish over the next 12 months.

PURPOSE-FOCUSED FINANCIAL PLAN ™

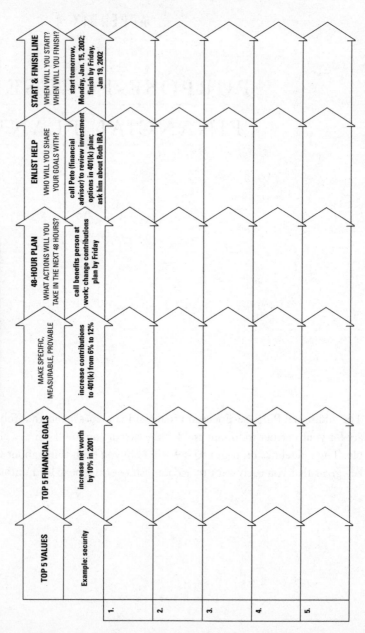

TOP 5 VALUES	TOP 5 FINANCIAL GOALS	MAKE SPECIFIC, MEASURABLE, PROVABLE	48-HOUR PLAN WHAT ACTIONS WILL YOU TAKE IN THE NEXT 48 HOURS?	ENLIST HELP WHO WILL YOU SHARE YOUR GOALS WITH?	START & FINISH LINE WHEN WILL YOU START? WHEN WILL YOU FINISH?
Example: security	increase net worth by 10% in 2001	increase contributions to 401(k) from 6% to 12%	call benefits person at work; change contributions plan by Friday	call Pete (financial advisor) to review investment options in 401(k) plan; ask him about Roth IRA	start tomorrow, Monday, Jan. 15, 2002; finish by Friday, Jan 19, 2002
1.					
2.					
3.					
4.					
5.					

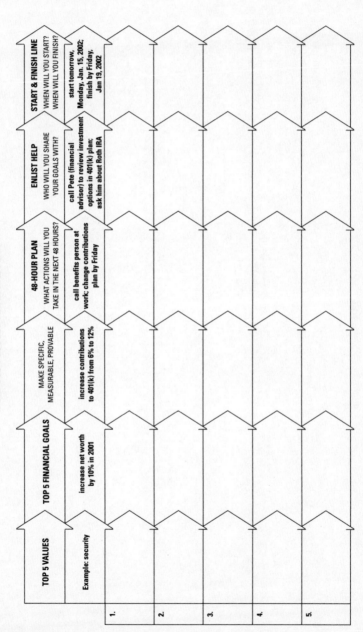

PURPOSE-FOCUSED FINANCIAL PLAN ™

	TOP 5 VALUES	TOP 5 FINANCIAL GOALS	MAKE SPECIFIC, MEASURABLE, PROVABLE	48-HOUR PLAN WHAT ACTIONS WILL YOU TAKE IN THE NEXT 48 HOURS?	ENLIST HELP WHO WILL YOU SHARE YOUR GOALS WITH?	START & FINISH LINE WHEN WILL YOU START? WHEN WILL YOU FINISH?
	Example: security	increase net worth by 10% in 2001	increase contributions to 401(k) from 6% to 12%	call benefits person at work; change contributions plan by Friday	call Pete (financial advisor) to review investment options in 401(k) plan; ask him about Roth IRA	start tomorrow, Monday, Jan. 15, 2002; finish by Friday, Jan 19, 2002
1.						
2.						
3.						
4.						
5.						

DAVID BACH is the author of the national bestsellers *Smart Women Finish Rich* and *Smart Couples Finish Rich*. The host of his own PBS special, "Smart Women Finish Rich." Bach is an internationally recognized financial advisor, author, and educator.

Bach is the creator of the FinishRich™ book and seminar series from which millions of people have benefited from his quick and easy-to-use financial strategies. In just the last few years, over 250,000 people have attended his Smart Women Finish Rich™ and Smart Couples Finish Rich™ Seminars, which have been taught coast to coast by thousands of financial advisors in over 1,500 cities. Each month, through these seminars, men and women continue to learn firsthand how to take smart financial action to live a life in line with their values.

Regularly featured on television and on radio as well as in newspapers and magazines, Bach has appeared on ABC's *The View*, Fox News Channel's *The O'Reilly Factor*, CNBC, and MSNBC, and he has been profiled in major publications, including *BusinessWeek*, *USA Today*, *People*, the *Financial Times*, the *Washington Post*, *The Wall Street Journal*, the *Los Angeles Times*, the *San Francisco Chronicle*, *Working Woman*, and *Family Circle*. Bestseller lists that have featured *Smart Women Finish Rich* include the *New York Times* and *Wall Street Journal* business lists, *Business Week*, the *Washington Post*, the *Boston Globe*, and the *San Francisco Chronicle*. *Smart Couples Finish Rich* has also appeared on the *New York Times* business, *BusinessWeek* and *San Francisco Chronicle* bestseller lists. His books are currently printed in five languages.

Today, Bach is the CEO of FinishRich™ Inc., a company dedicated to revolutionizing the way people learn about money. Prior to founding FinishRich™ Inc., Bach was a senior president of a major New York brokerage firm and a partner of The Bach Group, which, during his tenure (1993 to 2001), managed over a half-billion dollars for individual investors.

David Bach lives in New York with his wife, Michelle. Please visit his website at www.finishrich.com.

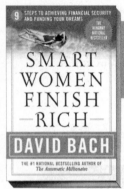
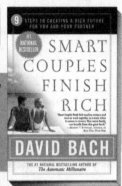

Attend a FinishRich™ Seminar

My grandmother taught me anyone could be rich if they had the right tools and the right motivation. Now I want to teach you! Come to a Smart Women Finish Rich™ or Smart Couples Finish Rich™ Seminar—or both!

They have been taught to thousands of people who have learned—just as you can—that improving their financial lives can be easy and fun. You will also learn how to focus on your values so that the money you do spend enhances the life you always dreamed of living.

Both seminars are usually offered at no cost and include a free workbook.

To see David live or attend a FinishRich™ Seminar in your area, please visit:

www.finishrich.com

. . . go to *FinishRich.com*

If you would like more information about *Smart Women Finish Rich* or other financial-management products and services we have developed, please contact us at *www.finishrich.com*. There you will find information on:

- My free online FinishRich™ newsletter
- How to attend a Smart Couples Finish Rich™ and/or Smart Women Finish Rich™ Seminar
- How to hire David Bach to speak at your next event
- Books
- Audiotapes
- Videos
- Interactive CD-rom
- FinishRich™ QuickStart Program
- For financial advisors: How to become licensed to teach FinishRich™ Seminars
- Coming soon . . . information on *Smart Kids Finish Rich* and *Smart Teens Finish Rich* and the *FinishRich Workbook*

To everyone who has written and e-mailed me . . . THANK YOU from the bottom of my heart . . . I am incredibly grateful and humbled by the amount of letters and e-mails I have received thus far. If this book has made a significant impact on you, please know that I would like to hear about your successes!

Maybe your personal story (if you give us permission) will become part of a future edition. Also, I am working on *Smart Teens Finish Rich*, and we are actively looking for success stories of teenagers who are involved in managing their money. If you have a teen or know of one that manages his or her money, please share their stories with us. To share success stories, e-mail us at *success@finishrich.com*.

Lastly, I am no longer taking financial planning clients, and due to legal liabilities, I unfortunately cannot answer personal financial questions. If you have specific financial questions, I strongly recommend meeting with a professional. Visit our website resource center, where we have created a section on how to find a financial advisor.

INDEX

Action mode versus complaint mode, 255–57

American Stock Exchange, web site, 197

Annual renewable term life insurance, 166

Annuities, variable, 203–4, 224

Appreciation, shown toward financial advisors and other professionals, 244–45

Asset allocation of retirement funds, 138–39

Assumptions couples make about each other and money, 3–4, 15, 27

Attorney, power of, 151

Bach, Marty (author's father), 226–27

Bach, Rose (author's grandmother), 6–7, 226–27, 245–46

Balanced mutual funds (stocks and bonds), 193

Bank accounts. *See* Checking accounts

"Being" and money, 39

Bill-paying, assumptions and
  agreements about, 1–5, 233–34
Blaming, avoidance of, 12
Bond funds, dream basket in short-
  term, 192–93
Borrowing from retirement accounts,
  110–11
Business owners, retirement basket for,
  131–42

Cash cushion, 145–49
Cash flow, worksheet for determining,
  275–78
Cash-value life insurance, 167–70
Certificates of deposit (CDs)
  as fixed-rate investment, 137
  Individual Retirement Accounts
    (IRAs) versus, 130–31
Change, commitment to, 12, 32
Charitable Remainder Trust, 153
Checking accounts
  cash cushion in money-market,
    147–49
  managing records on, 65–66
  partners' separate and joint,
    233–34
Children
  college-savings plans for, 220–25
  as dreamers, 181–82
  financial education of, 224–29
  IRAs for, 128, 129
  managing financial records of, 67
Christopher Reeve Paralysis
  Foundation, 171
"Churning," 241
Clarity Question, 81
Clutter, cleaning up, 258–62
College-savings plans, 220–25
Commission-based financial advisors,
  241–42

Complaint mode versus action mode,
  255–57
Compound interest, miracle of, 93–96,
  227
Consumer Credit Counseling Services,
  215
Contingent beneficiary, 118
Couple(s). *See also* Partners, financial
  in age 50 plus group, 20–21
  assumptions made by, 3–4, 15, 27
  attitudes of, toward money, 26–27
  avoiding money stresses by working
    together as, 8, 16–17, 60
  cooperating, on financial goal-setting,
    79–80
  establishing financial responsibility of
    each person in, 232–34
  facts and myths about money and,
    13–32
  financial management for (*see*
    Financial management)
  finding greater purpose beyond
    relationship of, 231–32
  non-cooperative, on financial
    planning, 9–10, 27–28, 60,
    68–71
  prenuptial agreements for, 229–31
  retirement goals of, 13–15
  spending by (*see* Couples' Latté
    Factor)
  taking control of financial future as,
    1–12
  teamwork of, as financial partners,
    9–10, 24–31, 57–60
  three words that make a difference
    for, 273–74
Couples' Latté Factor, 20–21, 85–96
  analyzing spending habits and
    finding, 87–91
  miracle of compound interest on
    savings from, 93–96

Seven-Day Financial Challenge to find, 91–93
spending and debt problem in U.S. and, 85–87
Credit-card debt, 212–15
credit rating, credit records and, 212–15
managing records on, 66
taking seriously, 212
Credit ratings, 214–15
Credit records, 212–13
Critical income, 22
"Cubicle copying" of investment decisions, 113–14
Current financial condition. *See* Financial condition, current
Custodial care, long-term coverage for, 175–79

Day-trading, dangers of, 215–18
Death benefit, 162, 165
Debt
American problem of overspending and, 85–87
credit-card, 66, 212–15
inheriting, 163
managing records on, 67
Debt Counselors of America, 215
Defined Contribution Plans (Keough Plans), 132, 133–35
Defined-benefits plans, 135
Disability insurance, 171–75
assumptions about employer-provided, 172–73
how much to purchase, 172
information about, 175
questions to ask about, 173–75
self-employment and, 173, 175
Dividend Reinvestment Program (DRIP), 205

Divorce, 38
money stresses as cause of, 8
"Doing" and money, 39
Dow Jones Industrial Average, 193
Dow Jones Industrial Average Model Depositary Shares (Diamonds), 196
Dream basket, 97, 98, 181–206
avoiding "I don't have a dream" trap, 187
how much and how to invest to create, 189
individual stocks for creation of, 204–5
learning how to dream and how to create, 181–84
for long-term dreams (four to ten years), 193–203
for mid-term dreams (two to four years), 192–93
mutual funds for creation of, 190–203
for short-term dreams (less than two years), 191–92
systematic investing as key to creating, 187–89, 201
variable annuities for creation of, 203–4
worksheet for, 185–86 *fig*

Early payment of mortgages, 209–11
Earnings outlook, 22 *table*
Economic Growth and Tax Relief Reconciliation Act of 2001, 97, 132, 133–34
Education, financial, 105
for children, 224–29
Educational IRAs, 223–24
80/20 rule (80% of revenue from 20% of customers), 263–64

Einstein, Albert, 93

Emergency accounts, 145–49

Employer-sponsored retirement plans, 107–21
  changing jobs and handling, 117–18
  401(k) plan basics, 107–14
  investing, 112–16
  joining, 116–17
  lack of, 118–19

Employers
  assessing future of, 255
  reasons for giving pay raise, 251

Equities. *See* Stocks

Estate planning, 118, 128, 149–56

Exchange Traded Funds (ETFs), 196–97, 224

Expenses, cash cushion based on three months of, 145–46. *See also* Spending habits

Facts and myths about couples and money, 16–32
  on communicating about money, 24–31
  on investing, 21–23
  on love and money, 16–17
  quizzing your knowledge on, 28–31

Fee-based financial advisors, 242

Fee-for-service health insurance plans, 157–58

File folder system for financial records, 64–71

Financial advisors, 235–36
  advantages of hiring, 235–36
  be prepared before meeting, 238
  check out background of, 237–38
  determine philosophy of, 239–40
  get referrals for, 237
  go with gut feelings about, 240
  hire locally, 236–37

payment of, 240–42
  researching, 242–44
  rules for hiring, 236–45
  showing appreciation for, 244–45

Financial condition, current
  determining current cash flow, 275–78
  inventory of, 61–71, 279–83

Financial education, 105, 224–29

Financial hardships, preparing for. *See* Security basket

Financial information, web sites for, 114–16, 227–29

Financial knowledge quiz, 28–31

Financial management
  avoiding mistakes of, 141, 207–44
  for dream fulfillment, 181–206
  facts and myths about, 13–32
  increasing income by 10 percent in nine weeks, 247–71
  on money requirements, 17–21
  planning together (*see* Financial planning)
  for retirement, 97–142
  for security, 143–79
  spending habits, saving habits, and, 85–96
  taking control of, 1–11
  on taxes and inflation, 23–24
  this book about, 5, 11–13
  values-based, 33–55

Financial planning, 57–84
  achieving dreams through, 184–89
  designing Purpose-Focused Financial Plan, 73–83
  determining current financial situation, 61–62
  failure of, effect on couple's relationship, 60
  goal-setting based on values in, 71–81

organizing financial documents for, 62–71

rewards of, 59–60

taking charge by cooperating on, 10–11

three fundamental truths of, 60–61

values-based (*see* Values-based financial planning)

Financial responsibilities of each partner, 232–34

FinishRich File Folder System, 64–71

FinishRich Inventory Planner, 62–63, 67, 238, 279–83

FinishRich Rules of Retirement Investing, 137–42

48-hour action step toward goals, 76–77

401(k) retirement accounts, 107–21
  basics of, 107–8
  borrowing from, 110–11
  changing jobs and, 117–18
  funding IRAs and, 121–22, 125, 126
  investing, 112–16
  joining, 116–17
  lack of, 118–19
  maximum contributions to, 108–11, 109 *table*
  "rolling over" into IRA, 117–18
  self-directed, 107
  SIMPLE IRA vs., 135
  withdrawals from, 110

Friends, job hunting and role of, 268

Goals, 71–81
  cooperating on values and, 79–80
  determining money required to achieve, 78–79
  enlisting help in attaining, 77–78
  putting in writing, 76
  setting specific, detailed, and ending, 74–76

setting value-based, 74, 79–80

taking action on, within 48 hours, 76–77

values versus, 36, 43, 52, 53 *table*

writing down pay raise, 257–58, 284

Government, retirement funds and role of U.S., 98

Growth
  investing dream basket for (*see* Mutual funds)
  investing retirement money for, 137–38

Guaranteed fixed-rate investments, 113

Happiness
  cooperative financial management and fostering, 26
  dreams and, 183

"Having" and money, 39

Health insurance coverage, 156–62
  choosing best, 160
  fee-for-service plans, 157–58
  information about, 161–62
  managed-care plans, 158–60
  maternity coverage, 160–61
  for self-employed persons, 161–62

Help, achieving goals and asking for, 77–78

HMO (health maintenance organizations) health coverage, 158–59

Home, cleaning your, 261–62

Household accounts, managing records on, 66

Hunt, Helen, 236

"I don't have a dream" trap, 187

IBM Corporation, 140

Income. *See also* Money
building dream basket by investing at
least 3 percent of after-tax, 189
critical, 22
increasing (see Pay raises)
life insurance and, 163–64
lifetime outlook for, 22 *table*
"pay yourself first" 10 percent of
pretax, 102–3
reducing spending and investing
disposable, 21–23
saving 15 percent of, 103–4
savings from reducing gross, 104–6
Indemnity plans, health insurance,
157–58
Indexed mutual funds, 193–97, 224
Individual Retirement Accounts (IRAs),
120–31
certificates of deposit (CDs) versus,
130–31
converting traditional IRA to Roth,
127–28
educational, 223–24
guidelines for choosing Roth versus
traditional, 126
maximum contribution to, 120 *table*
rolling over 401(k) funds into,
117–18
Roth, 120 *table*, 124–29
for self-employed and business
owners, 132–33, 135–36, 136 *table*
traditional, 120–24
in trusts, 154
Inflation, facts and myths about,
23–24
Insurance
disability, 171–75
health, 156–62
life, 162–71
long-term care, 175–79
managing records on, 67

Interest
on checking accounts, 147–49
miracle of compound, 93–96, 227
on mortgages, 208
International (global) funds, 199
Investments
building dream basket by making
systematic, 187–89, 201
building wealth by saving and
making, 17–23
day-trading versus long-term,
216–17
managing records on, 65–66
research on, 114–16
types of, for retirement accounts,
112–13 (*see also* Retirement basket)
value of tax-deferred versus taxable,
102 *table*
Investor kits, 140
Investors
"cubicle copying" by, 113–14
mistakes of (*see* Mistakes, ten biggest
financial)
prior riches not required to be, 8–9
Rose Bach as, 6–7, 245–46
using disposable income to become,
21–23
Irrevocable Life Insurance Trust, 153

Jackson, Phil, 236
Job fairs, 266–67
Job hunting, 265–68
job fairs for, 266–67
online searching for, 267
talking to friends as, 268
Job market, during economic
recessions, 249
Jobs, retirement plans and change of,
117–18
Jordan, Michael, 73, 236

Keough Plans (Defined Contribution
Plans), 132, 133–35

Large capitalization growth funds, 198
Large capitalization value funds,
197–98
Level term life insurance, 167
basics of, 176–77
questions to ask about, 178–79
rating companies which sell, 179
reducing premiums for, 177–78
shortcomings of Medicare and need
for, 176
Life expectancy and IRA withdrawals,
123
Life insurance, 162–71
how much to purchase, 162–64
information about, 170–71
portable, 164
for "stay-at-home" parent, 164–65
types of, 165–70
Living trusts, 151–53
Living wills, 150–51
Loans from retirement accounts,
110–11
Long-term care coverage, 175–79
Love, relationship of money to, 16–17

Managed-care health coverage, 158–60
Margin, buying stocks on, 219–20
Margin call, 219
Marital and Bypass Trust, 152
Marriage, prenuptial agreements
before, 229–31
Maternity coverage, 160–61
McDonald's Corporation, 205, 227
Medicare, myths and
misunderstandings about, 176
Medium capitalization funds, 198

Messes, cleaning up, 258–62
Midlife crisis, 38
Mistakes, ten biggest financial, 141,
207–44
Money. *See also* Income
attitudes toward, 26–27
compound interest on saved, 93–96,
227
determining true purpose of (*see*
Values-based financial planning)
facts and myths about, 13–32
myth of "it takes money to make
money," 17–21
pretax retirement savings as free,
104–6
relationship of love to, 16–17
relationship problems caused by non-
cooperation about, 8
as taboo subject, 25–26
time value of, 95 *table*
Money-market accounts
checking accounts, 147–49
short-term dream basket in, 191–92
Money-purchase plans, 133–34
Mortgage calculators, 210
Mortgages, 208–12
early payment of, 209–11
mistakes on statements of, 66 *note*,
210
paying off immediately, 212
taxes and, 211–12
30-year versus 15-year, 208–9
Mutual funds, 21, 113, 189–203
advantages of, 190–91
average performance of select, 200
table
balanced funds, 193
bond funds, 192–93
building dream basket by investing
in, 189–91
"core" funds, 197–99

defined, 190
finding the right, 200–1
indexed, 193–97
investing in, for college, 224–25
"load" and "no-load," 201, 202–3
minimum investment in, 201–3
Myths. *See* Facts and myths about
    couples and money
Myvesta, 215

NASDAQ 100 Trust (Cubes), 196
National Association of Securities
    Dealers (NASD), 238
Net worth, determining, 279–83
Non-cooperating couples, 9–10, 27–28,
    60, 68–71
Nursing homes, long-term care
    coverage for, 175–79

Office, cleaning your, 259–61
Online job searching, 267
Organization, improving office and
    home, 258–62
Overspending. *See* Couples' Latté
    Factor

Parents, life insurance for stay-at-
    home, 164–65
Pareto Principle, 263
Partners, financial. *See also* Couple(s)
    couples as, 9–10, 24–31, 57–60
    establishing responsibilities of each,
        232–34
    non-cooperative, 9–10, 27–28, 60,
        68–71
Pay raises, 247–71. *See also* Income
    asking for, 269–70

deserving and acting on need for,
    247–53
    during bad economies, 249
    practice asking for, 268–69
    ProActive Income Nine-Week Plan
        for getting, 248–50, 254–71, 284
    for self-employed, 248, 250, 270
Pay yourself first, 11, 24, 98–106, 142
    maximum contributions to
        retirement accounts as, 108–11,
        109 *table*, 120 *table*
    returns from, 94 *table*
    three principles of, 99–104
Penalties
    on retirement-account withdrawals,
        110, 122–23
    on selling variable annuities, 204
Permanent life insurance, 167–70
Personal finance. *See* Financial
    management
Planning. *See* Financial planning
POS (point of service) health coverage,
    159–60
Power of attorney, 151
PPO (preferred-provider organization)
    health coverage, 159
Prenuptial agreements, 229–31
Prepaid tuition programs, 222
Pretax retirement accounts
    employer-sponsored, 107–21
    investing, 112–16, 137–42
    IRAs, 120–31
    pay yourself first in, 99–104, 108–11,
        142
    for self-employed, 132–37
ProActive Income Nine-Week Plan,
    248–71
    asking for raise in week eight of, 270
    celebrating success in week nine of,
        270–71

cleaning up messes in week three of, 258–62

determining how you add value in week four of, 262–63

focus on 80/20 rule (Pareto Principle) in week five of, 263–64

power of, 250

practice asking for raise in week seven of, 268–69

putting yourself in play (job hunting) in week six of, 265–68

reality assessment in week one of, 257–58

writing down goals in week two of, 257–58, 284

Profit-Sharing Plans, 134–35

Purpose, finding greater, 231–32

Purpose-Focused Financial Plan, 57, 73–81

  goal-setting in, 74–81

  values and, 33, 41, 49–50, 74

  worksheets, 82, 83, 285–87 *figs*

Put yourself in play (job hunting), 265–68

Qualified Terminable Interest Property Trust (QTIP), 152–53

Quiz on current financial condition, 28–31

Reality assessment in ProActive Income plan, 254–57

Recession, job market during, 249

Records management

  on investments, 64–68

  on wills and trusts, 155–56

Reeve, Christopher, 171

Relationships. *See* Couple(s)

Replating, 153

Retirement accounts. *See* Retirement basket

Retirement basket, 97–142

  employer-sponsored (401[k]) accounts for, 107–21

  first one million dollars and, 20

  Individual Retirement Accounts (IRAs), 120–31

  investing, 112–16, 137–42

  pay yourself first to build, 98–106, 108–12, 142

  role of Social Security and government in, 98

  for self-employed and business owners, 132–37

  two types of retirement accounts, 107

  withdrawals and borrowing from, 110–11, 122–23

  your first one million dollars and, 20

Retirement goals

  couple's agreement on, 13–15

  financial planning and achievement of, 57–60

Revocable Living Trust, 152

Robbins, Tony, 32

Roth IRAs, 124–29

  conversion of traditional IRAs to, 127–28

  guidelines for choosing traditional IRA or, 126

  maximum contribution to, 120 *table*

  working teens eligible for opening, 128

Salary increases. *See* Pay raises

Savings, 85–96

  building wealth with, 17–21

failure of most Americans to create, 25–26

finding, from overspending (*see* Couples' Latté Factor)

managing records on, 66

miracle of compound interest on, 93–96, 227

paying yourself first to create (*see* Pay yourself first)

as percent of income, 102–4

for retirement (*see* Retirement basket)

Rose Bach's lessons about, 6

Savings Incentive Match Plan for Employees (SIMPLE IRA), 132, 135–36, 136 *table*

Savings rate in United States, 25

Section 529 college-savings plans, 222–23

Security basket, 97–98, 143–79

cash cushion in, 145–49

disability insurance in, 171–75

health coverage in, 156–62

life insurance in, 162–71

long-term care coverage in, 175–79

preparing for unexpected hardships and creating, 143–44

priority of, over college-savings plans, 220–21

wills and living trusts in, 149–56

Self-directed retirement plans, 107

Self-employed persons

determining how you add value for clients, 263

disability insurance and, 173, 175

health coverage for, 161–62

pay raise for, 248, 250, 270

retirement basket for, 131–42

Self-made person, myth of, 77

SEP-IRA, 132–33, 135

Seven-Day Financial Challenge, 91–93

72T rule, 123

Short-term bond funds, 192–93

Sign-up package for 401(k) plans, 108

SIMPLE IRA, 132, 135–36, 136 *table*

Simplified Employee Pension Plan (SEP-IRA), 132–33, 135

"Sleeping well at night," cash cushion for, 146

Small capitalization funds, 199

Smart Women Finish Rich (Bach), 9

Social Security

managing records on, 65

role of, in retirement funds, 98

Social Security integration, 133

Socrates, 53

Spending habits, 20–21, 85–93

American consumer debt and, 85–87

analyzing, 87–91, 275–78

setting aside cash cushion based on three months of, 145–46

Standard & Poor's (S&P) 500 index funds, 193, 194–95

Index Depositary Receipts (Spiders), 196

Midcap 400 Depositary Receipts (MDY), 196

Stocks. *See also* Mutual funds

buying on margin, 219–20

day-trading, 215–18

investing dream basket in individual, 204–5

investing in your own company's, 139–41

investing retirement funds in, 138–42

web sites for investigating, 141

in your own company, 113

Subchapter S corporation, retirement account for, 132

Success, celebrating your pay increase, 270–71

Talking with partner about money, 27–28, 68–71

Tax returns, filing, 64–65

Tax-reform bill, Economic Growth and Tax Relief Reconciliation Act of 2001, 97, 132, 133–34

Taxes
facts and myths about, 23–24, 211–12
Individual Retirement Accounts (IRAs) and, 121–23, 125, 127
mortgages and, 211–12

Teamwork, financial, 9–10, 24–31, 57–60

Technology funds, 199

Teenagers, Roth IRAs and, 128

10-K reports, 140

Term life insurance, 165–67

Trusts, 118, 149–56
avoiding putting IRA into, 154
college savings in UGMA and UTMA, 221–22, 223
correct funding of, 153–54
living, 151–53
managing records on, 67
most common mistakes made with, 154–56

Uniform Gift to Minors Act (UGMA) accounts, 221–22, 223

Uniform Transfers to Minors Act (UTMA), 221–22, 223

United States
overspending, savings, and debt problem in, 25, 85–87
retirement funds and role of, 98

Universal life insurance, 168

Value, determining how you add, for employers, 262–63

Value Circle, 41, 46–49
creating your own, 50–51, 52 *fig*
examples of clients, 42–50, 52
goal-setting and use of, 74

Values. *See also* Values-based financial planning
creating financial goals based on, 71–81
finding greater purpose as, 231–32
goals versus, 36, 43, 52, 53 *table*
importance of knowing your own, 53–55
life decisions based on personal, 33–35, 53–55

Values-based financial planning, 33–55
constructing Values Circle for, 42–46, 50–52
financial planning, personal values and, 39–42, 53–55
goals versus values and, 52, 53 *table*
knowing your purpose in life, 33–35
matching financial behavior to values and, 46–50
purpose of money in your life, 35–39
Purpose-Focused Financial Plan and, 33, 41, 49–50

Variable annuities
building dream basket with, 203–4
saving for college with, 224

Variable universal life insurance, 168–70

Vesting schedule, for Money-purchase plans, 134

Web sites
American Stock Exchange, 197
author's FinishRich.com, 288
college planning, 223, 224–25
credit rating, 214
disability insurance, 175

financial advisors, 243–44

financial information, 114–16

financial information for children, 227–29

health coverage for self-employed people, 161–62

individual stocks, 141

job searching, 267

life insurance, 170–71

long-term care coverage, 179

money-market checking accounts, 148–49

mortgage calculators, 210

mutual funds, 194–96, 202–3

for worthy causes, 232

Whole life insurance, 168

Wills, 149–56

living, 150–51

managing records on, 67

most common mistakes made with, 154–56

Wilshire 5000 Index Fund, 194, 195–96

Winfrey, Oprah, 73

Withdrawals from retirement accounts, 110, 122–23

Woods, Tiger, 235